AWS X-Ray Developer Guide

A catalogue record for this book is available from the Hong Kong Public Libraries.

Published in Hong Kong by Samurai Media Limited.

Email: info@samuraimedia.org

ISBN 9789888407798

Contents

What Is AWS X-Ray?

AWS X-Ray is a service that collects data about requests that your application serves, and provides tools you can use to view, filter, and gain insights into that data to identify issues and opportunities for optimization. For any traced request to your application, you can see detailed information not only about the request and response, but also about calls that your application makes to downstream AWS resources, microservices, databases and HTTP web APIs.

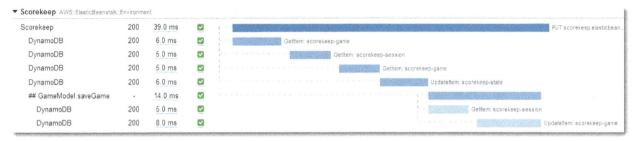

The X-Ray SDK provides:

- **Interceptors** to add to your code to trace incoming HTTP requests
- **Client handlers** to instrument AWS SDK clients that your application uses to call other AWS services
- An **HTTP client** to use to instrument calls to other internal and external HTTP web services

The SDK also supports instrumenting calls to SQL databases, automatic AWS SDK client instrumentation, and other features.

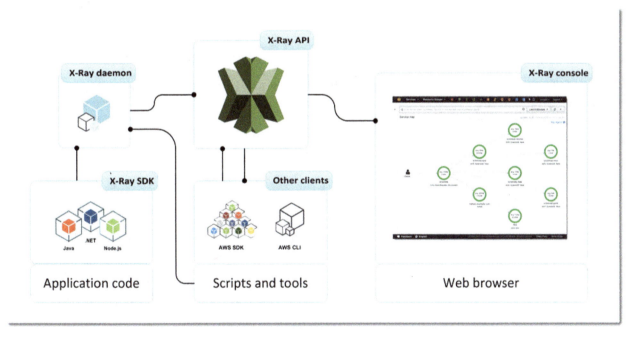

Instead of sending trace data directly to X-Ray, the SDK sends JSON segment documents to a daemon process listening for UDP traffic. The **X-Ray daemon** buffers segments in a queue and uploads them to X-Ray in batches. The daemon is available for Linux, Windows, and macOS, and is included on AWS Elastic Beanstalk and AWS Lambda platforms.

X-Ray uses trace data from the AWS resources that power your cloud applications to generate a detailed **service graph**. The service graph shows the client, your front-end service, and backend services that your front-end service calls to process requests and persist data. Use the service graph to identify bottlenecks, latency spikes, and other issues to solve to improve the performance of your applications.

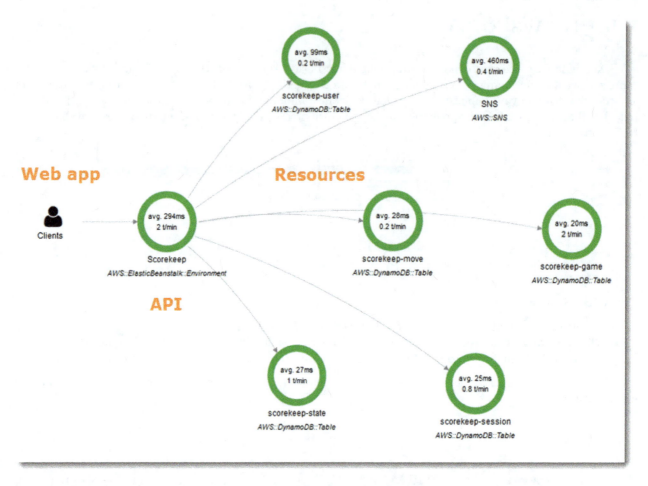

See the getting started tutorial to start using X-Ray in just a few minutes with an instrumented sample application. Or keep reading to learn about the languages, frameworks, and services that work with X-Ray.

AWS X-Ray Use Cases and Requirements

You can use the X-Ray SDK and AWS service integration to instrument requests to your applications that are running locally or on AWS compute services such as Amazon EC2, Elastic Beanstalk, Amazon ECS and AWS Lambda.

To instrument your application code, you use the **X-Ray SDK**. The SDK records data about incoming and outgoing requests and sends it to the X-Ray daemon, which relays the data in batches to X-Ray. For example, when your application calls DynamoDB to retrieve user information from a DynamoDB table, the X-Ray SDK records data from both the client request and the downstream call to DynamoDB.

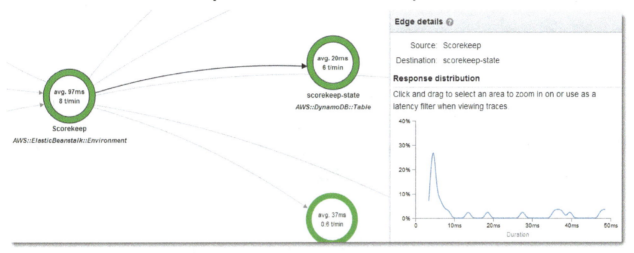

Other AWS services make it easier to instrument your application's components by integrating with X-Ray. **Service integration** can include adding tracing headers to incoming requests, sending trace data to X-Ray, or running the X-Ray daemon. For example, AWS Lambda can send trace data about requests to your Lambda functions, and run the X-Ray daemon on workers to make it easier to use the X-Ray SDK.

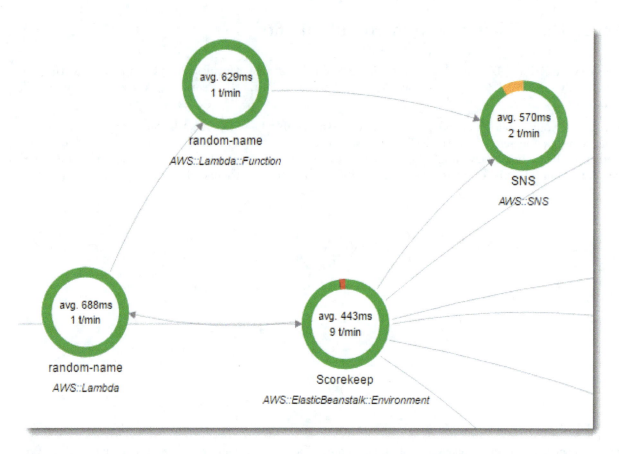

Many instrumentation scenarios require only configuration changes. For example, you can instrument all incoming HTTP requests and downstream calls to AWS services that your Java application makes. To do this, you add the X-Ray SDK for Java's filter to your servlet configuration, and take the AWS SDK for Java Instrumentor submodule as a build dependency. For advanced instrumentation, you can modify your application code to customize and annotate the data that the SDK sends to X-Ray.

Topics

- Supported Languages and Frameworks
- Supported AWS Services
- Code and Configuration Changes

Supported Languages and Frameworks

AWS X-Ray provides tools and integration to support a variety of languages, frameworks, and platforms.

C#

On Windows Server, you can use the X-Ray SDK for .NET to instrument incoming requests, AWS SDK clients, SQL clients, and HTTP clients. On AWS Lambda, you can use the Lambda X-Ray integration to instrument incoming requests.

See AWS X-Ray SDK for .NET for more information.

- **.NET on Windows Server** – Add a message handler to your HTTP configuration to instrument incoming requests.
- **C# .NET Core on AWS Lambda** – Enable X-Ray on your Lambda function configuration to instrument incoming requests.

Go

In any Go application, you can use the X-Ray SDK for Go classes to instrument incoming requests, AWS SDK clients, SQL clients, and HTTP clients. Automatic request instrumentation is available for applications that use HTTP handlers.

On AWS Lambda, you can use the Lambda X-Ray integration to instrument incoming requests. Add the X-Ray SDK for Go to your function for full instrumentation.

See AWS X-Ray SDK for Go for more information.

- **Go web applications** – Use the X-Ray SDK for Go HTTP handler to process incoming requests on your routes.
- **Go on AWS Lambda** – Enable X-Ray on your Lambda function configuration to instrument incoming requests. Add the X-Ray SDK for Go to instrument AWS SDK, HTTP, and SQL clients.

Java

In any Java application, you can use the X-Ray SDK for Java classes to instrument incoming requests, AWS SDK clients, SQL clients, and HTTP clients. Automatic request instrumentation is available for frameworks that support Java servlets. Automatic SDK instrumentation is available through the Instrumentor submodule.

On AWS Lambda, you can use the Lambda X-Ray integration to instrument incoming requests. Add the X-Ray SDK for Java to your function for full instrumentation.

See AWS X-Ray SDK for Java for more information.

- **Tomcat** – Add a servlet filter to your deployment descriptor (`web.xml`) to instrument incoming requests.
- **Spring Boot** – Add a servlet filter to your `WebConfig` class to instrument incoming requests.
- **Java on AWS Lambda** – Enable X-Ray on your Lambda function to instrument incoming requests. Add the X-Ray SDK for Java to instrument AWS SDK, HTTP, and SQL clients.
- **Other frameworks** – Add a servlet filter if your framework supports servlets, or manually create a segment for each incoming request.

Node.js

In any Node.js application, you can use the X-Ray SDK for Node.js classes to instrument incoming requests, AWS SDK clients, SQL clients, and HTTP clients. Automatic request instrumentation is available for applications that use the Express and Restify frameworks.

On AWS Lambda, you can use the Lambda X-Ray integration to instrument incoming requests. Add the X-Ray SDK for Node.js to your function for full instrumentation.

See The X-Ray SDK for Node.js for more information.

- **Express or Restify** – Use the X-Ray SDK for Node.js middleware to instrument incoming requests.
- **Node.js on AWS Lambda** – Enable X-Ray on your Lambda function to instrument incoming requests. Add the X-Ray SDK for Node.js to instrument AWS SDK, HTTP, and SQL clients
- **Other frameworks** – Manually create a segment for each incoming request.

Python

In any Python application, you can use the X-Ray SDK for Python classes to instrument incoming requests, AWS SDK clients, SQL clients, and HTTP clients. Automatic request instrumentation is available for applications that use the Django and Flask frameworks.

On AWS Lambda, you can use the Lambda X-Ray integration to instrument incoming requests. Add the X-Ray SDK for Python to your function for full instrumentation.

See AWS X-Ray SDK for Python for more information.

- **Django or Flask** – Use the X-Ray SDK for Python middleware to instrument incoming requests.
- **Python on AWS Lambda** – Enable X-Ray on your Lambda function configuration to instrument incoming requests. Add the X-Ray SDK for Python to instrument AWS SDK, HTTP, and SQL clients.
- **Other frameworks** – Manually create a segment for each incoming request.

Ruby

In any Ruby application, you can use the X-Ray SDK for Ruby classes to instrument incoming requests, AWS SDK clients, SQL clients, and HTTP clients. Automatic request instrumentation is available for applications that use the Rails framework.

- **Rails** – Add the X-Ray SDK for Ruby gem and railtie to your gemfile, and configure the recorder in an initializer to instrument incoming requests.
- **Other frameworks** – Manually create a segment for each incoming request.

If the X-Ray SDK isn't available for your language or platform, you can generate trace data manually and send it to the X-Ray daemon, or directly to the X-Ray API.

Supported AWS Services

Several AWS services provide **X-Ray integration**. Integrated services offer varying levels of integration that can include sampling and adding headers to incoming requests, running the X-Ray daemon, and automatically sending trace data to X-Ray.

- **Active instrumentation** – Samples and instruments incoming requests.
- **Passive instrumentation** – Instruments requests that have been sampled by another service.
- **Request tracing** – Adds a tracing header to all incoming requests and propagates it downstream.
- **Tooling** – Runs the AWS X-Ray daemon to receive segments from the X-Ray SDK.

Services with X-Ray integration include:

- **AWS Lambda** – Active and passive instrumentation of incoming requests on all runtimes. When you enable instrumentation, AWS Lambda also runs the X-Ray daemon on Java and Node.js runtimes for use with the X-Ray SDK. Learn more.

- **Amazon API Gateway** – Request tracing. API Gateway passes the trace ID to AWS Lambda and adds it to the request header for other downstream services. Learn more.

- **Elastic Load Balancing** – Request tracing on application load balancers. The application load balancer adds the trace ID to the request header before sending it to a target group. Learn more.

- **AWS Elastic Beanstalk** – Tooling. Elastic Beanstalk includes the X-Ray daemon on the following platforms:

  - **Java SE** – 2.3.0 and newer configurations
  - **Tomcat** – 2.4.0 and newer configurations
  - **Node.js** – 3.2.0 and newer configurations
  - **Windows Server** – All configurations other than Windows Server Core released since December 9th, 2016.

  You can tell Elastic Beanstalk to run the daemon on these platforms in the Elastic Beanstalk console, or by using the `XRayEnabled` option in the `aws:elasticbeanstalk:xray` namespace. Learn more.

Code and Configuration Changes

A large amount of tracing data can be generated without any functional changes to your code. Detailed tracing of front-end and downstream calls requires only minimal changes to build and deploy-time configuration.

Examples of Code and Configuration Changes

- **AWS resource configuration** – Change AWS resource settings to instrument requests to a Lambda function. Run the X-Ray daemon on the instances in your Elastic Beanstalk environment by changing an option setting.

- **Build configuration** – Take X-Ray SDK for Java submodules as a compile-time dependency to instrument all downstream requests to AWS services, and to resources such as Amazon DynamoDB tables, Amazon SQS queues, and Amazon S3 buckets.
- **Application configuration** – To instrument incoming HTTP requests, add a servlet filter to your Java application, or use the X-Ray SDK for Node.js as middleware on your Express application. Change sampling rules and enable plugins to instrument the Amazon EC2, Amazon ECS, and AWS Elastic Beanstalk resources that run your application.
- **Class or object configuration** – To instrument outgoing HTTP calls in Java, import the X-Ray SDK for Java version of `HttpClientBuilder` instead of the Apache.org version.
- **Functional changes** – Add a request handler to an AWS SDK client to instrument calls that it makes to AWS services. Create subsegments to group downstream calls, and add debug information to segments with annotations and metadata.

Getting Started with AWS X-Ray

To get started with AWS X-Ray, launch a sample app in Elastic Beanstalk that is already instrumented to generate trace data. In a few minutes, you can launch the sample app, generate traffic, send segments to X-Ray, and view a service graph and traces in the AWS Management Console.

This tutorial uses a sample Java application to generate segments and send them to X-Ray. The application uses the Spring framework to implement a JSON web API and the AWS SDK for Java to persist data to Amazon DynamoDB. A servlet filter in the application instruments all incoming requests served by the application, and a request handler on the AWS SDK client instruments downstream calls to DynamoDB.

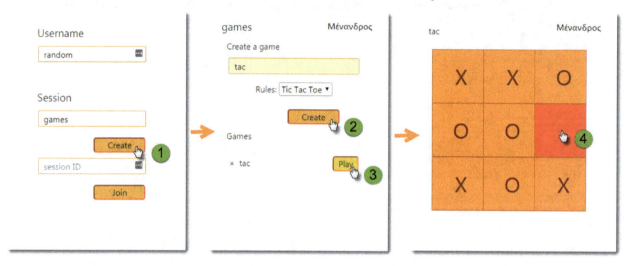

You use the X-Ray console to view the connections among client, server, and DynamoDB in a service map. The service map is a visual representation of the services that make up your web application, generated from the trace data that it generates by serving requests.

With the X-Ray SDK for Java, you can trace all of your application's primary and downstream AWS resources by making two configuration changes:

- Add the X-Ray SDK for Java's tracing filter to your servlet configuration in a `WebConfig` class or `web.xml` file.
- Take the X-Ray SDK for Java's submodules as build dependencies in your Maven or Gradle build configuration.

You can also access the raw service map and trace data by using the AWS CLI to call the X-Ray API. The service map and trace data are JSON that you can query to ensure that your application is sending data, or to check specific fields as part of your test automation.

Topics

- Prerequisites
- Deploy to Elastic Beanstalk and Generate Trace Data
- View the Service Map in the X-Ray Console
- Configuration Amazon SNS Notifications
- Explore the Sample Application
- Clean Up
- Next Steps

Prerequisites

This tutorial uses Elastic Beanstalk to create and configure the resources that run the sample application and X-Ray daemon. If you use an IAM user with limited permissions, add the Elastic Beanstalk managed user policy to grant your IAM user permission to use Elastic Beanstalk, and the `AWSXrayReadOnlyAccess` managed policy for permission to read the service map and traces in the X-Ray console.

Create an Elastic Beanstalk environment for the sample application. If you haven't used Elastic Beanstalk before, this will also create a service role and instance profile for your application.

To create an Elastic Beanstalk environment

1. Open the Elastic Beanstalk Management Console with this preconfigured link: https://console.aws.amazon.com/elasticbeanstalk/#/newApplication?applicationName=scorekeep&solutionStackName=Java

2. Choose **Create application** to create an application with an environment running the Java 8 SE platform.

3. When your environment is ready, the console redirects you to the environment Dashboard.

4. Click the URL at the top of the page to open the site.

The instances in your environment need permission to send data to the AWS X-Ray service. Additionally, the sample application uses Amazon S3 and DynamoDB. Modify the default Elastic Beanstalk instance profile to include permissions to use these services.

To add X-Ray, Amazon S3 and DynamoDB permissions to your Elastic Beanstalk environment

1. Open the Elastic Beanstalk instance profile in the IAM console: aws-elasticbeanstalk-ec2-role.

2. Choose **Attach Policy**.

3. Attach **AWSXrayFullAccess**, **AmazonS3FullAccess**, and **AmazonDynamoDBFullAccess** to the role.

Deploy to Elastic Beanstalk and Generate Trace Data

Deploy the sample application to your Elastic Beanstalk environment. The sample application uses Elastic Beanstalk configuration files to configure the environment for use with X-Ray and create the DynamoDB that it uses automatically.

To deploy the source code

1. Download the sample app: eb-java-scorekeep-xray-gettingstarted-v1.3.zip

2. Open the Elastic Beanstalk console.

3. Navigate to the management console for your environment.

4. Choose **Upload and Deploy**.

5. Upload eb-java-scorekeep-xray-gettingstarted-v1.3.zip, and then choose **Deploy**.

The sample application includes a front-end web app. Use the web app to generate traffic to the API and send trace data to X-Ray.

To generate trace data

1. In the environment Dashboard, click the URL to open the web app.

2. Choose **Create** to create a user and session.

3. Type a **game name**, set the **Rules** to **Tic Tac Toe**, and then choose **Create** to create a game.

4. Choose **Play** to start the game.

5. Choose a tile to make a move and change the game state.

Each of these steps generates HTTP requests to the API, and downstream calls to DynamoDB to read and write user, session, game, move, and state data.

View the Service Map in the X-Ray Console

You can see the service map and traces generated by the sample application in the X-Ray console.

To use the X-Ray console

1. Open the service map page of the X-Ray console.

2. The console shows a representation of the service graph that X-Ray generates from the trace data sent by the application.

The service map shows the web app client, the API running in Elastic Beanstalk, the DynamoDB service, and each DynamoDB table that the application uses. Every request to the application, up to a configurable maximum number of requests per second, is traced as it hits the API, generates requests to downstream services, and completes.

You can choose any node in the service graph to view traces for requests that generated traffic to that node. Currently, the Amazon SNS node is red. Drill down to find out why.

To find the cause of the error

1. Choose the node named **SNS**.

2. Choose the trace from the **Trace list**. This trace doesn't have a method or URL because it was recorded during startup instead of in response to an incoming request.

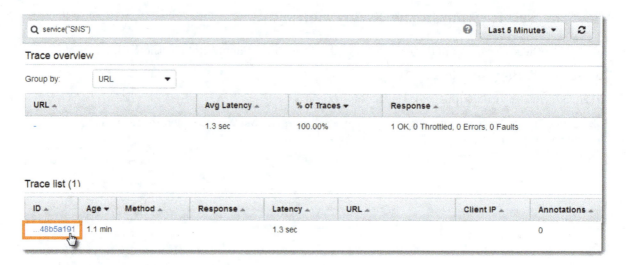

3. Choose the red status icon to open the **Exceptions** page for the SNS subsegment.

4. The X-Ray SDK automatically captures exceptions thrown by instrumented AWS SDK clients and records the stack trace.

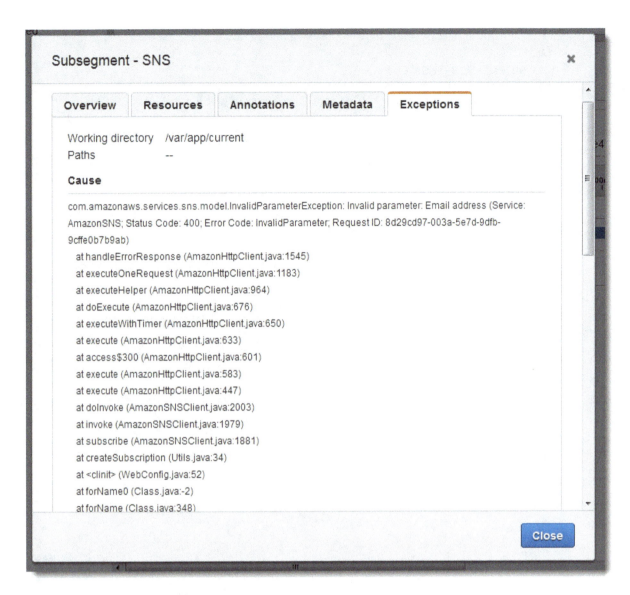

The cause indicates that the email address provided in a call to `createSubscription` made in the `WebConfig` class was invalid. Let's fix that.

Configuration Amazon SNS Notifications

Scorekeep uses Amazon SNS to send notifications when users complete a game. When the application starts up, it tries to create a subscription for an email address defined in an environment variable. That call is currently failing, causing the Amazon SNS node in your service map to be red. Configure a notification email in an environment variable to enable notifications and make the service map green.

To configure Amazon SNS notifications for Scorekeep

1. Open the Elastic Beanstalk console.

2. Navigate to the management console for your environment.

3. Choose **Configuration**.

4. Choose **Software Configuration**.

5. Under **Environment Properties**, replace the default value with your email address.

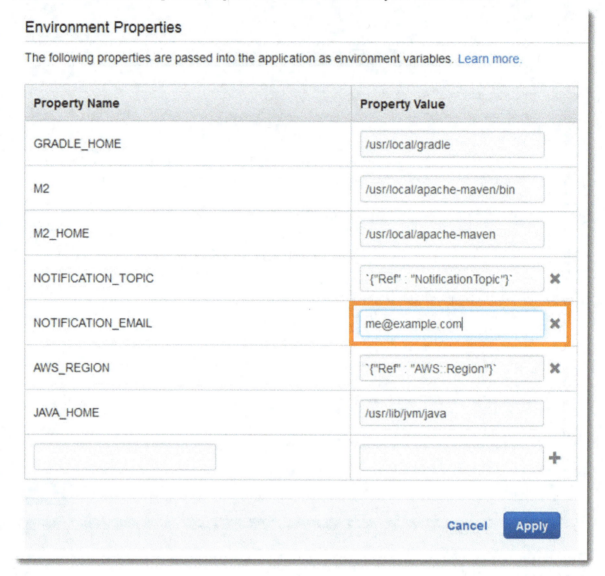

Note

The default value uses an AWS CloudFormation function to retrieve a parameter stored in a configuration file (a dummy value in this case).

6. Choose **Apply**.

When the update completes, Scorekeep restarts and creates a subscription to the SNS topic. Check your email and confirm the subscription to see updates when you complete a game.

Explore the Sample Application

The sample application is an HTTP web API in Java that is configured to use the X-Ray SDK for Java. When you deploy the application to Elastic Beanstalk, it creates the DynamoDB tables, compiles the API with Gradle, and configures the nginx proxy server to serve the web app statically at the root path. At the same time, Elastic Beanstalk routes requests to paths starting with /api to the API.

To instrument incoming HTTP requests, the application adds the `TracingFilter` provided by the SDK.

Example src/main/java/scorekeep/WebConfig.java - Servlet Filter

```
1 import javax.servlet.Filter;
2 import [com\.amazonaws\.xray\.javax\.servlet\.AWSXRayServletFilter](http://docs.aws.amazon.com/
      xray-sdk-for-java/latest/javadoc/com/amazonaws/xray/javax/servlet/AWSXRayServletFilter.html)
      ;
3 ...
4
5 @Configuration
6 public class WebConfig {
7
8   @Bean
9   public Filter TracingFilter() {
10    return new AWSXRayServletFilter("Scorekeep");
11  }
12 ...
```

This filter sends trace data about all incoming requests that the application serves, including request URL, method, response status, start time, and end time.

The application also makes downstream calls to DynamoDB using the AWS SDK for Java. To instrument these calls, the application simply takes the AWS SDK-related submodules as dependencies, and the X-Ray SDK for Java automatically instruments all AWS SDK clients.

The application uses a `Buildfile` file to build the source code on-instance with `Gradle` and a `Procfile` file to run the executable JAR that Gradle generates. `Buildfile` and `Procfile` support is a feature of the Elastic Beanstalk Java SE platform.

Example Buildfile

```
1 build: gradle build
```

Example Procfile

```
1 web: java -Dserver.port=5000 -jar build/libs/scorekeep-api-1.0.0.jar
```

The `build.gradle` file downloads the SDK submodules from Maven during compilation by declaring them as dependencies.

Example build.gradle -- Dependencies

```
1  ...
2  dependencies {
3      compile("org.springframework.boot:spring-boot-starter-web")
4      testCompile('org.springframework.boot:spring-boot-starter-test')
5      compile('com.amazonaws:aws-java-sdk-dynamodb')
6      compile("com.amazonaws:aws-xray-recorder-sdk-core")
7      compile("com.amazonaws:aws-xray-recorder-sdk-aws-sdk")
8      compile("com.amazonaws:aws-xray-recorder-sdk-aws-sdk-instrumentor")
9      ...
10 }
11 dependencyManagement {
12     imports {
13         mavenBom("com.amazonaws:aws-java-sdk-bom:1.11.67")
14         mavenBom("com.amazonaws:aws-xray-recorder-sdk-bom:1.3.1")
15     }
16 }
```

The core, AWS SDK, and AWS SDK Instrumentor submodules are all that's required to automatically instrument any downstream calls made with the AWS SDK.

To run the X-Ray daemon, the application uses another feature of Elastic Beanstalk, configuration files. The configuration file tells Elastic Beanstalk to run the daemon and send its log on demand.

Example .ebextensions/xray.config

```
1 option_settings:
2   aws:elasticbeanstalk:xray:
3     XRayEnabled: true
4
5 files:
6   "/opt/elasticbeanstalk/tasks/taillogs.d/xray-daemon.conf" :
7     mode: "000644"
8     owner: root
9     group: root
10    content: |
11      /var/log/xray/xray.log
```

The X-Ray SDK for Java provides a class named `AWSXRay` that provides the global recorder, a `TracingHandler` that you can use to instrument your code. You can configure the global recorder to customize the `AWSXRayServletFilter` that creates segments for incoming HTTP calls. The sample includes a static block in the `WebConfig` class that configures the global recorder with plugins and sampling rules.

Example src/main/java/scorekeep/WebConfig.java - Recorder

```
1 import [com\.amazonaws\.xray\.AWSXRay](http://docs.aws.amazon.com/xray-sdk-for-java/latest/
      javadoc/com/amazonaws/xray/AWSXRay.html);
2 import [com\.amazonaws\.xray\.AWSXRayRecorderBuilder](http://docs.aws.amazon.com/xray-sdk-for-
      java/latest/javadoc/com/amazonaws/xray/AWSXRayRecorderBuilder.html);
3 import [com\.amazonaws\.xray\.plugins\.EC2Plugin](http://docs.aws.amazon.com/xray-sdk-for-java/
      latest/javadoc/com/amazonaws/xray/plugins/EC2Plugin.html);
4 import [com\.amazonaws\.xray\.plugins\.ElasticBeanstalkPlugin](http://docs.aws.amazon.com/xray-
      sdk-for-java/latest/javadoc/com/amazonaws/xray/plugins/ElasticBeanstalkPlugin.html);
5 import [com\.amazonaws\.xray\.strategy\.sampling\.LocalizedSamplingStrategy](http://docs.aws.
      amazon.com/xray-sdk-for-java/latest/javadoc/com/amazonaws/xray/strategy/sampling/
      LocalizedSamplingStrategy.html);
6
7 @Configuration
8 public class WebConfig {
9 ...
10  static {
11    AWSXRayRecorderBuilder builder = AWSXRayRecorderBuilder.standard().withPlugin(new EC2Plugin
          ()).withPlugin(new ElasticBeanstalkPlugin());
12
13    URL ruleFile = WebConfig.class.getResource("/sampling-rules.json");
14    builder.withSamplingStrategy(new LocalizedSamplingStrategy(ruleFile));
15
16    AWSXRay.setGlobalRecorder(builder.build());
17  }
18 }
```

This example uses the builder to load sampling rules from a file named `sampling-rules.json`. Sampling rules determine the rate at which the SDK records segments for incoming requests.

Example src/main/java/resources/sampling-rules.json

```
1  {
2    "version": 1,
3    "rules": [
4      {
5        "description": "Resource creation.",
6        "service_name": "*",
7        "http_method": "POST",
8        "url_path": "/api/*",
9        "fixed_target": 1,
10       "rate": 1.0
11     },
12     {
13       "description": "Session polling.",
14       "service_name": "*",
15       "http_method": "GET",
16       "url_path": "/api/session/*",
17       "fixed_target": 0,
18       "rate": 0.05
19     },
20     {
21       "description": "Game polling.",
22       "service_name": "*",
23       "http_method": "GET",
24       "url_path": "/api/game/*/*",
25       "fixed_target": 0,
26       "rate": 0.05
27     },
28     {
29       "description": "State polling.",
30       "service_name": "*",
31       "http_method": "GET",
32       "url_path": "/api/state/*/*/*",
33       "fixed_target": 0,
34       "rate": 0.05
35     }
36   ],
37   "default": {
38     "fixed_target": 1,
39     "rate": 0.1
40   }
41 }
```

The sampling rules file defines four custom sampling rules and the default rule. For each incoming request, the SDK evaluates the custom rules in the order in which they are defined. The SDK applies the first rule that matches the request's method, path, and service name. For Scorekeep, the first rule catches all POST requests (resource creation calls) by applying a fixed target of one request per second and a rate of 1.0, or 100 percent of requests after the fixed target is satisfied.

The other three custom rules apply a five percent rate with no fixed target to session, game, and state reads (GET requests). This minimizes the number of traces for periodic calls that the front end makes automatically every few seconds to ensure the content is up to date. For all other requests, the file defines a default rate of one request per second and a rate of 10 percent.

The sample application also shows how to use advanced features such as manual SDK client instrumentation, creating additional subsegments, and outgoing HTTP calls. For more information, see AWS X-Ray Sample Application.

Clean Up

Terminate your Elastic Beanstalk environment to shut down the Amazon EC2 instances, DynamoDB tables, and other resources.

To terminate your Elastic Beanstalk environment

1. Open the Elastic Beanstalk console.

2. Navigate to the management console for your environment.

3. Choose **Actions**.

4. Choose **Terminate Environment**.

5. Choose **Terminate**.

Trace data is automatically deleted from X-Ray after 30 days.

Next Steps

Learn more about X-Ray in the next chapter, AWS X-Ray Concepts.

To instrument your own app, learn more about the X-Ray SDK for Java or one of the other X-Ray SDKs:

- **X-Ray SDK for Java** – AWS X-Ray SDK for Java
- **X-Ray SDK for Node.js** – The X-Ray SDK for Node.js
- **X-Ray SDK for .NET** – AWS X-Ray SDK for .NET

To run the X-Ray daemon locally or on AWS, see AWS X-Ray Daemon.

To contribute to the sample application on GitHub, see eb-java-scorekeep.

AWS X-Ray Concepts

AWS X-Ray receives data from services as *segments*. X-Ray then groups segments that have a common request into *traces*. X-Ray processes the traces to generate a *service graph* that provides a visual representation of your application.

Topics

- Segments
- Subsegments
- Service Graph
- Traces
- Sampling
- Tracing Header
- Filter Expressions
- Annotations and Metadata
- Errors, Faults, and Exceptions

Segments

The compute resources running your application logic send data about their work as **segments**. A segment provides the resource's name, details about the request, and details about the work done. For example, when an HTTP request reaches your application, it can record the following data about:

- **The host** – hostname, alias or IP address
- **The request** – method, client address, path, user agent
- **The response** – status, content
- **The work done** – start and end times, subsegments
- **Issues that occur** – errors, faults and exceptions, including automatic capture of exception stacks.

The X-Ray SDK gathers information from request and response headers, the code in your application, and metadata about the AWS resources on which it runs. You choose the data to collect by modifying your application configuration or code to instrument incoming requests, downstream requests, and AWS SDK clients.

Forwarded Requests

If a load balancer or other intermediary forwards a request to your application, X-Ray takes the client IP from the `X-Forwarded-For` header in the request instead of from the source IP in the IP packet. The client IP that is recorded for a forwarded request can be forged, so it should not be trusted.

You can use the X-Ray SDK to record additional information such as annotations and metadata. For details about the structure and information that is recorded in segments and subsegments, see AWS X-Ray Segment Documents. Segment documents can be up to 64 kB in size.

Subsegments

A segment can break down the data about the work done into **subsegments**. Subsegments provide more granular timing information and details about downstream calls that your application made to fulfill the original request. A subsegment can contain additional details about a call to an AWS service, an external HTTP API, or an SQL database. You can even define arbitrary subsegments to instrument specific functions or lines of code in your application.

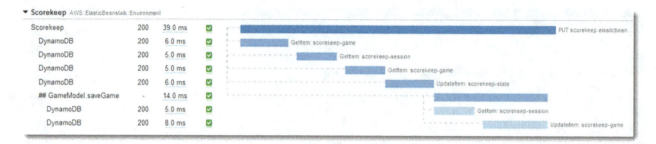

For services that don't send their own segments, like Amazon DynamoDB, X-Ray uses subsegments to generate *inferred segments* and downstream nodes on the service map. This lets you see all of your downstream dependencies, even if they don't support tracing, or are external.

Subsegments represent your application's view of a downstream call as a client. If the downstream service is also instrumented, the segment that it sends replaces the inferred segment generated from the uptsream client's subsegment. The node on the service graph always uses information from the service's segment, if it's available, while the edge between the two nodes uses the upstream service's subsegment.

For example, when you call DynamoDB with an instrumented AWS SDK client, the X-Ray SDK records a subsegment for that call. DynamoDB doesn't send a segment, so the inferred segment in the trace, the DynamoDB node on the service graph, and the edge between your service and DynamoDB all contain information from the subsegment.

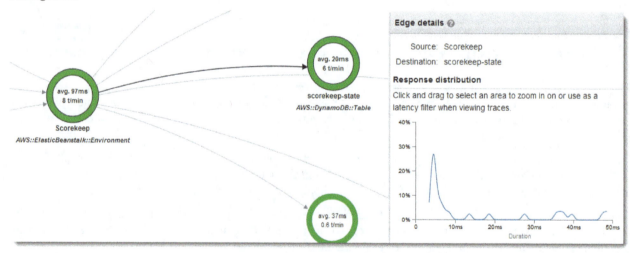

When you call another instrumented service with an instrumented application, the downstream service sends its own segment to record its view of the same call that the upstream service recorded in a subsegment. In the service graph, both services' nodes contain timing and error information from those services' segments, while the edge between them contains information from the upstream service's subsegment.

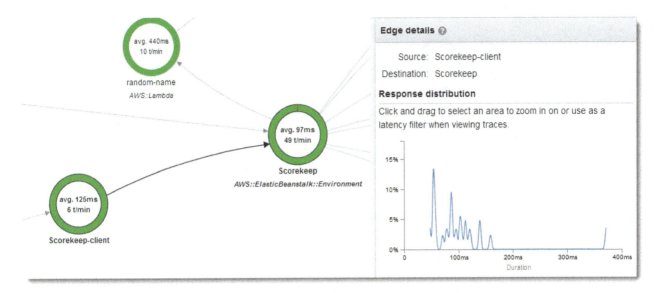

Both viewpoints are useful, as the downstream service records precisely when it started and ended work on the request, and the upstream service records the round trip latency, including time that the request spent traveling between the two services.

Service Graph

X-Ray uses the data that your application sends to generate a **service graph**. Each AWS resource that sends data to X-Ray appears as a service in the graph. **Edges** connect the services that work together to serve requests. Edges connect clients to your application, and your application to the downstream services and resources that it uses.

Service Names

A segment's `name` should match the domain name or logical name of the service that generates the segment. However, this is not enforced. Any application that has permission to http://docs.aws.amazon.com/xray/latest/api/API_PutTraceSegments.html can send segments with any name.

A service graph is a JSON document that contains information about the services and resources that make up your application. The X-Ray console uses the service graph to generate a visualization or *service map*.

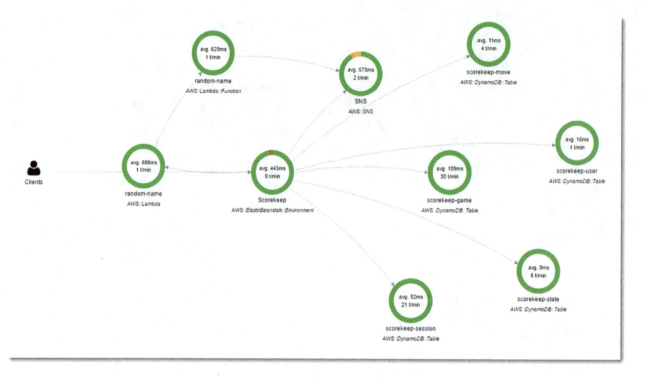

For a distributed application, X-Ray combines nodes from all services that process requests with the same trace ID into a single service graph. The first service that the request hits adds a tracing header that is propagated between the front end and services that it calls.

For example, Scorekeep runs a web API that calls a microservice (an AWS Lambda function) to generate a random name by using a Node.js library. The X-Ray SDK for Java generates the trace ID and includes it in calls to Lambda. Lambda sends tracing data and passes the trace ID to the function. The X-Ray SDK for Node.js also uses the trace ID to send data. As a result, nodes for the API, the Lambda service, and the Lambda function all appear as separate, but connected, nodes on the service map.

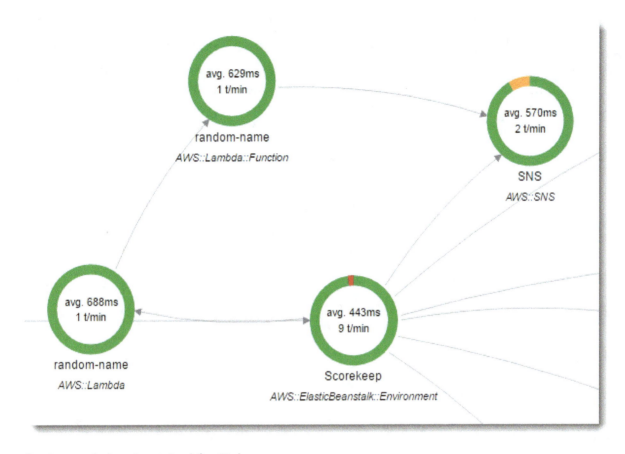

Service graph data is retained for 30 days.

Traces

A **trace ID** tracks the path of a request through your application. A trace collects all the segments generated by a single request. That request is typically an HTTP GET or POST request that travels through a load balancer, hits your application code, and generates downstream calls to other AWS services or external web APIs. The first supported service that the HTTP request interacts with adds a trace ID header to the request, and propagates it downstream to track the latency, disposition, and other request data.

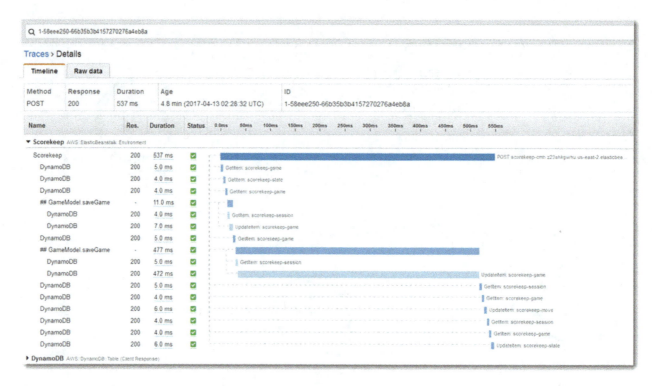

Service graph data is retained for 30 days.

Sampling

To ensure efficient tracing and provide a representative sample of the requests that your application serves, the X-Ray SDK applies a **sampling** algorithm to determine which requests get traced. By default, the X-Ray SDK records the first request each second, and five percent of any additional requests.

To avoid incurring service charges when you are getting started, the default sampling rate is conservative. You can configure the SDK to modify the default sampling rules and configure different sampling rates for different routes that your application serves.

For example, you may want to disable sampling and trace all requests for calls that modify state or deal with user accounts or transactions. For high volume read-only calls, like background polling, health checks, or connection maintenance, you can sample at a low rate and still get enough data to see any issues that arise.

Learn more about sampling configuration with a hands-on example in the Getting Started tutorial.

Tracing Header

All requests are traced, up to a configurable minimum. After reaching that minimum, a percentage of requests are traced to avoid unnecessary cost. The sampling decision and trace ID are added to HTTP requests in **tracing headers** named `X-Amzn-Trace-Id`. The first X-Ray-integrated service that the request hits adds a tracing header, which is read by the X-Ray SDK and included in the response.

Example Tracing header with root trace ID and sampling decision

```
1  X-Amzn-Trace-Id: Root=1-5759e988-bd862e3fe1be46a994272793;Sampled=1
```

Tracing Header Security
A tracing header can originate from the X-Ray SDK, an AWS service, or the client request. Your application can

remove `X-Amzn-Trace-Id` from incoming requests to avoid issues caused by users adding trace IDs or sampling decisions to their requests.

The tracing header can also contain a parent segment ID if the request originated from an instrumented application. For example, if your application calls a downstream HTTP web API with an instrumented HTTP client, the X-Ray SDK adds the segment ID for the original request to the tracing header of the downstream request. An instrumented application that serves the downstream request can record the parent segment ID to connect the two requests.

Example Tracing header with root trace ID, parent segment ID and sampling decision

```
1  X-Amzn-Trace-Id: Root=1-5759e988-bd862e3fe1be46a994272793;Parent=53995c3f42cd8ad8;Sampled=1
```

Filter Expressions

Even with sampling, a complex application generates a lot of data. The AWS X-Ray console provides an easy-to-navigate view of the service graph. It shows health and performance information that helps you identify issues and opportunities for optimization in your application. For advanced tracing, you can drill down to traces for individual requests, or use **filter expressions** to find traces related to specific paths or users.

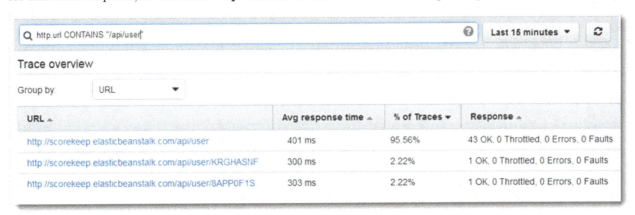

Annotations and Metadata

When you instrument your application, the X-Ray SDK records information about incoming and outgoing requests, the AWS resources used, and the application itself. You can add other information to the segment document as annotations and metadata.

Annotations are simple key-value pairs that are indexed for use with filter expressions. Use annotations to record data that you want to use to group traces in the console, or when calling the http://docs.aws.amazon.com/xray/latest/api/API_GetTraceSummaries.html API.

X-Ray indexes up to 50 annotations per trace.

Metadata are key-value pairs with values of any type, including objects and lists, but that are not indexed. Use metadata to record data you want to store in the trace but don't need to use for searching traces.

You can view annotations and metadata in the segment or subsegment details in the X-Ray console.

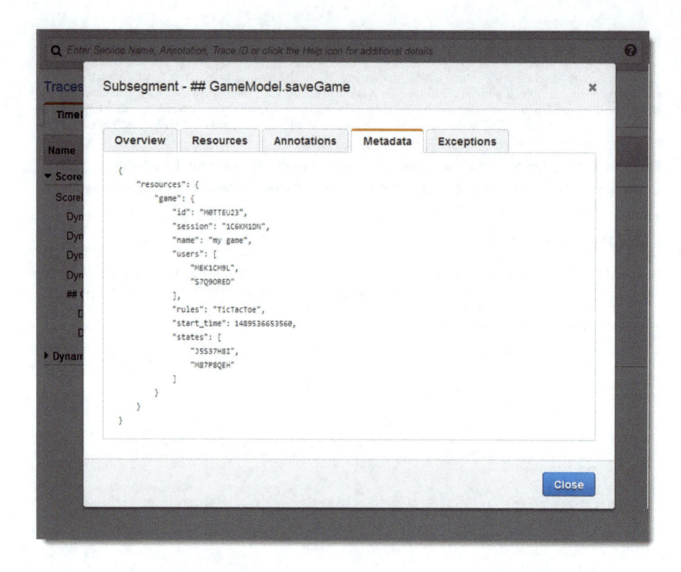

Errors, Faults, and Exceptions

X-Ray tracks errors that occur in your application code, and errors that are returned by downstream services. Errors are categorized as follows.

- **Error** – Client errors (400 series errors)
- **Fault** – Server faults (500 series errors)
- **Throttle** – Throttling errors (429 Too Many Requests)

When an exception occurs while your application is serving an instrumented request, the X-Ray SDK records details about the exception, including the stack trace, if available. You can view exceptions under segment details in the X-Ray console.

AWS X-Ray Console

The AWS X-Ray console enables you to view service maps and traces for requests that your applications serve.

The console's service map is a visual representation of the JSON service graph that X-Ray generates from the trace data generated by your applications. The map consists of service nodes for each application in your account that serves requests, upstream client nodes that represent the origins of the requests, and downstream service nodes that represent web services and resources used by an application while processing a request.

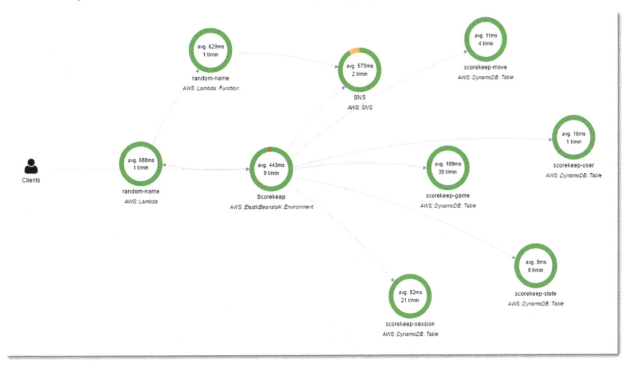

You can use filters to view a service map or traces for a specific request, service, connection between two services (an edge), or requests that satisfy a condition. X-Ray provides a filter expression language for filtering requests, services, and edges based on data in request headers, response status, and indexed fields on the original segments.

Viewing the Service Map

View the service map in the X-Ray console to identify services where errors are occurring, connections with high latency, or traces for requests that were unsuccessful.

To view the service map

1. Open the service map page of the X-Ray console.

2. Choose a service node to view requests for that node, or an edge between two nodes to view requests that traveled that connection.

3. Use the histogram to filter traces by duration, and select status codes for which you want to view traces. Then choose **View traces** to open the trace list with the filter expression applied.

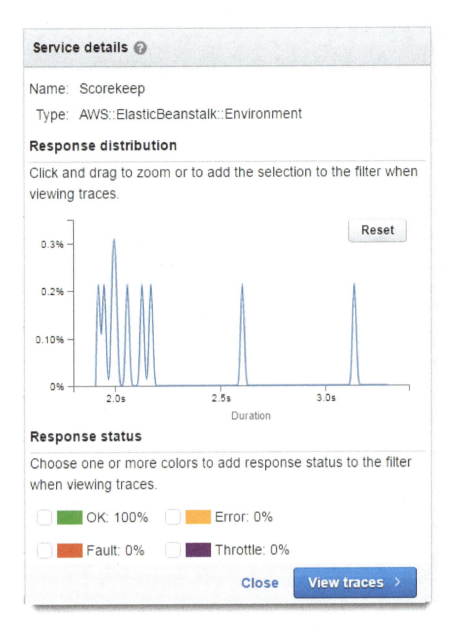

The service map indicates the health of each node by coloring it based on the ratio of successful calls to errors and faults:

- **Green** for successful calls
- **Red** for server faults (500 series errors)
- **Yellow** for client errors (400 series errors)
- **Purple** for throttling errors (429 Too Many Requests)

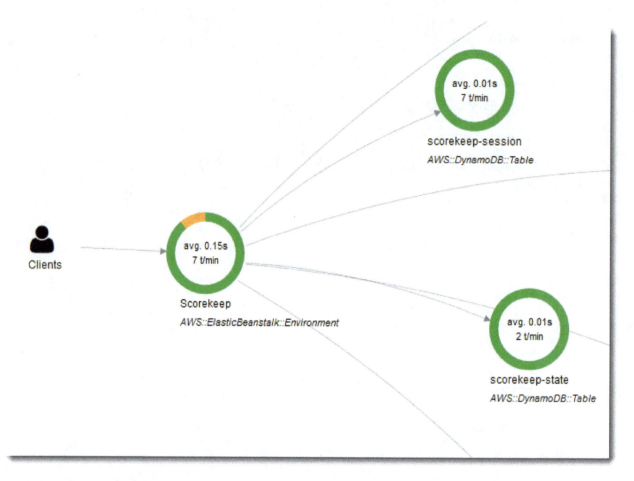

In the center of each node, the console shows the average response time and number of traces that it sent per minute during the chosen time range.

If your service map is large, the console defaults to a zoomed out view. Use the on-screen controls or mouse to zoom in and out and move the image around.

Controls

- 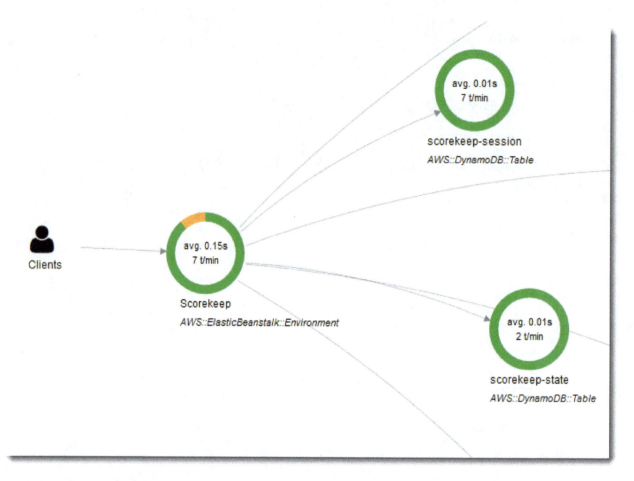 – zoom in or out. You can also use the mouse wheel to zoom in and out.
- – scroll the service map. Click and drag to scroll with the mouse.
- – frame the selected node or edge in the center of map.

Viewing Traces

Use the trace list in the X-Ray console to find traces by URL, response code, or other data from the trace summary.

To use the trace list

1. Open the traces page of the X-Ray console.

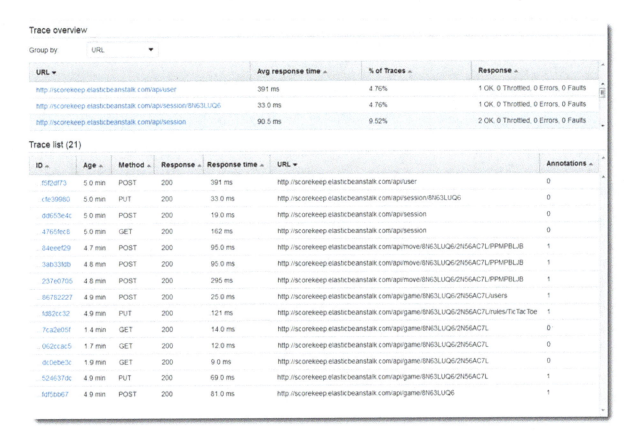

2. Choose a URL to filter the trace list.

3. Choose a trace ID to view the timeline for a trace.

The timeline view shows a hierarchy of segments and subsegments. The first entry in the list is the segment, which represents all data recorded by the service for a single request.

Below the segment are subsegments. This example shows subsegments recorded by instrumented Amazon DynamoDB clients, and a custom subsegment.

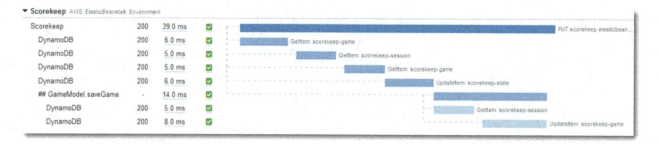

The X-Ray SDK records subsegments automatically when you use an instrumented AWS SDK, HTTP, or SQL client to make calls to external resources. You can also tell the SDK to record custom subsegments for any function or block of code. Additional subsegments recorded while a custom subsegment is open become children of the custom subsegment.

From the timeline view, you can also access the raw trace data that the console uses to generate the timeline. Choose **Raw data** to see the JSON document that contains all the segments and subsegments that make up the trace.

| Timeline | Raw data |

```
{
    "Duration": 0.04499983787536621,
    "Id": "1-58c88690-5b492bc62b0fc5a7c0b004de",
    "Segments": [
        {
            "Document": {
                "id": "69e25bb5bfe4c13f",
                "start_time": 1489536656.769,
                "end_time": 1489536656.814,
                "trace_id": "1-58c88690-5b492bc62b0fc5a7c0b004de",
                "name": "Scorekeep",
                "origin": "AWS::ElasticBeanstalk::Environment",
                "aws": {
                    "elastic_beanstalk": {
                        "version_label": "app-9952-170314_220507",
                        "deployment_id": 188,
                        "environment_name": "scorekeep"
                    },
                    "ec2": {
                        "availability_zone": "us-west-2a",
                        "instance_id": "i-0c8afa67249a5b7ea"
                    },
                    "xray": {
                        "sdk_version": "1.0.5-beta for Java"
                    }
                },
                "http": {
                    "request": {
                        "method": "PUT",
                        "client_ip": "205.255.255.255",
                        "url": "http://scorekeep.elasticbeanstalk.com/api/game/1C6KM1DN/M0TTEU23/rules/TicTacToe",
                        "user_agent": "Mozilla/5.0 (Windows NT 6.1; WOW64) AppleWebKit/537.36 (KHTML, like Gecko) Chrome/55.0.2883.87 Safari/537.36",
                        "x_forwarded_for": true
                    },
                    "response": {
                        "status": 200
                    }
                },
                "annotations": {
                    "gameid": "M0TTEU23"
                },
                "subsegments": [
                    {
                        "id": "21cfdfd9065bac32",
                        "start_time": 1489536656.77,
                        "end_time": 1489536656.775,
                        "name": "DynamoDB",
                        "namespace": "aws",
                        "http": {
                            "response": {
                                "content_length": 226,
                                "status": 200
                            }
                        },
                        "aws": {
                            "consistent_read": false,
                            "table_name": "scorekeep-game",
                            "operation": "GetItem",
                            "request_id": "O98S14KEI0FG06DMRNN7I8F64BVV4KQNSO5AEMVJF66Q9ASUAAJG",
                            "resource_names": [
```

Viewing Segment Details

From the trace timeline, choose the name of a segment to view its details. The **Overview** shows information about the request and response.

The **Resources** tab for a segment shows information about the AWS resources running your application and the X-Ray SDK. Use the Amazon EC2, AWS Elastic Beanstalk, or Amazon ECS plugin for the SDK to record service-specific resource information.

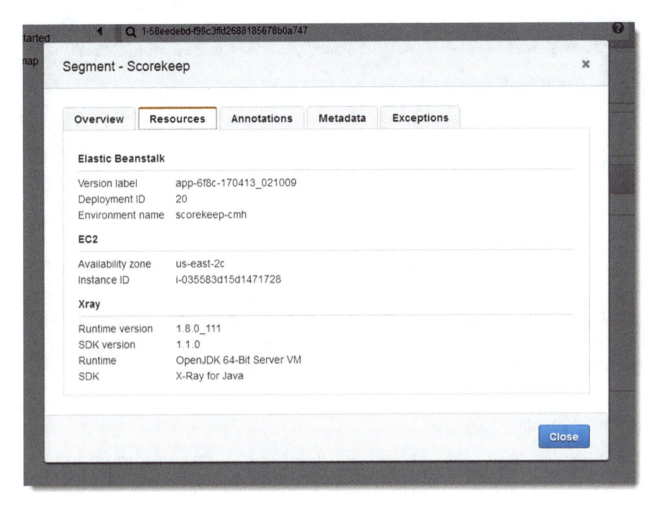

The remaining tabs show **Annotations**, **Metadata**, and **Exceptions** recorded on the segment. Exceptions are captured automatically when thrown from an instrumented request. Annotations and metadata contain additional information that you record by using the methods provided by the SDK.

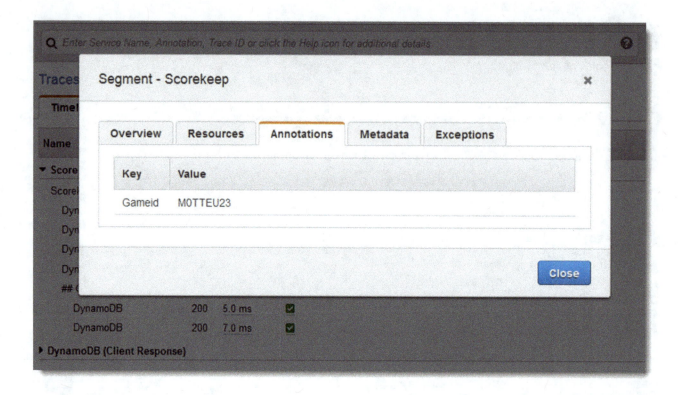

Viewing Subsegment Details

From the trace timeline, choose the name of a segment to view its details. For subsegments generated with instrumented clients, the **Overview** contains information about the request and response from your application's point of view. This example shows a subsegment from an instrumented call to DynamoDB.

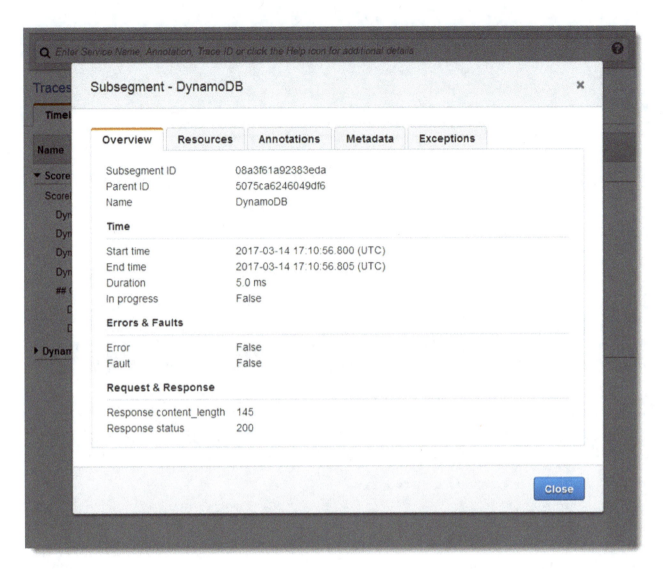

The **Resources** tab for subsegment showing details about the DynamoDB table, operation called, and request ID.

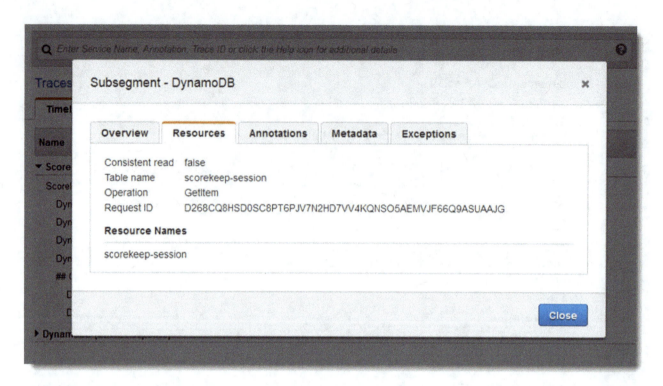

For custom subsegments, the **Overview** shows the name of the subsegment, which you can set to specify the area of the code or function that it records.

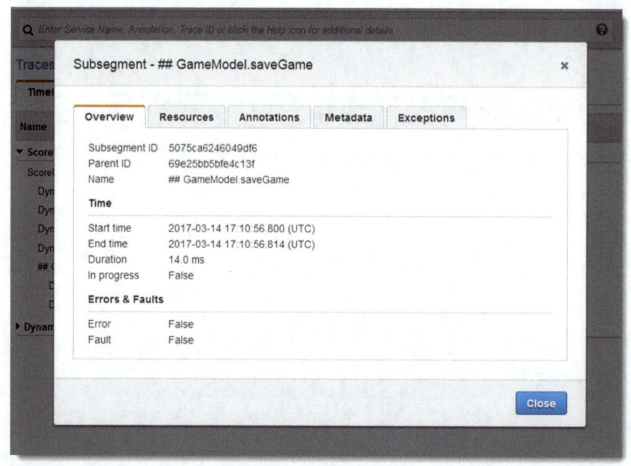

Use custom subsegments to organize subsegments from instrumented clients into groups. You can also record metadata and annotations on subsegments, which can help you debug functions.

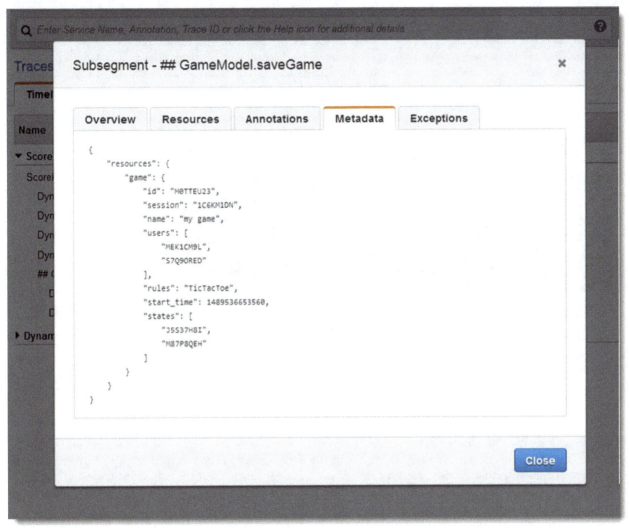

In this example, the application records the state of each `Game` object that it saves to DynamoDB, simply by passing the object into the `putMetadata` method on the subsegment. The X-Ray SDK serializes the object into JSON and adds it to the segment document.

Searching for Traces in the AWS X-Ray Console with Filter Expressions

When you choose a time period of traces to view in the X-Ray console, you might get more results than the console can display. In the top-right corner, the console shows the number of traces that it scanned and, whether there are more traces available. You can narrow the results to just the traces that you want to find by using a **filter expression**.

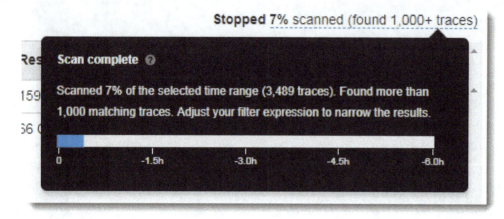

When you choose a node in the service map, the console constructs a filter expression based on the service name of the node, and the types of error present based on your selection. To find traces that show performance issues or that relate to specific requests, you can adjust the expression provided by the console, or create your own. If you add annotations with the X-Ray SDK, you can also filter based on the presence of an annotation key or the value of a key.

Note
If you choose a relative time range in the service map, the console converts it to an absolute start and end time when you choose a node. To ensure that the traces for the node appear in the search results, and avoid scanning times when the node was not active, the time range only includes times when the node sent traces. If you want to search relative to the current time, you can switch back to a relative time range in the traces page and re-scan.

If there are still more results available than the console can show, the console shows you how many traces matched and the number of traces scanned. The percentage shown is the percentage of the selected time frame that was scanned. Narrow your filter expression further, or choose a shorter time frame, to ensure that you see all matching traces represented in the results.

To get the freshest results first, the console starts scanning at the end of the time range and works backwards. If there are a large number of traces, but few results, the console splits the time range into chunks and scans them in parallel. The progress bar shows the parts of the time range that have been scanned.

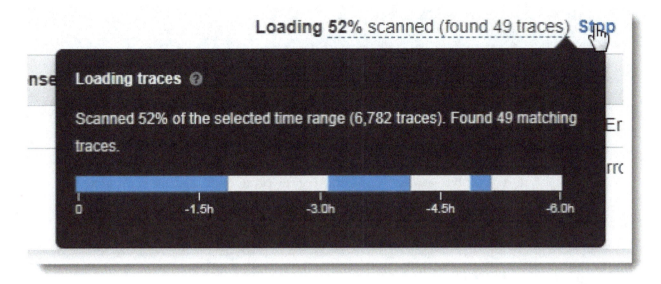

Topics

- Filter Expression Syntax
- Boolean Keywords
- Number Keywords
- String Keywords
- Complex Keywords
- The ID Function

Filter Expression Syntax

Filter expressions can contain a *keyword*, a unary or binary *operator*, and a *value* for comparison.

```
1  keyword operator value
```

Different operators are available for different types of keyword. For example, `responsetime` is a number keyword and can be compared with operators related to numbers.

Example Requests where response time was more than 5 seconds

```
1  responsetime > 5
```

You can combine multiple expressions in a compound expression with the `AND` and `OR` operators.

Example Requests where the total duration was 5 to 8 seconds

```
1  duration >= 5 AND duration <= 8
```

Simple keywords and operators only find issues at the trace level. If an error occurs downstream, but is handled by your application and not returned to the user, a search for `error` will not find it.

To find traces with downstream issues, you can use the complex keywords `service()` and `edge()`. These keywords let you apply a filter expression to all downstream nodes, a single downstream node, or an edge between two nodes. For even more granularity, you can filter services and edges by type with the id() function.

Boolean Keywords

Boolean keywords are either true or false. Use these keywords to find traces that resulted in errors.

Boolean Keywords

- `ok` – Response status code was 2XX Success.
- `error` – Response status code was 4XX Client Error.
- `throttle` – Response status code was *429 Too Many Requests*.
- `fault` – Response status code was 5XX Server Error.
- `partial` – Request has incomplete segments.

Boolean operators find segments where the specified key is `true` or `false`.

Boolean Operators

- `none` – The expression is true if the keyword is true.
- `!` – The expression is true if the keyword is false.
- `=,!=` – Compare the value of the keyword to the string `true` or `false`. Acts the same as the other operators but is more explicit.

Example Response status is 2XX OK

```
1 ok
```

Example Response status is not 2XX OK

```
1 !ok
```

Example Response status is not 2XX OK

```
1 ok = false
```

Number Keywords

Number keywords let you search for requests with a specific response time, duration, or response status.

Number Keywords

- `responsetime` – Time that the server took to send a response.
- `duration` – Total request duration, including all downstream calls.
- `http.status` – Response status code.

Number keywords use standard equality and comparison operators.

Number Operators

- `=,!=` – The keyword is equal to or not equal to a number value.
- `<,<=, >,>=` – The keyword is less than or greater than a number value.

Example Response status is not 200 OK

```
1 http.status != 200
```

Example Request where the total duration was 5 to 8 seconds

```
1 duration >= 5 AND duration <= 8
```

Example Requests that completed successfully in under 3 seconds, including all downstream calls

```
1 ok !partial duration <3
```

String Keywords

String keywords let you find traces with specific text in the request headers, or user IDs.

String Keywords

- `http.url` – Request URL.
- `http.method` – Request method.
- `http.useragent` – Request user agent string.
- `http.clientip` – Requestor's IP address.
- `user` – Value of user field on any segment in the trace.

String operators find values that are equal to or contain specific text. Values must always be specified in quotation marks.

String Operators

- `=,!=` – The keyword is equal to or not equal to a number value.
- `CONTAINS` – The keyword contains a specific string.
- `BEGINSWITH ,ENDSWITH` – The keyword starts or ends with a specific string.

Example User filter

```
1 http.url CONTAINS "/api/game/"
```

To test if a field exists on a trace, regardless of its value, check to see if it contains the empty string.

Example User filter
Find all traces with user IDs.

```
1 user CONTAINS ""
```

Complex Keywords

Complex keywords let you find requests based on service name, edge name, or annotation value. For services and edges, you can specify an additional filter expression that applies to the service or edge. For annotations, you can filter on the value of an annotation with a specific key using boolean, number or string operators.

Complex Keywords

- `service(name) {filter}` – Service with name *name*. Optional curly braces can contain a filter expression that applies to segments created by the service.
- `edge(name) {filter}` – Connection between services *source* and *destination*. Optional curly braces can contain a filter expression that applies to segments on this connection.
- `annotation.key` – Value of annotation with field *key*. The value of an annotation can be a boolean, number, or string, so you can use any of those type's comparison operators. You cannot use this keyword in combination with the `service` or `edge` keywords.

Use the service keyword to find traces for requests that hit a certain node on your service map.

Example Service filter
Requests that included a call to `api.example.com` with a fault (500 series error).

```
1 service("api.example.com") { fault }
```

You can exclude the service name to apply a filter expression to all nodes on your service map.

Example Service filter
Requests that caused a fault anywhere on your service map.

```
1 service() { fault }
```

The edge keyword applies a filter expression to a connection between two nodes.

Example Edge filter

Request where the service `api.example.com` made a call to `backend.example.com` that failed with an error.

```
1 edge("api.example.com", "backend.example.com") { error }
```

You can also use the ! operator with service and edge keywords to exclude a service or edge from the results of another filter expression.

Example Service and request filter

Request where the URL begins with `http://api.example.com/` and contains `/v2/` but does not reach a service named `api.example.com`.

```
1 http.url BEGINSWITH "http://api.example.com/" AND http.url CONTAINS "/v2/" AND !service("api.
    example.com")
```

For annotations, use the comparison operators that correspond to the type of value.

Example Annotation with string value

Requests with an annotation named `gameid` with string value `"817DL6VO"`.

```
1 annotation.gameid = "817DL6VO"
```

Example Annotation with number value

Requests with annotation age with numerical value greater than 29.

```
1 annotation.age > 29
```

The ID Function

When you provide a service name to the `service` or `edge` keywords, you get results for all nodes that have that name. For more precise filtering, you can use the `id` function to specify a service type in addition to a name to distinguish between nodes with the same name.

```
1 id(name: "service-name", type:"service::type")
```

You can use the `id` function in place of a service name in service and edge filters.

```
1 service(id(name: "service-name", type:"service::type")) { filter }
```

```
1 edge(id(name: "service-one", type:"service::type"), id(name: "service-two", type:"service::type
    ")) { filter }
```

For example, the Scorekeep sample application includes an AWS Lambda function named `random-name`. This creates two nodes in the service map, one for the function invocation, and one for the Lambda service.

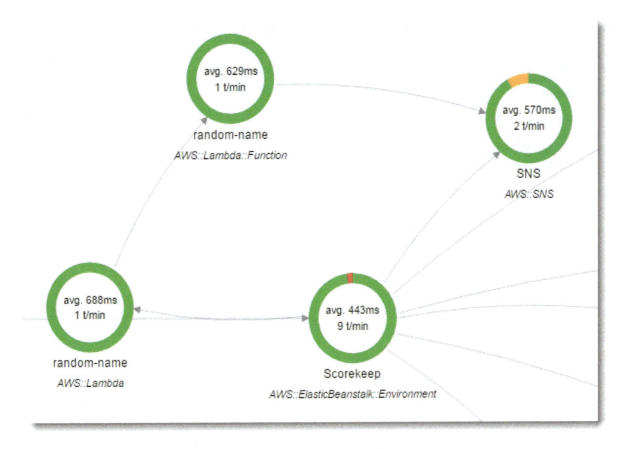

The two nodes have the same name but different types. A standard service filter will find traces for both.

Example Service filter

Requests that include an error on any service named `random-name`.

```
1 service("random-name") { error }
```

Use the `id` function to narrow the search down to errors on the function itself, excluding errors from the service.

Example Service filter with id function

Requests that include an error on a service named `random-name` with type `AWS::Lambda::Function`.

```
1 service(id(name: "random-name", type: "AWS::Lambda::Function")) { error }
```

You can also exclude the name entirely, to search for nodes by type.

Example Service filter with id() function

Requests that include an error on a service with type `AWS::Lambda::Function`.

```
1 service(id(type: "AWS::Lambda::Function")) { error }
```

Deep Linking

You can use routes and queries to deep link into specific traces, or filtered views of traces and the service map.

Console Pages

- Welcome Page – xray/home#/welcome
- Getting Started – xray/home#/getting-started
- Service Map – xray/home#/service-map
- Traces – xray/home#/traces

Traces

You can generate links for timeline, raw, and map views of individual traces.

Trace timeline – xray/home#/traces/trace-id

Raw trace data – xray/home#/traces/trace-id/raw

Example Raw trace data

```
1 https://console.aws.amazon.com/xray/home#/traces/1-57f5498f-d91047849216d0f2ea3b6442/raw
```

Filter Expressions

Link to a filtered list of traces.

Filtered traces view – xray/home#/traces?filter=filter-expression

Example Filter expression

```
1 https://console.aws.amazon.com/xray/home#/traces?filter=service("api.amazon.com") { fault = true
      OR responsetime > 2.5 } AND annotation.foo = "bar"
```

Example Filter expression (URL encoded)

```
1 https://console.aws.amazon.com/xray/home#/traces?filter=service(%22api.amazon.com%22)%20%7B%20
      fault%20%3D%20true%20OR%20responsetime%20%3E%202.5%20%7D%20AND%20annotation.foo%20%3D%20%22
      bar%22
```

For more information on filter expressions, see Searching for Traces in the AWS X-Ray Console with Filter Expressions.

Time Range

Specify a length of time or start and end time in ISO8601 format. Time ranges are in UTC and can be up to 6 hours long.

Length of time – xray/home#/page?timeRange=range-in-minutes

Example Service map for the last hour

```
1 https://console.aws.amazon.com/xray/home#/service-map?timeRange=PT1H
```

Start and end time – xray/home#/page?timeRange=start~end

Example Time range accurate to seconds

```
1 https://console.aws.amazon.com/xray/home#/traces?timeRange=2018-3-01T16:00:00~2018-3-01T22:00:00
```

Example Time range accurate to minutes

```
1 https://console.aws.amazon.com/xray/home#/traces?timeRange=2018-3-01T16:00~2018-3-01T22:00
```

Region

Specify a region to link to pages in that region. If you don't specify a region, the console redirects you to the last visited region.

Region – xray/home?region=region#/page

Example Service map in Oregon (us-west-2)

```
1 https://console.aws.amazon.com/xray/home?region=us-west-2#/service-map
```

When you include a region with other query parameters, the region query goes before the hash, and the X-Ray-specific queries go after the page name.

Example Service map for the last hour in Oregon (us-west-2)

```
1 https://console.aws.amazon.com/xray/home?region=us-west-2#/service-map?timeRange=PT1H
```

Combined

Example Recent traces with duration filter

```
1 https://console.aws.amazon.com/xray/home#/traces?timeRange=PT15M&filter=duration%20%3E%3D%205%20
    AND%20duration%20%3C%3D%208
```

Output

- Page – Traces
- Time Range – Last 15 minutes
- Filter – duration >= 5 AND duration <= 8

Using Latency Histograms in the AWS X-Ray Console

When you select a node or edge on an AWS X-Ray service map, the X-Ray console shows a latency distribution histogram. Latency is the amount of time between when a request starts and when it completes. A histogram shows a distribution of latencies. It shows duration on the x-axis, and the percentage of requests that match each duration on the y-axis.

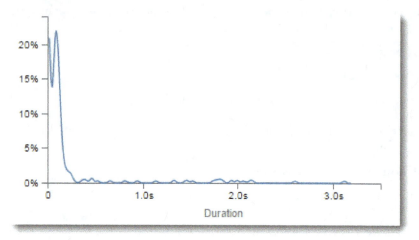

This histogram shows a service that completes most requests in less than 300 ms. A small percentage of requests take up to 2 seconds, and a few outliers take more time.

Service histograms and edge histograms provide a visual representation of latency from the viewpoint of a service or requester.

- Choose a *service node* by clicking the circle. X-Ray shows a histogram for requests served by the service. The latencies are those recorded by the service, and do not include any network latency between the service and the requester.
- Choose an *edge* by clicking the line or arrow tip of the edge between two services. X-Ray shows a histogram for requests from the requester that were served by the downstream service. The latencies are those recorded by the requester, and include latency in the network connection between the two services.

To interpret the **Service details** panel histogram, you can look for values that differ the most from the majority of values in the histogram. These *outliers* can be seen as peaks or spikes in the histogram, and you can view the traces for a specific area to investigate what's going on.

To view traces filtered by latency, select a range on the histogram. Click where you want to start the selection and drag from left to right to highlight a range of latencies to include in the trace filter.

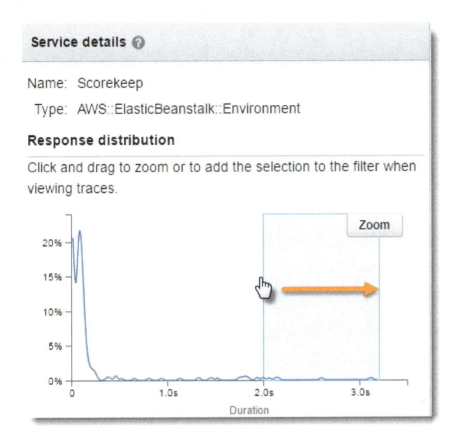

After selecting a range, you can choose **Zoom** to view just that portion of the histogram and refine your selection.

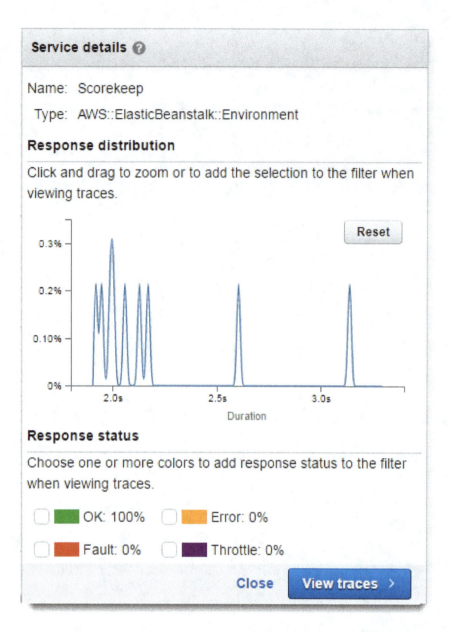

Once you have the focus set to the area you're interested in, choose **View traces**.

AWS X-Ray API

The X-Ray API provides access to all X-Ray functionality through the AWS SDK, AWS Command Line Interface, or directly over HTTPS. The X-Ray API Reference documents input parameters each API action, and the fields and data types that they return.

You can use the AWS SDK to develop programs that use the X-Ray API. The X-Ray console and X-Ray daemon both use the AWS SDK to communicate with X-Ray. The AWS SDK for each language has a reference document for classes and methods that map to X-Ray API actions and types.

AWS SDK References

- **Java** – AWS SDK for Java
- **JavaScript** – AWS SDK for JavaScript
- **.NET** – AWS SDK for .NET
- **Ruby** – AWS SDK for Ruby
- **Go** – AWS SDK for Go
- **PHP** – AWS SDK for PHP
- **Python** – AWS SDK for Python (Boto)

The AWS Command Line Interface is a command line tool that uses the SDK for Python to call AWS APIs. When you are first learning an AWS API, the AWS CLI provides an easy way to explore the available parameters and view the service output in JSON or text form.

See the AWS CLI Command Reference for details on `aws xray` subcommands.

Topics

- Using the AWS X-Ray API with the AWS CLI
- Sending Trace Data to AWS X-Ray
- Getting Data from AWS X-Ray
- AWS X-Ray Segment Documents

Using the AWS X-Ray API with the AWS CLI

The AWS CLI lets your access the X-Ray service directly and use the same APIs that the X-Ray console uses to retrieve the service graph and raw traces data. The sample application includes scripts that show how to use these APIs with the AWS CLI.

Prerequisites

This tutorial uses the Scorekeep sample application and included scripts to generate tracing data and a service map. Follow the instructions in the getting started tutorial to launch the application.

This tutorial uses the AWS CLI to show basic use of the X-Ray API. The AWS CLI, available for Windows, Linux, and OS-X, provides command line access to the public APIs for all AWS services.

Scripts included to test the sample application uses cURL to send traffic to the API and jq to parse the output. You can download the jq executable from stedolan.github.io, and the curl executable from https://curl.haxx.se/download.html. Most Linux and OS X installations include cURL.

Generate Trace Data

The web app continues to generate traffic to the API every few seconds while the game is in-progress, but only generates one type of request. Use the test-api.sh script to run end to end scenarios and generate more diverse trace data while you test the API.

To use the test-api.sh script

1. Open the Elastic Beanstalk console.

2. Navigate to the management console for your environment.

3. Copy the environment **URL** from the page header.

4. Open bin/test-api.sh and replace the value for API with your environment's URL.

```
1  #!/bin/bash
2  API=scorekeep.9hbtbm23t2.us-west-2.elasticbeanstalk.com
```

5. Run the script to generate traffic to the API.

```
1  ~/debugger-tutorial$ ./bin/test-api.sh
2  Creating users,
3  session,
4  game,
5  configuring game,
6  playing game,
7  ending game,
8  game complete.
9  {"id":"MTBP8BAS","session":"HUF6IT64","name":"tic-tac-toe-test","users":["QFF3HBGM","
     KL6JR98D"],"rules":"102","startTime":1476314241,"endTime":1476314245,"states":["
     JQVLEOM2","D67QLPIC","VF9BM9NC","OEAA6GK9","2A705073","1U2LFTLJ","HUKIDD70","BAN1C8FI
     ","G3UDJTUF","AB70HVEV"],"moves":["BS8F8LQ","4MTTSPKP","4630ETES","SVEBCL3N","N7CQ1GHP
     ","0840NEPD","EG4BPROQ","V4BLIDJ3","9RL3NPMV"]}
```

Use the X-Ray API

The AWS CLI provides commands for all of the API actions that X-Ray provides, including http://docs.aws.amazon.com/xray/latest/api/API_GetServiceGraph.html and http://docs.aws.amazon.com/xray/latest/api/API_GetTraceSummaries.html. See the AWS X-Ray API Reference for more information on all of the supported actions and the data types that they use.

Example bin/service-graph.sh

```
EPOCH=$(date +%s)
aws xray get-service-graph --start-time $(($EPOCH-600)) --end-time $EPOCH
```

The script retrieves a service graph for the last 10 minutes.

```
~/eb-java-scorekeep$ ./bin/service-graph.sh | less
{
    "StartTime": 1479068648.0,
    "Services": [
        {
            "StartTime": 1479068648.0,
            "ReferenceId": 0,
            "State": "unknown",
            "EndTime": 1479068651.0,
            "Type": "client",
            "Edges": [
                {
                    "StartTime": 1479068648.0,
                    "ReferenceId": 1,
                    "SummaryStatistics": {
                        "ErrorStatistics": {
                            "ThrottleCount": 0,
                            "TotalCount": 0,
                            "OtherCount": 0
                        },
                        "FaultStatistics": {
                            "TotalCount": 0,
                            "OtherCount": 0
                        },
                        "TotalCount": 2,
                        "OkCount": 2,
                        "TotalResponseTime": 0.054000139236450195
                    },
                    "EndTime": 1479068651.0,
                    "Aliases": []
                }
            ]
        },
        {
            "StartTime": 1479068648.0,
            "Names": [
                "scorekeep.elasticbeanstalk.com"
            ],
            "ReferenceId": 1,
            "State": "active",
            "EndTime": 1479068651.0,
            "Root": true,
```

```
43          "Name": "scorekeep.elasticbeanstalk.com",
44 ...
```

Example bin/trace-urls.sh

```
1 EPOCH=$(date +%s)
2 aws xray get-trace-summaries --start-time $(($EPOCH-120)) --end-time $(($EPOCH-60)) --query '
    TraceSummaries[*].Http.HttpURL'
```

The script retrieves the URLs of traces generated between one and two minutes ago.

```
1 ~/eb-java-scorekeep$ ./bin/trace-urls.sh
2 [
3     "http://scorekeep.elasticbeanstalk.com/api/game/6Q0UE1DG/5FGLM9U3/endtime/1479069438",
4     "http://scorekeep.elasticbeanstalk.com/api/session/KH4341QH",
5     "http://scorekeep.elasticbeanstalk.com/api/game/GLQBJ3K5/153AHDIA",
6     "http://scorekeep.elasticbeanstalk.com/api/game/VPDL672J/G2V41HM6/endtime/1479069466"
7 ]
```

Example bin/full-traces.sh

```
1 EPOCH=$(date +%s)
2 TRACEIDS=$(aws xray get-trace-summaries --start-time $(($EPOCH-120)) --end-time $(($EPOCH-60))
    --query 'TraceSummaries[*].Id' --output text)
3 aws xray batch-get-traces --trace-ids $TRACEIDS --query 'Traces[*]'
```

The script retrieves full traces generated between one and two minutes ago.

```
1 ~/eb-java-scorekeep$ ./bin/full-traces.sh | less
2 [
3   {
4     "Segments": [
5       {
6         "Id": "3f212bc237bafd5d",
7         "Document": "{\"id\":\"3f212bc237bafd5d\",\"name\":\"DynamoDB\",\"trace_id
            \":\"1-5828d9f2-a90669393f4343211bc1cf75\",\"start_time\":1.479072242459E9
            ,\"end_time\":1.479072242477E9,\"parent_id\":\"72a08dcf87991ca9\",\"http
            \":{\"response\":{\"content_length\":60,\"status\":200}},\"inferred\":true
            ,\"aws\":{\"consistent_read\":false,\"table_name\":\"scorekeep-session-xray
            \",\"operation\":\"GetItem\",\"request_id\":\"
            QAKE0S8DD0LJM245KAOPMA746BVV4KQNSO5AEMVJF66Q9ASUAAJG\",\"resource_names
            \":[\"scorekeep-session-xray\"]},\"origin\":\"AWS::DynamoDB::Table\"}"
8       },
9       {
10        "Id": "309e355f1148347f",
11        "Document": "{\"id\":\"309e355f1148347f\",\"name\":\"DynamoDB\",\"trace_id
            \":\"1-5828d9f2-a90669393f4343211bc1cf75\",\"start_time\":1.479072242477E9
            ,\"end_time\":1.479072242494E9,\"parent_id\":\"37f14ef837f00022\",\"http
            \":{\"response\":{\"content_length\":606,\"status\":200}},\"inferred\":true
            ,\"aws\":{\"table_name\":\"scorekeep-game-xray\",\"operation\":\"UpdateItem
            \",\"request_id\":\"388GEROC4PCA6D59ED3CTI5EEJVV4KQNSO5AEMVJF66Q9ASUAAJG
            \",\"resource_names\":[\"scorekeep-game-xray\"]},\"origin\":\"AWS::DynamoDB
            ::Table\"}"
12      }
13    ],
14    "Id": "1-5828d9f2-a90669393f4343211bc1cf75",
15    "Duration": 0.05099987983703613
```

```
16     }
17 ...
```

Cleanup

Terminate your Elastic Beanstalk environment to shut down the Amazon EC2 instances, DynamoDB tables and other resources.

To terminate your Elastic Beanstalk environment

1. Open the Elastic Beanstalk console.

2. Navigate to the management console for your environment.

3. Choose **Actions**.

4. Choose **Terminate Environment**.

5. Choose **Terminate**.

Trace data is automatically deleted from X-Ray after 30 days.

Sending Trace Data to AWS X-Ray

You can send trace data to X-Ray in the form of segment documents. A segment document is a JSON formatted string that contains information about the work that your application does in service of a request. Your application can record data about the work that it does itself in segments, or work that uses downstream services and resources in subsegments.

Segments record information about the work that your application does. A segment, at a minimum, records the time spent on a task, a name, and two IDs. The trace ID tracks the request as it travels between services. The segment ID tracks the work done for the request by a single service.

Example Minimal complete segment

```
1 {
2   "name" : "Scorekeep",
3   "id" : "70de5b6f19ff9a0a",
4   "start_time" : 1.478293361271E9,
5   "trace_id" : "1-581cf771-a006649127e371903a2de979",
6   "end_time" : 1.478293361449E9
7 }
```

When a request is received, you can send an in-progress segment as a placeholder until the request is completed.

Example In-progress segment

```
1 {
2   "name" : "Scorekeep",
3   "id" : "70de5b6f19ff9a0b",
4   "start_time" : 1.478293361271E9,
5   "trace_id" : "1-581cf771-a006649127e371903a2de979",""
6   in_progress: true
7 }
```

You can send segments to X-Ray directly, with `PutTraceSegments`, or through the X-Ray daemon.

Most applications call other services or access resources with the AWS SDK. Record information about downstream calls in *subsegments*. X-Ray uses subsegments to identify downstream services that don't send segments and create entries for them on the service graph.

A subsegment can be embedded in a full segment document, or sent separately. Send subsegments separately to asynchronously trace downstream calls for long-running requests, or to avoid exceeding the maximum segment document size (64 kB).

Example Subsegment
A subsegment has a `type` of `subsegment` and a `parent_id` that identifies the parent segment.

```
1 {
2   "name" : "www2.example.com",
3   "id" : "70de5b6f19ff9a0c",
4   "start_time" : 1.478293361271E9,
5   "trace_id" : "1-581cf771-a006649127e371903a2de979"""
6   end_time : 1.478293361449E9,""
7   type : ""subsegment,""
8   parent_id : "70"de5b6f19ff9a0b
9 }
```

For more information on the fields and values that you can include in segments and subsegments, see AWS X-Ray Segment Documents.

Topics

- Generating Trace IDs
- Using PutTraceSegments
- Sending Segment Documents to the X-Ray Daemon

Generating Trace IDs

To send data to X-Ray, you need to generate a unique trace ID for each request. Trace IDs must meet the following requirements.

Trace ID Format

A `trace_id` consists of three numbers separated by hyphens. For example, `1-58406520-a006649127e371903a2de979`. This includes:

- The version number, that is, `1`.

- The time of the original request, in Unix epoch time, in **8 hexadecimal digits**.

  For example, 10:00AM December 1st, 2016 PST in epoch time is 1480615200 seconds, or 58406520 in hexadecimal.

- A 96-bit identifier for the trace, globally unique, in **24 hexadecimal digits**.

You can write a script to generate trace IDs for testing. Here are two examples.

Python

```
1 import time
2 import os
3 import binascii
4
5 START_TIME = time.time()
6 HEX=hex(int(START_TIME))[2:]
7 TRACE_ID="1-" + HEX + "-" + binascii.b2a_hex(os.urandom(12))
```

Bash

```
1 START_TIME=$(date +%s)
2 HEX_TIME=$(printf '%x\n' $START_TIME)
3 GUID=$(dd if=/dev/random bs=12 count=1 2>/dev/null | od -An -tx1 | tr -d ' \t\n')
4 TRACE_ID="1-$HEX_TIME-$GUID"
```

See the Scorekeep sample application for scripts that create trace IDs and send segments to the X-Ray daemon.

- Python – https://github.com/awslabs/eb-java-scorekeep/blob/xray/bin/xray_start.py
- Bash – https://github.com/awslabs/eb-java-scorekeep/blob/xray/bin/xray_start.sh

Using PutTraceSegments

You can upload segment documents with the http://docs.aws.amazon.com/xray/latest/api/API_PutTraceSegments.html API. The API has a single parameter, `TraceSegmentDocuments`, that takes a list of JSON segment documents.

With the AWS CLI, use the `aws xray put-trace-segments` command to send segment documents directly to X-Ray.

```
1 $ DOC='{"trace_id": "1-5960082b-ab52431b496add878434aa25", "id": "6226467e3f845502", "start_time
    ": 1498082657.37518, "end_time": 1498082695.4042, "name": "test.elasticbeanstalk.com"}'
2 $ aws xray put-trace-segments --trace-segment-documents $DOC
```

```
3 {
4     "UnprocessedTraceSegments": []
5 }
```

Note

Windows Command Processor and Windows PowerShell have different requirements for quoting and escaping quotes in JSON strings. See Quoting Strings in the AWS CLI User Guide for details.

The output lists any segments that failed processing. For example, if the date in the trace ID is too far in the past, you see an error like the following.

```
1 {
2     "UnprocessedTraceSegments": [
3         {
4             "ErrorCode": "InvalidTraceId",
5             "Message": "Invalid segment. ErrorCode: InvalidTraceId",
6             "Id": "6226467e3f845502"
7         }
8     ]
9 }
```

You can pass multiple segment documents at the same time, separated by spaces.

```
1 $ aws xray put-trace-segments --trace-segment-documents $DOC1 $DOC2
```

Sending Segment Documents to the X-Ray Daemon

Instead of sending segment documents to the X-Ray API, you can send segments and subsegments to the X-Ray daemon, which will buffer them and upload to the X-Ray API in batches. The X-Ray SDK sends segment documents to the daemon to avoid making calls to AWS directly.

Note

See Running the X-Ray Daemon Locally for instructions on running the daemon.

Send the segment in JSON over UDP port 2000, prepended by the daemon header, {"format": "json", "version": 1}\n

```
1 {"format": "json", "version": 1}\n{"trace_id": "1-5759e988-bd862e3fe1be46a994272793", "id": "
    defdfd9912dc5a56", "start_time": 1461096053.37518, "end_time": 1461096053.4042, "name": "
    test.elasticbeanstalk.com"}
```

On Linux, you can send segment documents to the daemon from a Bash terminal. Save the header and segment document to a text file and pipe it to /dev/udp with cat.

```
1 $ cat segment.txt > /dev/udp/127.0.0.1/2000
```

Example segment.txt

```
1 {"format": "json", "version": 1}
2 {"trace_id": "1-594aed87-ad72e26896b3f9d3a27054bb", "id": "6226467e3f845502", "start_time":
    1498082657.37518, "end_time": 1498082695.4042, "name": "test.elasticbeanstalk.com"}
```

Check the daemon log to verify that it sent the segment to X-Ray.

```
1 2017-07-07T01:57:24Z [Debug] processor: sending partial batch
2 2017-07-07T01:57:24Z [Debug] processor: segment batch size: 1. capacity: 50
3 2017-07-07T01:57:24Z [Info] Successfully sent batch of 1 segments (0.020 seconds)
```

Getting Data from AWS X-Ray

AWS X-Ray processes the trace data that you send to it to generate full traces, trace summaries, and service graphs in JSON. You can retrieve the generated data directly from the API with the AWS CLI.

Topics

- Retrieving the Service Graph
- Retrieving Traces

Retrieving the Service Graph

You can use the http://docs.aws.amazon.com/xray/latest/api/API_GetServiceGraph.html API to retrieve the JSON service graph. The API requires a start time and end time, which you can calculate from a Linux terminal with the `date` command.

```
1 $ date +%s
2 1499394617
```

`date +%s` prints a date in seconds. Use this number as an end time and subtract time from it to get a start time.

Example Script to retrieve a service graph for the last 10 minutes

```
1 EPOCH=$(date +%s)
2 aws xray get-service-graph --start-time $(($EPOCH-600)) --end-time $EPOCH
```

Retrieving Traces

You can use the http://docs.aws.amazon.com/xray/latest/api/API_GetTraceSummaries.html API to get a list of trace summaries. Trace summaries include information that you can use to identify traces that you want to download in full, including annotations, request and response information, and IDs.

Use the `aws xray get-trace-summaries` command to get a list of trace summaries. The following commands get a list of trace summaries from between 1 and 2 minutes in the past.

```
1 $ EPOCH=$(date +%s)
2 $ aws xray get-trace-summaries --start-time $(($EPOCH-120)) --end-time $(($EPOCH-60))
```

```
1  {
2      "TraceSummaries": [
3          {
4              "HasError": false,
5              "Http": {
6                  "HttpStatus": 200,
7                  "ClientIp": "205.255.255.183",
8                  "HttpURL": "http://scorekeep.elasticbeanstalk.com/api/session",
9                  "UserAgent": "Mozilla/5.0 (Windows NT 6.1; Win64; x64) AppleWebKit/537.36 (KHTML
                       , like Gecko) Chrome/59.0.3071.115 Safari/537.36",
10                 "HttpMethod": "POST"
11             },
12             "Users": [],
13             "HasFault": false,
14             "Annotations": {},
15             "ResponseTime": 0.084,
16             "Duration": 0.084,
```

```
17              "Id": "1-59602606-a43a1ac52fc7ee0eea12a82c",
18              "HasThrottle": false
19          },
20          {
21              "HasError": false,
22              "Http": {
23                  "HttpStatus": 200,
24                  "ClientIp": "205.255.255.183",
25                  "HttpURL": "http://scorekeep.elasticbeanstalk.com/api/user",
26                  "UserAgent": "Mozilla/5.0 (Windows NT 6.1; Win64; x64) AppleWebKit/537.36 (KHTML
                        , like Gecko) Chrome/59.0.3071.115 Safari/537.36",
27                  "HttpMethod": "POST"
28              },
29              "Users": [
30                  {
31                      "UserName": "5M388M1E"
32                  }
33              ],
34              "HasFault": false,
35              "Annotations": {
36                  "UserID": [
37                      {
38                          "AnnotationValue": {
39                              "StringValue": "5M388M1E"
40                          }
41                      }
42                  ],
43                  "Name": [
44                      {
45                          "AnnotationValue": {
46                              "StringValue": "Ola"
47                          }
48                      }
49                  ]
50              },
51              "ResponseTime": 3.232,
52              "Duration": 3.232,
53              "Id": "1-59602603-23fc5b688855d396af79b496",
54              "HasThrottle": false
55          }
56      ],
57      "ApproximateTime": 1499473304.0,
58      "TracesProcessedCount": 2
59  }
```

Use the trace ID from the output to retrieve a full trace with the http://docs.aws.amazon.com/xray/latest/api/API_BatchGetTraces.html API.

```
1 $ aws xray batch-get-traces --trace-ids 1-596025b4-7170afe49f7aa708b1dd4a6b
```

```
1 {
2     "Traces": [
3         {
4             "Duration": 3.232,
5             "Segments": [
```

```
6          {
7              "Document": "{\"id\":\"1fb07842d944e714\",\"name\":\"random-name\",\"
                   start_time\":1.499473411677E9,\"end_time\":1.499473414572E9,\"parent_id
                   \":\"0c544c1b1bbff948\",\"http\":{\"response\":{\"status\":200}},\"aws
                   \":{\"request_id\":\"ac086670-6373-11e7-a174-f31b3397f190\"},\"trace_id
                   \":\"1-59602603-23fc5b688855d396af79b496\",\"origin\":\"AWS::Lambda\",\"
                   resource_arn\":\"arn:aws:lambda:us-west-2:123456789012:function:random-
                   name\"}",
8              "Id": "1fb07842d944e714"
9          },
10         {
11             "Document": "{\"id\":\"194fcc8747581230\",\"name\":\"Scorekeep\",\"
                   start_time\":1.499473411562E9,\"end_time\":1.499473414794E9,\"http\":{\"
                   request\":{\"url\":\"http://scorekeep.elasticbeanstalk.com/api/user\",\"
                   method\":\"POST\",\"user_agent\":\"Mozilla/5.0 (Windows NT 6.1; Win64;
                   x64) AppleWebKit/537.36 (KHTML, like Gecko) Chrome/59.0.3071.115 Safari
                   /537.36\",\"client_ip\":\"205.251.233.183\"},\"response\":{\"status
                   \":200}},\"aws\":{\"elastic_beanstalk\":{\"version_label\":\"app-abb9
                   -170708_002045\",\"deployment_id\":406,\"environment_name\":\"scorekeep-
                   dev\"},\"ec2\":{\"availability_zone\":\"us-west-2c\",\"instance_id\":\"i
                   -0cd9e448944061b4a\"},\"xray\":{\"sdk_version\":\"1.1.2\",\"sdk\":\"X-
                   Ray for Java\"}},\"service\":{},\"trace_id\":\"1-59602603-23
                   fc5b688855d396af79b496\",\"user\":\"5M388M1E\",\"origin\":\"AWS::
                   ElasticBeanstalk::Environment\",\"subsegments\":[{\"id\":\"0
                   c544c1b1bbff948\",\"name\":\"Lambda\",\"start_time\":1.499473411629E9,\"
                   end_time\":1.499473414572E9,\"http\":{\"response\":{\"status\":200,\"
                   content_length\":14}},\"aws\":{\"log_type\":\"None\",\"status_code
                   \":200,\"function_name\":\"random-name\",\"invocation_type\":\"
                   RequestResponse\",\"operation\":\"Invoke\",\"request_id\":\"ac086670
                   -6373-11e7-a174-f31b3397f190\",\"resource_names\":[\"random-name\"]},\"
                   namespace\":\"aws\"},{\"id\":\"071684f2e555e571\",\"name\":\"##
                   UserModel.saveUser\",\"start_time\":1.499473414581E9,\"end_time
                   \":1.499473414769E9,\"metadata\":{\"debug\":{\"test\":\"Metadata string
                   from UserModel.saveUser\"}},\"subsegments\":[{\"id\":\"4cd3f10b76c624b4
                   \",\"name\":\"DynamoDB\",\"start_time\":1.49947341469E9,\"end_time
                   \":1.499473414769E9,\"http\":{\"response\":{\"status\":200,\"
                   content_length\":57}},\"aws\":{\"table_name\":\"scorekeep-user\",\"
                   operation\":\"UpdateItem\",\"request_id\":\"
                   MFQ8CGJ3JTDDVVVASUAAJGQ6NJ82F738BOB4KQNSO5AEMVJF66Q9\",\"resource_names
                   \":[\"scorekeep-user\"]},\"namespace\":\"aws\"}]}]}",
12             "Id": "194fcc8747581230"
13         },
14         {
15             "Document": "{\"id\":\"00f91aa01f4984fd\",\"name\":\"random-name\",\"
                   start_time\":1.49947341283E9,\"end_time\":1.49947341457E9,\"parent_id
                   \":\"1fb07842d944e714\",\"aws\":{\"function_arn\":\"arn:aws:lambda:us-
                   west-2:123456789012:function:random-name\",\"resource_names\":[\"random-
                   name\"],\"account_id\":\"123456789012\"},\"trace_id\":\"1-59602603-23
                   fc5b688855d396af79b496\",\"origin\":\"AWS::Lambda::Function\",\"
                   subsegments\":[{\"id\":\"e6d2fe619f827804\",\"name\":\"annotations\",\"
                   start_time\":1.499473413012E9,\"end_time\":1.499473413069E9,\"
                   annotations\":{\"UserID\":\"5M388M1E\",\"Name\":\"Ola\"}},{\"id\":\"
                   b29b548af4d54a0f\",\"name\":\"SNS\",\"start_time\":1.499473413112E9,\"
                   end_time\":1.499473414071E9,\"http\":{\"response\":{\"status\":200}},\"
```

```
                       aws\":{\"operation\":\"Publish\",\"region\":\"us-west-2\",\"request_id
                       \":\"a2137970-f6fc-5029-83e8-28aadeb99198\",\"retries\":0,\"topic_arn
                       \":\"arn:aws:sns:us-west-2:123456789012:awseb-e-ruag3jyweb-stack-
                       NotificationTopic-6B829NT9V5O9\"},\"namespace\":\"aws\"},{\"id\":\"2279
                       c0030c955e52\",\"name\":\"Initialization\",\"start_time\":1.499473412064
                       E9,\"end_time\":1.499473412819E9,\"aws\":{\"function_arn\":\"arn:aws:
                       lambda:us-west-2:123456789012:function:random-name\"}}]}",
16                    "Id": "00f91aa01f4984fd"
17               },
18               {
19                    "Document": "{\"id\":\"17ba309b32c7fbaf\",\"name\":\"DynamoDB\",\"start_time
                       \":1.49947341469E9,\"end_time\":1.499473414769E9,\"parent_id\":\"4
                       cd3f10b76c624b4\",\"inferred\":true,\"http\":{\"response\":{\"status
                       \":200,\"content_length\":57}},\"aws\":{\"table_name\":\"scorekeep-user
                       \",\"operation\":\"UpdateItem\",\"request_id\":\"
                       MFQ8CGJ3JTDDVVVASUAAJGQ6NJ82F738BOB4KQNSO5AEMVJF66Q9\",\"resource_names
                       \":[\"scorekeep-user\"]},\"trace_id\":\"1-59602603-23
                       fc5b688855d396af79b496\",\"origin\":\"AWS::DynamoDB::Table\"}",
20                    "Id": "17ba309b32c7fbaf"
21               },
22               {
23                    "Document": "{\"id\":\"1ee3c4a523f89ca5\",\"name\":\"SNS\",\"start_time
                       \":1.499473413112E9,\"end_time\":1.499473414071E9,\"parent_id\":\"
                       b29b548af4d54a0f\",\"inferred\":true,\"http\":{\"response\":{\"status
                       \":200}},\"aws\":{\"operation\":\"Publish\",\"region\":\"us-west-2\",\"
                       request_id\":\"a2137970-f6fc-5029-83e8-28aadeb99198\",\"retries\":0,\"
                       topic_arn\":\"arn:aws:sns:us-west-2:123456789012:awseb-e-ruag3jyweb-
                       stack-NotificationTopic-6B829NT9V5O9\"},\"trace_id\":\"1-59602603-23
                       fc5b688855d396af79b496\",\"origin\":\"AWS::SNS\"}",
24                    "Id": "1ee3c4a523f89ca5"
25               }
26          ],
27          "Id": "1-59602603-23fc5b688855d396af79b496"
28     }
29   ],
30   "UnprocessedTraceIds": []
31 }
```

The full trace includes a document for each segment, compiled from all of the segment documents received with the same trace ID. These documents don't represent the data as it was sent to X-Ray by your application. Instead, they represent the processed documents generated by the X-Ray service. X-Ray creates the full trace document by compiling segment documents sent by your application, and removing data that doesn't comply with the segment document schema.

X-Ray also creates *inferred segments* for downstream calls to services that don't send segments themselves. For example, when you call DynamoDB with an instrumented client, the X-Ray SDK records a subsegment with details about the call from its point of view. However, DynamoDB doesn't send a corresponding segment. X-Ray uses the information in the subsegment to create an inferred segment to represent the DynamoDB resource in the service map, and adds it to the trace document.

To get multiple traces from the API, you need a list of trace IDs, which you can extract from the output of `get-trace-summaries` with an AWS CLI query. Redirect the list to the intput of `batch-get-traces` to get full traces for a specific time period.

Example Script to get full traces for a one minute period

```
1 EPOCH=$(date +%s)
```

```
2 TRACEIDS=$(aws xray get-trace-summaries --start-time $(($EPOCH-120)) --end-time $(($EPOCH-60))
    --query 'TraceSummaries[*].Id' --output text)
3 aws xray batch-get-traces --trace-ids $TRACEIDS --query 'Traces[*]'
```

AWS X-Ray Segment Documents

A **trace segment** is a JSON representation of a request that your application serves. A trace segment records information about the original request, information about the work that your application does locally, and **subsegments** with information about downstream calls that your application makes to AWS resources, HTTP APIs, and SQL databases.

A **segment document** conveys information about a segment to X-Ray. A segment document can be up to 64 kB and contain a whole segment with subsegments, a fragment of a segment that indicates that a request is in progress, or a single subsegment that is sent separately. You can send segment documents directly to X-Ray by using the http://docs.aws.amazon.com/xray/latest/api/API_PutTraceSegments.html API.

X-Ray compiles and processes segment documents to generate queryable **trace summaries** and **full traces** that you can access by using the http://docs.aws.amazon.com/xray/latest/api/API_GetTraceSummaries.html and http://docs.aws.amazon.com/xray/latest/api/API_BatchGetTraces.html APIs, respectively. In addition to the segments and subsegments that you send to X-Ray, the service uses information in subsegments to generate **inferred segments** and adds them to the full trace. Inferred segments represent downstream services and resources in the service map.

X-Ray provides a **JSON schema** for segment documents. You can download the schema here: xray-segmentdocument-schema-v1.0.0. The fields and objects listed in the schema are described in more detail in the following sections.

A subset of segment fields are indexed by X-Ray for use with filter expressions. For example, if you set the `user` field on a segment to a unique identifier, you can search for segments associated with specific users in the X-Ray console or by using the `GetTraceSummaries` API. For more information, see Searching for Traces in the AWS X-Ray Console with Filter Expressions.

When you instrument your application with the X-Ray SDK, the SDK generates segment documents for you. Instead of sending segment documents directly to X-Ray, the SDK transmits them over a local UDP port to the X-Ray daemon. For more information, see Sending Segment Documents to the X-Ray Daemon.

Topics

- Segment Fields
- Subsegments
- HTTP Request Data
- Annotations
- Metadata
- AWS Resource Data
- Errors and Exceptions
- SQL Queries

Segment Fields

A segment records tracing information about a request that your application serves. At a minimum, a segment records the name, ID, start time, trace ID, and end time of the request.

Example Minimal Complete Segment

```
1 {
2   "name" : "example.com",
3   "id" : "70de5b6f19ff9a0a",
4   "start_time" : 1.478293361271E9,
5   "trace_id" : "1-581cf771-a006649127e371903a2de979",
6   "end_time" : 1.478293361449E9
7 }
```

74

The following fields are required, or conditionally required, for segments.

Note

Values must be strings (up to 250 characters) unless noted otherwise.

Required Segment Fields

- `name` – The logical name of the service that handled the request, up to **200 characters**. For example, your application's name or domain name. Names can contain Unicode letters, numbers, and whitespace, and the following symbols: _, ., :, /, %, &, #, =, +, \, -, @
- `id` – A 64-bit identifier for the segment, unique among segments in the same trace, in **16 hexadecimal digits**.
- `trace_id` – A unique identifier that connects all segments and subsegments originating from a single client request.

Trace ID Format

A `trace_id` consists of three numbers separated by hyphens. For example, 1-58406520-a006649127e371903a2de979. This includes:

- The version number, that is, 1.

- The time of the original request, in Unix epoch time, in **8 hexadecimal digits**.

  For example, 10:00AM December 1st, 2016 PST in epoch time is 1480615200 seconds, or 58406520 in hexadecimal.

- A 96-bit identifier for the trace, globally unique, in **24 hexadecimal digits. Trace ID Security**
  Trace IDs are visible in response headers. Generate trace IDs with a secure random algorithm to ensure that attackers cannot calculate future trace IDs and send requests with those IDs to your application.

- `start_time` – **number** that is the time the segment was created, in floating point seconds in epoch time. For example, 1480615200.010 or 1.480615200010E9. Use as many decimal places as you need. Microsecond resolution is recommended when available.

- `end_time` – **number** that is the time the segment was closed. For example, 1480615200.090 or 1.480615200090E9. Specify either an `end_time` or `in_progress`.

- `in_progress` – **boolean**, set to `true` instead of specifying an `end_time` to record that a segment is started, but is not complete. Send an in-progress segment when your application receives a request that will take a long time to serve, to trace the request receipt. When the response is sent, send the complete segment to overwrite the in-progress segment. Only send one complete segment, and one or zero in-progress segments, per request.

Service Names

A segment's `name` should match the domain name or logical name of the service that generates the segment. However, this is not enforced. Any application that has permission to http://docs.aws.amazon.com/xray/latest/api/API_PutTraceSegments.html can send segments with any name.

The following fields are optional for segments.

Optional Segment Fields

- `service` – An object with information about your application.
  - `version` – A string that identifies the version of your application that served the request.
- `user` – A string that identifies the user who sent the request.
- `origin` – The type of AWS resource running your application.

Supported Values

- `AWS::EC2::Instance` – An Amazon EC2 instance.
- `AWS::ECS::Container` – An Amazon ECS container.
- `AWS::ElasticBeanstalk::Environment` – An Elastic Beanstalk environment.

When multiple values are applicable to your application, use the one that is most specific. For example, a Multicontainer Docker Elastic Beanstalk environment runs your application on an Amazon ECS container, which in turn runs on an Amazon EC2 instance. In this case you would set the origin to `AWS::ElasticBeanstalk::Environment` as the environment is the parent of the other two resources.

- `parent_id` – A subsegment ID you specify if the request originated from an instrumented application. The X-Ray SDK adds the parent subsegment ID to the tracing header for downstream HTTP calls.
- `http` – `http` objects with information about the original HTTP request.
- `aws` – `aws` object with information about the AWS resource on which your application served the request.
- `error`, `throttle`, `fault`, and `cause` – error fields that indicate an error occurred and that include information about the exception that caused the error.
- `annotations` – `annotations` object with key-value pairs that you want X-Ray to index for search.
- `metadata` – `metadata` object with any additional data that you want to store in the segment.
- `subsegments` – **array** of **subsegment** objects.

Subsegments

You can create subsegments to record calls to AWS services and resources that you make with the AWS SDK, calls to internal or external HTTP web APIs, or SQL database queries. You can also create subsegments to debug or annotate blocks of code in your application. Subsegments can contain other subsegments, so a custom subsegment that records metadata about an internal function call can contain other custom subsegments and subsegments for downstream calls.

A subsegment records a downstream call from the point of view of the service that calls it. X-Ray uses subsegments to identify downstream services that don't send segments and create entries for them on the service graph.

A subsegment can be embedded in a full segment document or sent independently. Send subsegments separately to asynchronously trace downstream calls for long-running requests, or to avoid exceeding the maximum segment document size.

Example Segment with Embedded Subsegment

An independent subsegment has a `type` of `subsegment` and a `parent_id` that identifies the parent segment.

```
1  {
2    "trace_id"   : "1-5759e988-bd862e3fe1be46a994272793",
3    "id"         : "defdfd9912dc5a56",
4    "start_time" : 1461096053.37518,
5    "end_time"   : 1461096053.4042,
6    "name"       : "www.example.com",
7    "http"       : {
8      "request"  : {
9        "url"        : "https://www.example.com/health",
10       "method"     : "GET",
11       "user_agent" : "Mozilla/5.0 (Macintosh; Intel Mac OS X 10_11_6) AppleWebKit/601.7.7",
12       "client_ip"  : "11.0.3.111"
13     },
14     "response" : {
15       "status"         : 200,
16       "content_length" : 86
17     }
18   },
19   "subsegments" : [
20     {
21       "id"         : "53995c3f42cd8ad8",
22       "name"       : "api.example.com",
```

```
23      "start_time"  : 1461096053.37769,
24      "end_time"    : 1461096053.40379,
25      "namespace"   : "remote",
26      "http"        : {
27        "request"   : {
28          "url"     : "https://api.example.com/health",
29          "method"  : "POST",
30          "traced"  : true
31        },
32        "response" : {
33          "status"         : 200,
34          "content_length" : 861
35        }
36      }
37    }
38  ]
39 }
```

For long-running requests, you can send an in-progress segment to notify X-Ray that the request was received, and then send subsegments separately to trace them before completing the original request.

Example In-Progress Segment

```
1 {
2   "name" : "example.com",
3   "id" : "70de5b6f19ff9a0b",
4   "start_time" : 1.478293361271E9,
5   "trace_id" : "1-581cf771-a006649127e371903a2de979",
6   "in_progress": true
7 }
```

Example Independent Subsegment

An independent subsegment has a `type` of `subsegment`, a `trace_id`, and a `parent_id` that identifies the parent segment.

```
1 {
2   "name" : "api.example.com",
3   "id" : "53995c3f42cd8ad8",
4   "start_time" : 1.478293361271E9,
5   "end_time" : 1.478293361449E9,
6   "type" : "subsegment",
7   "trace_id" : "1-581cf771-a006649127e371903a2de979"
8   "parent_id" : "defdfd9912dc5a56",
9   "namespace"   : "remote",
10  "http"        : {
11    "request"   : {
12      "url"     : "https://api.example.com/health",
13      "method"  : "POST",
14      "traced"  : true
15    },
16    "response" : {
17      "status"         : 200,
18      "content_length" : 861
19    }
20  }
21 }
```

77

When the request is complete, close the segment by resending it with an `end_time`. The complete segment overwrites the in-progress segment.

You can also send subsegments separately for completed requests that triggered asynchronous workflows. For example, a web API may return a `OK 200` response immediately prior to starting the work that the user requested. You can send a full segment to X-Ray as soon as the response is sent, followed by subsegments for work completed later. As with segments, you can also send a subsegment fragment to record that the subsegment has started, and then overwrite it with a full subsegment once the downstream call is complete.

The following fields are required, or are conditionally required, for subsegments.

Note
Values are strings up to 250 characters unless noted otherwise.

Required Subsegment Fields

- `id` – A 64-bit identifier for the subsegment, unique among segments in the same trace, in **16 hexadecimal digits**.
- `name` – The logical name of the subsegment. For downstream calls, name the subsegment after the resource or service called. For custom subsegments, name the subsegment after the code that it instruments (e.g., a function name).
- `start_time` – **number** that is the time the subsegment was created, in floating point seconds in epoch time, accurate to milliseconds. For example, 1480615200.010 or 1.480615200010E9.
- `end_time` – **number** that is the time the subsegment was closed. For example, 1480615200.090 or 1.480615200090E9. Specify an `end_time` or `in_progress`.
- `in_progress` – **boolean** that is set to `true` instead of specifying an `end_time` to record that a subsegment is started, but is not complete. Only send one complete subsegment, and one or zero in-progress subsegments, per downstream request.
- `trace_id` – Trace ID of the subsegment's parent segment. Required only if sending a subsegment separately.

Trace ID Format

A `trace_id` consists of three numbers separated by hyphens. For example, 1-58406520-a006649127e371903a2de979. This includes:

- The version number, that is, **1**.
- The time of the original request, in Unix epoch time, in **8 hexadecimal digits**.

  For example, 10:00AM December 1st, 2016 PST in epoch time is 1480615200 seconds, or 58406520 in hexadecimal.

- A 96-bit identifier for the trace, globally unique, in **24 hexadecimal digits**.

- `parent_id` – Segment ID of the subsegment's parent segment. Required only if sending a subsegment separately.

- `type` – subsegment. Required only if sending a subsegment separately.

The following fields are optional for subsegments.

Optional Subsegment Fields

- `namespace` – `aws` for AWS SDK calls; `remote` for other downstream calls.
- `http` – `http` object with information about an outgoing HTTP call.
- `aws` – `aws` object with information about the downstream AWS resource that your application called.
- `error`, `throttle`, `fault`, and `cause` – error fields that indicate an error occurred and that include information about the exception that caused the error.
- `annotations` – `annotations` object with key-value pairs that you want X-Ray to index for search.
- `metadata` – `metadata` object with any additional data that you want to store in the segment.
- `subsegments` – **array** of `subsegment` objects.

- precursor_ids – **array** of subsegment IDs that identifies subsegments with the same parent that completed prior to this subsegment.

HTTP Request Data

Use an HTTP block to record details about an HTTP request that your application served (in a segment) or that your application made to a downstream HTTP API (in a subsegment). Most of the fields in this object map to information found in an HTTP request and response.

http

All fields are optional.

- request – Information about a request.
  - method – The request method. For example, GET.
  - url – The full URL of the request, compiled from the protocol, hostname, and path of the request.
  - user_agent – The user agent string from the requester's client.
  - client_ip – The IP address of the requester. Can be retrieved from the IP packet's Source Address or, for forwarded requests, from an X-Forwarded-For header.
  - x_forwarded_for – (segments only) **boolean** indicating that the client_ip was read from an X-Forwarded-For header and is not reliable as it could have been forged.
  - traced – (subsegments only) **boolean** indicating that the downstream call is to another traced service. If this field is set to true, X-Ray considers the trace to be broken until the downstream service uploads a segment with a parent_id that matches the id of the subsegment that contains this block.
- response – Information about a response.
  - status – **number** indicating the HTTP status of the response.
  - content_length – **number** indicating the length of the response body in bytes.

When you instrument a call to a downstream web api, record a subsegment with information about the HTTP request and response. X-Ray uses the subsegment to generate an inferred segment for the remote API.

Example Segment for HTTP Call Served by an Application Running on Amazon EC2

```
1  {
2    "id": "6b55dcc497934f1a",
3    "start_time": 1484789387.126,
4    "end_time": 1484789387.535,
5    "trace_id": "1-5880168b-fd5158284b67678a3bb5a78c",
6    "name": "www.example.com",
7    "origin": "AWS::EC2::Instance",
8    "aws": {
9      "ec2": {
10       "availability_zone": "us-west-2c",
11       "instance_id": "i-0b5a4678fc325bg98"
12     },
13     "xray": {
14         "sdk_version": "1.3.1 for Java"
15     },
16   },
17   "http": {
18     "request": {
19       "method": "POST",
20       "client_ip": "78.255.233.48",
21       "url": "http://www.example.com/api/user",
22       "user_agent": "Mozilla/5.0 (Windows NT 6.1; WOW64; rv:45.0) Gecko/20100101 Firefox/45.0",
23       "x_forwarded_for": true
24     },
```

```
25      "response": {
26        "status": 200
27      }
28    }
```

Example Subsegment for a Downstream HTTP Call

```
1  {
2    "id": "004f72be19cddc2a",
3    "start_time": 1484786387.131,
4    "end_time": 1484786387.501,
5    "name": "names.example.com",
6    "namespace": "remote",
7    "http": {
8      "request": {
9        "method": "GET",
10       "url": "https://names.example.com/"
11     },
12     "response": {
13       "content_length": -1,
14       "status": 200
15     }
16   }
17 }
```

Example Inferred Segment for a Downstream HTTP Call

```
1  {
2    "id": "168416dc2ea97781",
3    "name": "names.example.com",
4    "trace_id": "1-5880168b-fd5153bb58284b67678aa78c",
5    "start_time": 1484786387.131,
6    "end_time": 1484786387.501,
7    "parent_id": "004f72be19cddc2a",
8    "http": {
9      "request": {
10       "method": "GET",
11       "url": "https://names.example.com/"
12     },
13     "response": {
14       "content_length": -1,
15       "status": 200
16     }
17   },
18   "inferred": true
19 }
```

Annotations

Segments and subsegments can include an **annotations** object containing one or more fields that X-Ray indexes for use with filter expressions. Fields can have string, number, or Boolean values (no objects or arrays).

Example Segment for HTTP Call with Annotations

```
1  {
```

```
2    "id": "6b55dcc497932f1a",
3    "start_time": 1484789187.126,
4    "end_time": 1484789187.535,
5    "trace_id": "1-5880168b-fd515828bs07678a3bb5a78c",
6    "name": "www.example.com",
7    "origin": "AWS::EC2::Instance",
8    "aws": {
9      "ec2": {
10       "availability_zone": "us-west-2c",
11       "instance_id": "i-0b5a4678fc325bg98"
12     },
13     "xray": {
14        "sdk_version": "1.3.1 for Java"
15     },
16   },
17   "annotations": {
18     "customer_category" : 124,
19     "zip_code" : 98101,
20     "country" : "United States",
21     "internal" : false
22   },
23   "http": {
24     "request": {
25       "method": "POST",
26       "client_ip": "78.255.233.48",
27       "url": "http://www.example.com/api/user",
28       "user_agent": "Mozilla/5.0 (Windows NT 6.1; WOW64; rv:45.0) Gecko/20100101 Firefox/45.0",
29       "x_forwarded_for": true
30     },
31     "response": {
32       "status": 200
33     }
34   }
```

Keys must be alphanumeric in order to work with filters. Underscore is allowed. Other symbols and whitespace are not allowed.

Metadata

Segments and subsegments can include a `metadata` object containing one or more fields with values of any type, including objects and arrays. X-Ray does not index metadata, and values can be any size, as long as the segment document doesn't exceed the maximum size (64 kB). You can view metadata in the full segment document returned by the http://docs.aws.amazon.com/xray/latest/api/API_BatchGetTraces.html API. Field keys (`debug` in the following example) starting with `AWS.` are reserved for use by AWS-provided SDKs and clients.

Example Custom Subsegment with Metadata

```
1  {
2    "id": "0e58d2918e9038e8",
3    "start_time": 1484789387.502,
4    "end_time": 1484789387.534,
5    "name": "## UserModel.saveUser",
6    "metadata": {
7      "debug": {
```

```
 8          "test": "Metadata string from UserModel.saveUser"
 9        }
10      },
11      "subsegments": [
12        {
13          "id": "0f910026178b71eb",
14          "start_time": 1484789387.502,
15          "end_time": 1484789387.534,
16          "name": "DynamoDB",
17          "namespace": "aws",
18          "http": {
19            "response": {
20              "content_length": 58,
21              "status": 200
22            }
23          },
24          "aws": {
25            "table_name": "scorekeep-user",
26            "operation": "UpdateItem",
27            "request_id": "3AIENM5J4ELQ3SPODHKBIRVIC3VV4KQNSO5AEMVJF66Q9ASUAAJG",
28            "resource_names": [
29              "scorekeep-user"
30            ]
31          }
32        }
33      ]
34    }
```

AWS Resource Data

For segments, the `aws` object contains information about the resource on which your application is running. Multiple fields can apply to a single resource. For example, an application running in a multicontainer Docker environment on Elastic Beanstalk could have information about the Amazon EC2 instance, the Amazon ECS container running on the instance, and the Elastic Beanstalk environment itself.

aws (Segments)

All fields are optional.

- `account_id` – If your application sends segments to a different AWS account, record the ID of the account running your application.
- `ecs` – Information about an Amazon ECS container.
  - `container` – The container ID of the container running your application.
- `ec2` – Information about an EC2 instance.
  - `instance_id` – The instance ID of the EC2 instance.
  - `availability_zone` – The Availability Zone in which the instance is running.
    Example AWS Block with Plugins

```
1 "aws": {
2   "elastic_beanstalk": {
3     "version_label": "app-5a56-170119_190650-stage-170119_190650",
4     "deployment_id": 32,
5     "environment_name": "scorekeep"
```

```
 6    },
 7    "ec2": {
 8      "availability_zone": "us-west-2c",
 9      "instance_id": "i-075ad396f12bc325a"
10    },
11    "xray": {
12      "sdk": "1.3.1 for Java"
13    }
14  }
```

- elastic_beanstalk – Information about an Elastic Beanstalk environment. You can find this information in a file named /var/elasticbeanstalk/xray/environment.conf on the latest Elastic Beanstalk platforms.

  - environment_name – The name of the environment.
  - version_label – The name of the application version that is currently deployed to the instance that served the request.
  - deployment_id – **number** indicating the ID of the last successful deployment to the instance that served the request.

For subsegments, record information about the AWS services and resources that your application accesses. X-Ray uses this information to create inferred segments that represent the downstream services in your service map.

aws (Subsegments)

All fields are optional.

- operation – The name of the API action invoked against an AWS service or resource.
- account_id – If your application accesses resources in a different account, or sends segments to a different account, record the ID of the account that owns the AWS resource that your application accessed.
- region – If the resource is in a region different from your application, record the region. For example, us-west-2.
- request_id – Unique identifier for the request.
- queue_url – For operations on an Amazon SQS queue, the queue's URL.
- table_name – For operations on a DynamoDB table, the name of the table.

Example Subsegment for a Call to DynamoDB to Save an Item

```
 1  {
 2    "id": "24756640c0d0978a",
 3    "start_time": 1.480305974194E9,
 4    "end_time": 1.4803059742E9,
 5    "name": "DynamoDB",
 6    "namespace": "aws",
 7    "http": {
 8      "response": {
 9        "content_length": 60,
10        "status": 200
11      }
12    },
13    "aws": {
14      "table_name": "scorekeep-user",
15      "operation": "UpdateItem",
16      "request_id": "UBQNSO5AEM8T4FDA4RQDEB94OVTDRVV4K4HIRGVJF66Q9ASUAAJG",
17    }
18  }
```

Errors and Exceptions

When an error occurs, you can record details about the error and exceptions that it generated. Record errors in segments when your application returns an error to the user, and in subsegments when a downstream call returns an error.

error types

Set one or more of the following fields to `true` to indicate that an error occurred. Multiple types can apply if errors compound. For example, a `429 Too Many Requests` error from a downstream call may cause your application to return `500 Internal Server Error`, in which case all three types would apply.

- `error` – **boolean** indicating that a client error occurred (response status code was 4XX Client Error).
- `throttle` – **boolean** indicating that a request was throttled (response status code was *429 Too Many Requests*).
- `fault` – **boolean** indicating that a server error occurred (response status code was 5XX Server Error).

Indicate the cause of the error by including a **cause** object in the segment or subsegment.

cause

A cause can be either a **16 character** exception ID or an object with the following fields:

- `working_directory` – The full path of the working directory when the exception occurred.
- `paths` – The **array** of paths to libraries or modules in use when the exception occurred.
- `exceptions` – The **array** of **exception** objects.

Include detailed information about the error in one or more **exception** objects.

exception

All fields are optional except `id`.

- `id` – A 64-bit identifier for the exception, unique among segments in the same trace, in **16 hexadecimal digits**.
- `message` – The exception message.
- `type` – The exception type.
- `remote` – **boolean** indicating that the exception was caused by an error returned by a downstream service.
- `truncated` – **integer** indicating the number of stack frames that are omitted from the `stack`.
- `skipped` – **integer** indicating the number of exceptions that were skipped between this exception and its child, that is, the exception that it caused.
- `cause` – Exception ID of the exception's parent, that is, the exception that caused this exception.
- `stack` – **array** of **stackFrame** objects.

If available, record information about the call stack in **stackFrame** objects.

stackFrame

All fields are optional.

- `path` – The relative path to the file.
- `line` – The line in the file.
- `label` – The function or method name.

SQL Queries

You can create subsegments for queries that your application makes to an SQL database.

sql

All fields are optional.

- connection_string – For SQL Server or other database connections that don't use URL connection strings, record the connection string, excluding passwords.
- url – For a database connection that uses a URL connection string, record the URL, excluding passwords.
- sanitized_query – The database query, with any user provided values removed or replaced by a placeholder.
- database_type – The name of the database engine.
- database_version – The version number of the database engine.
- driver_version – The name and version number of the database engine driver that your application uses.
- user – The database username.
- preparation – call if the query used a PreparedCall; statement if the query used a PreparedStatement.

Example Subsegment with an SQL Query

```
1  {
2    "id": "3fd8634e78ca9560",
3    "start_time": 1484872218.696,
4    "end_time": 1484872218.697,
5    "name": "ebdb@aawijb5u25wdoy.cpamxznpdoq8.us-west-2.rds.amazonaws.com",
6    "namespace": "remote",
7    "sql" : {
8      "url": "jdbc:postgresql://aawijb5u25wdoy.cpamxznpdoq8.us-west-2.rds.amazonaws.com:5432/ebdb
         ",
9      "preparation": "statement",
10     "database_type": "PostgreSQL",
11     "database_version": "9.5.4",
12     "driver_version": "PostgreSQL 9.4.1211.jre7",
13     "user" : "dbuser",
14     "sanitized_query" : "SELECT  *  FROM  customers  WHERE  customer_id=?;"
15   }
16 }
```

AWS X-Ray Permissions

You can use AWS Identity and Access Management (IAM) to grant X-Ray permissions to users and compute resources in your account. IAM controls access to the X-Ray service at the API level to enforce permissions uniformly, regardless of which client (console, AWS SDK, AWS CLI) your users employ.

To use the X-Ray console to view service maps and segments, you only need read permissions. To enable console access, add the `AWSXrayReadOnlyAccess` managed policy to your IAM user.

For local development and testing, create an IAM user with read and write permissions. Generate access keys for the user and store them in the standard AWS SDK location. You can use these credentials with the X-Ray daemon, the AWS CLI, and the AWS SDK.

To deploy your instrumented app to AWS, create an IAM role with write permissions and assign it to the resources running your application.

Topics

- IAM Managed Policies for X-Ray
- Running Your Application Locally
- Running Your Application in AWS

IAM Managed Policies for X-Ray

To make granting permissions easy, IAM supports **managed policies** for each service. A service can update these managed policies with new permissions when it releases new APIs. AWS X-Ray provides managed policies for read only, write only, and read/write use cases.

- `AWSXrayReadOnlyAccess` – Read permissions for using the X-Ray console, AWS CLI, or AWS SDK to get trace data and service maps from the X-Ray API.

```
1  {
2      "Version": "2012-10-17",
3      "Statement": [
4          {
5              "Effect": "Allow",
6              "Action": [
7                  "xray:BatchGetTraces",
8                  "xray:GetServiceGraph",
9                  "xray:GetTraceGraph",
10                 "xray:GetTraceSummaries"
11             ],
12             "Resource": [
13                 "*"
14             ]
15         }
16     ]
17 }
```

- `AWSXrayWriteOnlyAccess` – Write permissions for using the X-Ray daemon, AWS CLI, or AWS SDK to upload segment documents and telemetry to the X-Ray API.

```
1  {
2      "Version": "2012-10-17",
3      "Statement": [
4          {
5              "Effect": "Allow",
```

```
6            "Action": [
7                "xray:PutTraceSegments",
8                "xray:PutTelemetryRecords"
9            ],
10           "Resource": [
11               "*"
12           ]
13       }
14   ]
15 }
```

- `AWSXrayFullAccess` – Read/write permissions.

```
1 {
2     "Version": "2012-10-17",
3     "Statement": [
4         {
5             "Effect": "Allow",
6             "Action": [
7                 "xray:*"
8             ],
9             "Resource": [
10                "*"
11            ]
12       }
13   ]
14 }
```

- `AmazonS3ReadOnlyAccess` – Permission for the user or resource to download the X-Ray daemon from Amazon S3.

To add a managed policy to an IAM user, group, or role

1. Open the IAM console.

2. Open the role associated with your instance profile, an IAM user, or an IAM group.

3. Under **Permissions**, attach the managed policy.

Running Your Application Locally

Your instrumented application sends trace data to the X-Ray daemon. The daemon buffers segment documents and uploads them to the X-Ray service in batches. The daemon needs write permissions to upload trace data and telemetry to the X-Ray service.

When you run the daemon locally, store your IAM user's access key and secret key in a file named `credentials` in a folder named `.aws` in your user folder.

Example ~/.aws/credentials

```
1 [default]
2 aws_access_key_id=AKIAIOSFODNN7EXAMPLE
3 aws_secret_access_key=wJalrXUtnFEMI/K7MDENG/bPxRfiCYEXAMPLEKEY
```

If you already configured credentials for use with the AWS SDK or AWS CLI, the daemon can use those. If multiple profiles are available, the daemon uses the default profile.

Running Your Application in AWS

When you run your application on AWS, use a role to grant permission to the Amazon EC2 instance or Lambda function that runs the daemon.

- **Amazon Elastic Compute Cloud** – Create an IAM role and attach it to the EC2 instance as an instance profile.
- **Amazon Elastic Container Service** – Create an IAM role and attach it to container instances as a container instance IAM role.
- **AWS Elastic Beanstalk** – Elastic Beanstalk includes X-Ray permissions in its default instance profile. You can use the default instance profile, or add write permissions to a custom instance profile.
- **AWS Lambda** – Add write permissions to your function's execution role.

To create a role for use with X-Ray

1. Open the IAM console.

2. Choose **Roles**.

3. Choose **Create New Role**.

4. For **Role Name**, type **xray-application**. Choose **Next Step**.

5. For **Role Type**, choose **Amazon EC2**.

6. Attach managed policies to give your application access to AWS services.

   - **AWSXrayWriteOnlyAccess** – Gives the X-Ray daemon permission to upload trace data.
   - **AmazonS3ReadOnlyAccess** (Amazon EC2 only) – Gives the instance permission to download the X-Ray daemon from Amazon S3.

   If your application uses the AWS SDK to access other services, add policies that grant access to those services.

7. Choose **Next Step**.

8. Choose **Create Role**.

AWS X-Ray Sample Application

The AWS X-Ray eb-java-scorekeep sample app, available on GitHub, shows the use of the AWS X-Ray SDK to instrument incoming HTTP calls, DynamoDB SDK clients, and HTTP clients. The sample app uses AWS Elastic Beanstalk features to create DynamoDB tables, compile Java code on instance, and run the X-Ray daemon without any additional configuration.

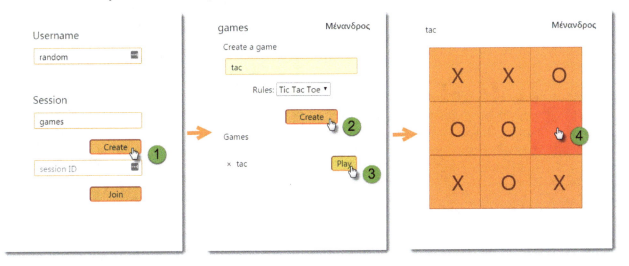

The sample is an instrumented version of the Scorekeep project on AWSLabs. It includes a front-end web app, the API that it calls, and the DynamoDB tables that it uses to store data. All the components are hosted in an Elastic Beanstalk environment for portability and ease of deployment.

Basic instrumentation with filters, plugins, and instrumented AWS SDK clients is shown in the project's `xray-gettingstarted` branch. This is the branch that you deploy in the getting started tutorial. Because this branch only includes the basics, you can diff it against the `master` branch to quickly understand the basics.

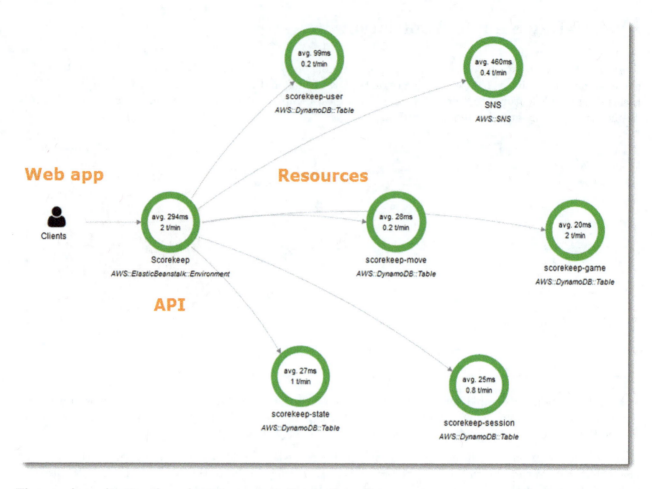

The sample application shows basic instrumentation in these files:

- **HTTP request filter** – https://github.com/awslabs/eb-java-scorekeep/tree/xray-gettingstarted/src/main/java/scorekeep/WebConfig.java
- **AWS SDK client instrumentation** – https://github.com/awslabs/eb-java-scorekeep/tree/xray-gettingstarted/build.gradle

The `xray` branch of the application adds the use of HTTPClient, Annotations, SQL queries, custom subsegments, an instrumented AWS Lambda function, and instrumented initialization code and scripts. This service map shows the `xray` branch running without a connected SQL database:

To support user log-in and AWS SDK for JavaScript use in the browser, the `xray-cognito` branch adds Amazon Cognito to support user authentication and authorization. With credentials retrieved from Amazon Cognito, the web app also sends trace data to X-Ray to record request information from the client's point of view. The browser client appears as its own node on the service map, and records additional information, including the URL of the page that the user is viewing, and the user's ID.

Finally, the `xray-worker` branch adds an instrumented Python Lambda function that runs independently, processing items from an Amazon SQS queue. Scorekeep adds an item to the queue each time a game ends. The Lambda worker, triggered by CloudWatch Events, pulls items from the queue every few minutes and processes them to store game records in Amazon S3 for analysis.

With all features enabled, Scorekeep's service map looks like this:

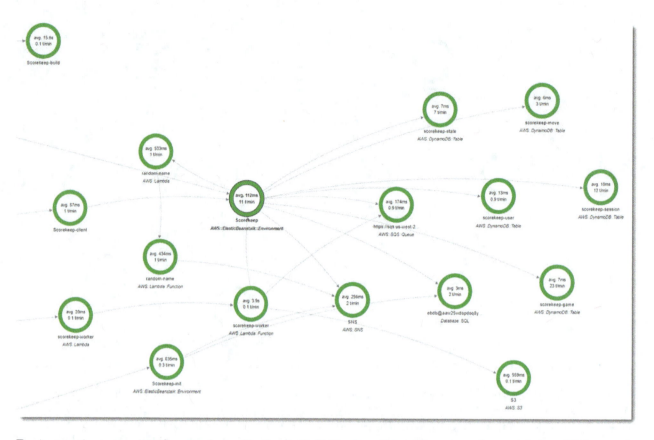

For instructions on using the sample application with X-Ray, see the getting started tutorial. In addition to the basic use of the X-Ray SDK for Java discussed in the tutorial, the sample also shows how to use the following features.

Topics

- Manually Instrumenting AWS SDK Clients
- Creating Additional Subsegments
- Recording Annotations, Metadata, and User IDs
- Instrumenting Outgoing HTTP Calls
- Instrumenting Calls to a PostgreSQL Database
- Instrumenting AWS Lambda Functions
- Instrumenting Amazon ECS Applications
- Instrumenting Startup Code
- Instrumenting Scripts
- Instrumenting a Web App Client
- Using Instrumented Clients in Worker Threads
- Deep Linking to the X-Ray Console

Manually Instrumenting AWS SDK Clients

The X-Ray SDK for Java automatically instruments all AWS SDK clients when you include the AWS SDK Instrumentor submodule in your build dependencies.

You can disable automatic client instrumentation by removing the Instrumentor submodule. This enables you to instrument some clients manually while ignoring others, or use different tracing handlers on different clients.

To illustrate support for instrumenting specific AWS SDK clients, the application passes a tracing handler to AmazonDynamoDBClientBuilder as a request handler in the user, game, and session model. This code change tells the SDK to instrument all calls to DynamoDB using those clients.

Example   https://github.com/awslabs/eb-java-scorekeep/tree/xray/src/main/java/scorekeep/
SessionModel.java – Manual AWS SDK Client Instrumentation

```
1  import [com\.amazonaws\.xray\.AWSXRay](http://docs.aws.amazon.com/xray-sdk-for-java/latest/
        javadoc/com/amazonaws/xray/AWSXRay.html);
2  import [com\.amazonaws\.xray\.handlers\.TracingHandler](http://docs.aws.amazon.com/xray-sdk-for-
        java/latest/javadoc/com/amazonaws/xray/handlers/TracingHandler.html);
3
4  public class SessionModel {
5    private AmazonDynamoDB client = AmazonDynamoDBClientBuilder.standard()
6          .withRegion(Constants.REGION)
7          .withRequestHandlers(new TracingHandler(AWSXRay.getGlobalRecorder()))
8          .build();
9    private DynamoDBMapper mapper = new DynamoDBMapper(client);
```

If you remove the AWS SDK Instrumentor submodule from project dependencies, only the manually instrumented AWS SDK clients appear in the service map.

Creating Additional Subsegments

Subsegments extend a trace's segment with details about work done in order to serve a request. Each time you make a call with an instrumented client, the X-Ray SDK records the information generated in a subsegment. You can create additional subsegments to group other subsegments, to measure the performance of a section of code, or to record annotations and metadata.

To manage subsegments, use the `BeginSubsegment` and `EndSubsegment` methods. Perform any work in the subsegment in a `try` block and use `AddException` to trace exceptions. Call `EndSubsegment` in a `finally` block to ensure that the subsegment is closed.

Example Controller.cs – Custom Subsegment

```
1 AWSXRayRecorder.Instance.BeginSubsegment("custom method");
2 try
3 {
4   DoWork();
5 }
6 catch (Exception e)
7 {
8   AWSXRayRecorder.Instance.AddException(e);
9 }
10 finally
11 {
12   AWSXRayRecorder.Instance.EndSubsegment();
13 }
```

When you create a subsegment within a segment or another subsegment, the X-Ray SDK for .NET generates an ID for it and records the start time and end time.

Example Subsegment with Metadata

```
1 "subsegments": [{
2   "id": "6f1605cd8a07cb70",
3   "start_time": 1.480305974194E9,
4   "end_time": 1.4803059742E9,
5   "name": "Custom subsegment for UserModel.saveUser function",
6   "metadata": {
7     "debug": {
8       "test": "Metadata string from UserModel.saveUser"
9     }
10   },
```

Recording Annotations, Metadata, and User IDs

In the game model class, the application records `Game` objects in a metadata block each time it saves a game in DynamoDB. Separately, the application records game IDs in annotations for use with filter expressions.

Example   https://github.com/awslabs/eb-java-scorekeep/tree/xray/src/main/java/scorekeep/ GameModel.java – Annotations and Metadata

```
1  import [com\.amazonaws\.xray\.AWSXRay](http://docs.aws.amazon.com/xray-sdk-for-java/latest/
       javadoc/com/amazonaws/xray/AWSXRay.html);
2  import [com\.amazonaws\.xray\.entities\.Segment](http://docs.aws.amazon.com/xray-sdk-for-java/
       latest/javadoc/com/amazonaws/xray/entities/Segment.html);
3  import [com\.amazonaws\.xray\.entities\.Subsegment](http://docs.aws.amazon.com/xray-sdk-for-java
       /latest/javadoc/com/amazonaws/xray/entities/Subsegment.html);
4  ...
5    public void saveGame(Game game) throws SessionNotFoundException {
6      // wrap in subsegment
7      Subsegment subsegment = AWSXRay.beginSubsegment("## GameModel.saveGame");
8      try {
9        // check session
10       String sessionId = game.getSession();
11       if (sessionModel.loadSession(sessionId) == null ) {
12         throw new SessionNotFoundException(sessionId);
13       }
14       Segment segment = AWSXRay.getCurrentSegment();
15       subsegment.putMetadata("resources", "game", game);
16       segment.putAnnotation("gameid", game.getId());
17       mapper.save(game);
18     } catch (Exception e) {
19       subsegment.addException(e);
20       throw e;
21     } finally {
22       AWSXRay.endSubsegment();
23     }
24   }
```

In the move controller, the application records user IDs with `setUser`. User IDs are recorded in a separate field on segments and are indexed for use with search.

Example src/main/java/scorekeep/MoveController.java – User ID

```
1  import [com\.amazonaws\.xray\.AWSXRay](http://docs.aws.amazon.com/xray-sdk-for-java/latest/
       javadoc/com/amazonaws/xray/AWSXRay.html);
2  ...
3    @RequestMapping(value="/{userId}", method=RequestMethod.POST)
4    public Move newMove(@PathVariable String sessionId, @PathVariable String gameId, @PathVariable
         String userId, @RequestBody String move) throws SessionNotFoundException,
       GameNotFoundException, StateNotFoundException, RulesException {
5      AWSXRay.getCurrentSegment().setUser(userId);
6      return moveFactory.newMove(sessionId, gameId, userId, move);
7    }
```

Instrumenting Outgoing HTTP Calls

The user factory class shows how the application uses the X-Ray SDK for Java's version of `HTTPClientBuilder` to instrument outgoing HTTP calls.

Example https://github.com/awslabs/eb-java-scorekeep/tree/xray/src/main/java/scorekeep/
UserFactory.java – HTTPClient Instrumentation

```
1  import [com\.amazonaws\.xray\.proxies\.apache\.http\.HttpClientBuilder](http://docs.aws.amazon.
      com/xray-sdk-for-java/latest/javadoc/com/amazonaws/xray/proxies/apache/http/
      HttpClientBuilder.html);
2
3   public String randomName() throws IOException {
4     CloseableHttpClient httpclient = HttpClientBuilder.create().build();
5     HttpGet httpGet = new HttpGet("http://uinames.com/api/");
6     CloseableHttpResponse response = httpclient.execute(httpGet);
7     try {
8       HttpEntity entity = response.getEntity();
9       InputStream inputStream = entity.getContent();
10      ObjectMapper mapper = new ObjectMapper();
11      Map<String, String> jsonMap = mapper.readValue(inputStream, Map.class);
12      String name = jsonMap.get("name");
13      EntityUtils.consume(entity);
14      return name;
15    } finally {
16      response.close();
17    }
18  }
```

If you currently use `org.apache.http.impl.client.HttpClientBuilder`, you can simply swap out the import statement for that class with one for `com.amazonaws.xray.proxies.apache.http.HttpClientBuilder`.

Instrumenting Calls to a PostgreSQL Database

The `application-pgsql.properties` file adds the X-Ray PostgreSQL tracing interceptor to the data source created in https://github.com/awslabs/eb-java-scorekeep/tree/xray/src/main/java/scorekeep/RdsWebConfig. java.

Example **https://github.com/awslabs/eb-java-scorekeep/tree/xray/src/main/resources/ application-pgsql.properties – PostgreSQL Database Instrumentation**

```
1 spring.datasource.continue-on-error=true
2 spring.jpa.show-sql=false
3 spring.jpa.hibernate.ddl-auto=create-drop
4 spring.datasource.jdbc-interceptors=com.amazonaws.xray.sql.postgres.TracingInterceptor
5 spring.jpa.database-platform=org.hibernate.dialect.PostgreSQL94Dialect
```

Note
See Configuring Databases with Elastic Beanstalk in the *AWS Elastic Beanstalk Developer Guide* for details on how to add a PostgreSQL database to the application environment.

The X-Ray demo page in the **xray** branch includes a demo that uses the instrumented data source to generate traces that show information about the SQL queries that it generates. Navigate to the **/#/xray** path in the running application or choose **Powered by AWS X-Ray** in the navigation bar to see the demo page.

Scorekeep

AWS X-Ray integration

This branch is integrated with the AWS X-Ray SDK for Java to record information about requests from this web app to the Scorekeep API, and calls that the API makes to Amazon DynamoDB and other downstream services

Trace game sessions

Create users and a session, and then create and play a game of tic-tac-toe with those users. Each call to Scorekeep is traced with AWS X-Ray, which generates a service map from the data.

Trace game sessions

View service map AWS X-Ray

Trace SQL queries

Simulate game sessions, and store the results in a PostgreSQL Amazon RDS database attached to the AWS Elastic Beanstalk environment running Scorekeep. This demo uses an instrumented JDBC data source to send details about the SQL queries to X-Ray.

For more information about Scorekeep's SQL integration, see the `sql` branch of this project.

Trace SQL queries

View traces in AWS X-Ray

ID	Winner	Loser
1	Mugur	Gheorghiță
2	Paula	Adorján
3	Αρχίας	Stela
4	付	Pərvanə

Choose **Trace SQL queries** to simulate game sessions and store the results in the attached database. Then, choose **View traces in AWS X-Ray** to see a filtered list of traces that hit the API's `/api/history` route. Choose one of the traces from the list to see the timeline, including the SQL query.

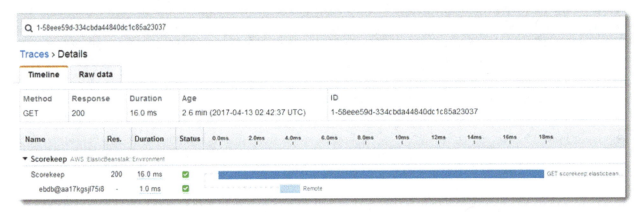

Instrumenting AWS Lambda Functions

Scorekeep uses two AWS Lambda functions. The first is a Node.js function from the `lambda` branch that generates random names for new users. When a user creates a session without entering a name, the application calls a function named `random-name` with the AWS SDK for Java. The X-Ray SDK for Java records information about the call to Lambda in a subsegment like any other call made with an instrumented AWS SDK client.

Note
Running the `random-name` Lambda function requires the creation of additional resources outside of the Elastic Beanstalk environment. See the readme for more information and instructions: AWS Lambda Integration.

The second function, `scorekeep-worker`, is a Python function that runs independently of the Scorekeep API. When a game ends, the API writes the session ID and game ID to an SQS queue. The worker function reads items from the queue, and calls the Scorekeep API to construct complete records of each game session for storage in Amazon S3.

Scorekeep includes AWS CloudFormation templates and scripts to create both functions. Because you need to bundle the X-Ray SDK with the function code, the templates create the functions without any code. When you deploy Scorekeep, a configuration file included in the `.ebextensions` folder creates a source bundle that includes the SDK, and updates the function code and configuration with the AWS Command Line Interface.

Topics
- Random Name
- Worker

Random Name

Scorekeep calls the random name function when a user starts a game session without signing in or specifying a user name. When Lambda processes the call to `random-name`, it reads the tracing header, which contains the trace ID and sampling decision written by the X-Ray SDK for Java.

For each sampled request, Lambda runs the X-Ray daemon and writes two segments. The first segment records information about the call to Lambda that invokes the function. This segment contains the same information as the subsegment recorded by Scorekeep, but from the Lambda point of view. The second segment represents the work that the function does.

Lambda passes the function segment to the X-Ray SDK through the function context. When you instrument a Lambda function, you don't use the SDK to create a segment for incoming requests. Lambda provides the segment, and you use the SDK to instrument clients and write subsegments.

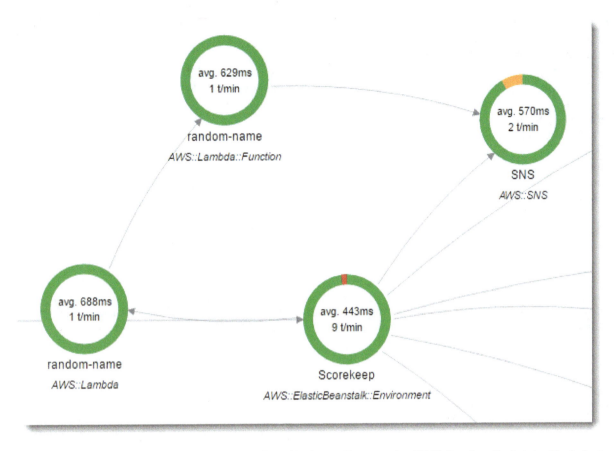

The `random-name` function is implemented in Node.js. It uses the SDK for JavaScript in Node.js to send notifications with Amazon SNS, and the X-Ray SDK for Node.js to instrument the AWS SDK client. To write annotations, the function creates a custom subsegment with `AWSXRay.captureFunc`, and writes annotations in the instrumented function. In Lambda, you can't write annotations directly to the function segment, only to a subsegment that you create.

Example   **https://github.com/awslabs/eb-java-scorekeep/tree/xray/_lambda/random-name/index.js -- Random Name Lambda Function**

```
1  var AWSXRay = require('aws-xray-sdk-core');
2  var AWS = AWSXRay.captureAWS(require('aws-sdk'));
3
4  AWS.config.update({region: process.env.AWS_REGION});
5  var Chance = require('chance');
6
7  var myFunction = function(event, context, callback) {
8    var sns = new AWS.SNS();
9    var chance = new Chance();
10   var userid = event.userid;
11   var name = chance.first();
12
13   AWSXRay.captureFunc('annotations', function(subsegment){
14     subsegment.addAnnotation('Name', name);
15     subsegment.addAnnotation('UserID', event.userid);
16   });
17
18   // Notify
19   var params = {
```

```
20      Message: 'Created randon name "' + name + '"" for user "' + userid + '".',
21      Subject: 'New user: ' + name,
22      TopicArn: process.env.TOPIC_ARN
23    };
24    sns.publish(params, function(err, data) {
25      if (err) {
26        console.log(err, err.stack);
27        callback(err);
28      }
29      else {
30        console.log(data);
31        callback(null, {"name": name});
32      }
33    });
34  };
35
36  exports.handler = myFunction;
```

This function is created automatically when you deploy the sample application to Elastic Beanstalk. The xray branch includes a script to create a blank Lambda function. Configuration files in the .ebextensions folder build the function package with npm install during deployment, and then update the Lambda function with the AWS CLI.

Worker

The instrumented worker function is provided in its own branch, xray-worker, as it cannot run unless you create the worker function and related resources first. See the branch readme for instructions.

The function is triggered by a bundled Amazon CloudWatch Events event every 5 minutes. When it runs, the function pulls an item from an Amazon SQS queue that Scorekeep manages. Each message contains information about a completed game.

The worker pulls the game record and documents from other tables that the game record references. For example, the game record in DynamoDB includes a list of moves that were executed during the game. The list does not contain the moves themselves, but rather IDs of moves that are stored in a separate table.

Sessions, and states are stored as references as well. This keeps the entries in the game table from being too large, but requires additional calls to get all of the information about the game. The worker dereferences all of these entries and constructs a complete record of the game as a single document in Amazon S3. When you want to do analytics on the data, you can run queries on it directly in Amazon S3 with Amazon Athena without running read-heavy data migrations to get your data out of DynamoDB.

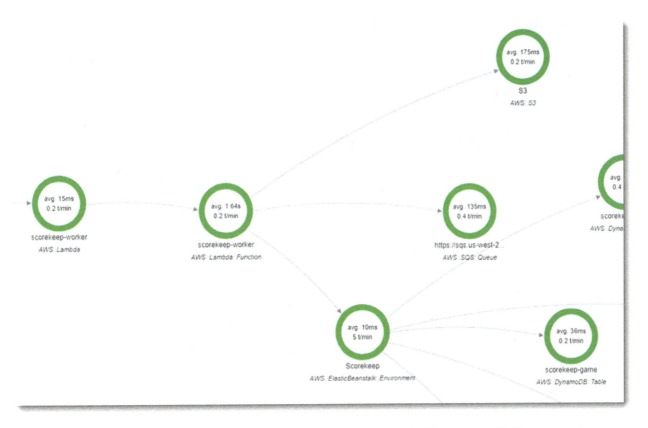

The worker function has active tracing enabled in its configuration in AWS Lambda. Unlike the random name function, the worker does not receive a request from an instrumented application, so AWS Lambda doesn't receive a tracing header. With active tracing, Lambda creates the trace ID and makes sampling decisions.

The X-Ray SDK for Python is just a few lines at the top of the function that import the SDK and run its `patch_all` function to patch the AWS SDK for Python (Boto) and HTTclients that it uses to call Amazon SQS and Amazon S3. When the worker calls the Scorekeep API, the SDK adds the tracing header to the request to trace calls through the API.

Example https://github.com/awslabs/eb-java-scorekeep/tree/xray-worker/_lambda/scorekeep-worker/scorekeep-worker.py -- Worker Lambda Function

```
1  import os
2  import boto3
3  import json
4  import requests
5  import time
6  from aws_xray_sdk.core import xray_recorder
7  from aws_xray_sdk.core import patch_all
8
9  patch_all()
10 queue_url = os.environ['WORKER_QUEUE']
11
12 def lambda_handler(event, context):
13     # Create SQS client
14     sqs = boto3.client('sqs')
15     s3client = boto3.client('s3')
16
17     # Receive message from SQS queue
18     response = sqs.receive_message(
19         QueueUrl=queue_url,
```

```
20        AttributeNames=[
21            'SentTimestamp'
22        ],
23        MaxNumberOfMessages=1,
24        MessageAttributeNames=[
25            'All'
26        ],
27        VisibilityTimeout=0,
28        WaitTimeSeconds=0
29    )
30    ...
```

Instrumenting Amazon ECS Applications

In the https://github.com/awslabs/eb-java-scorekeep/tree/xray-ecs branch, the Scorekeep sample application shows how to instrument an application running in Amazon Elastic Container Service (Amazon ECS). The branch provides scripts and configuration files for creating, uploading, and running Docker images in a Multicontainer Docker environment in AWS Elastic Beanstalk.

The project includes three Dockerfiles that define container images for the API, front end, and X-Ray daemon components.

- /Dockerfile – The Scorekeep API.
- /scorekeep-frontend/Dockerfile – The Angular web app client, and the nginx proxy that routes incoming traffic.
- /xray-daemon/Dockerfile – The X-Ray daemon.

The X-Ray daemon Dockerfile creates an image based on Amazon Linux that runs the X-Ray daemon.

Example Dockerfile – Amazon Linux

```
1 FROM amazonlinux
2 RUN yum install -y unzip
3 RUN curl -o daemon.zip https://s3.dualstack.us-east-2.amazonaws.com/aws-xray-assets.us-east-2/
    xray-daemon/aws-xray-daemon-linux-2.x.zip
4 RUN unzip daemon.zip && cp xray /usr/bin/xray
5 ENTRYPOINT ["/usr/bin/xray", "-b", "0.0.0.0:2000"]
6 EXPOSE 2000/udp
```

The makefile in the same directory defines commands for building the image, uploading it to Amazon ECR, and running it locally.

To run the containers on Amazon ECS, the branch includes a script to generate a Dockerrun.aws.json file, which you can deploy to a multicontainer Docker environment in Elastic Beanstalk. The template that the script uses shows how to write a task definition that configures networking between the containers in Amazon ECS.

Note
Dockerrun.aws.json is the Elastic Beanstalk version of an Amazon ECS task definition file. If you don't want to use Elastic Beanstalk to create your Amazon ECS cluster, you can modify the Dockerrun.aws.json file to run on Amazon ECS directly by removing the AWSEBDockerrunVersion key from the file.

See the branch README for instructions on how to deploy Scorekeep to Amazon ECS.

Instrumenting Startup Code

The X-Ray SDK for Java automatically creates segments for incoming requests. As long as a request is in scope, you can use instrumented clients and record subsegments without issue. If you try to use an instrumented client in startup code, though, you'll get a SegmentNotFoundException.

Startup code runs outside of the standard request/response flow of a web application, so you need to create segments manually to instrument it. Scorekeep shows the instrumentation of startup code in its `WebConfig` files. Scorekeep calls an SQL database and Amazon SNS during startup.

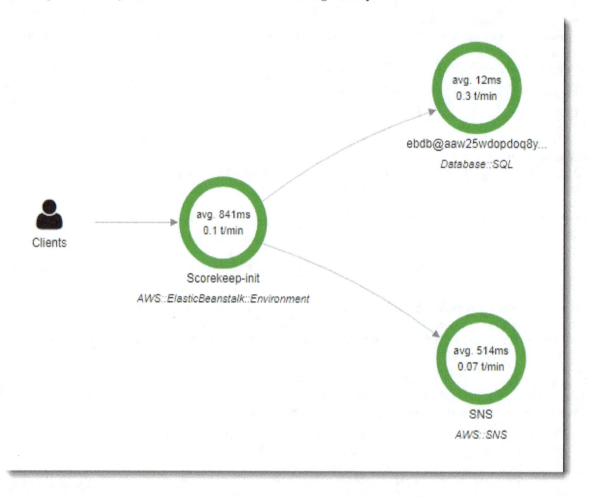

The default `WebConfig` class creates an Amazon SNS subscription for notifications. To provide a segment for the X-Ray SDK to write to when the Amazon SNS client is used, Scorekeep calls `beginSegment` and `endSegment` on the global recorder.

Example   https://github.com/awslabs/eb-java-scorekeep/tree/xray/src/main/java/scorekeep/ WebConfig.java#L49 – Instrumented AWS SDK client in startup code

```
1 AWSXRay.beginSegment("Scorekeep-init");
2 if ( System.getenv("NOTIFICATION_EMAIL") != null ){
3   try { Sns.createSubscription(); }
4   catch (Exception e ) {
5     logger.warn("Failed to create subscription for email "+  System.getenv("NOTIFICATION_EMAIL")
          );
6   }
7 }
```

```
8 AWSXRay.endSegment();
```

In `RdsWebConfig`, which Scorekeep uses when an Amazon RDS database is connected, the configuration also creates a segment for the SQL client that Hibernate uses when it applies the database schema during startup.

Example https://github.com/awslabs/eb-java-scorekeep/tree/xray/src/main/java/scorekeep/ **RdsWebConfig.java#L83 – Instrumented SQL database client in startup code**

```
1  @PostConstruct
2  public void schemaExport() {
3    EntityManagerFactoryImpl entityManagerFactoryImpl = (EntityManagerFactoryImpl)
        localContainerEntityManagerFactoryBean.getNativeEntityManagerFactory();
4    SessionFactoryImplementor sessionFactoryImplementor = entityManagerFactoryImpl.
        getSessionFactory();
5    StandardServiceRegistry standardServiceRegistry = sessionFactoryImplementor.
        getSessionFactoryOptions().getServiceRegistry();
6    MetadataSources metadataSources = new MetadataSources(new BootstrapServiceRegistryBuilder().
        build());
7    metadataSources.addAnnotatedClass(GameHistory.class);
8    MetadataImplementor metadataImplementor = (MetadataImplementor) metadataSources.buildMetadata(
        standardServiceRegistry);
9    SchemaExport schemaExport = new SchemaExport(standardServiceRegistry, metadataImplementor);
10
11   AWSXRay.beginSegment("Scorekeep-init");
12   schemaExport.create(true, true);
13   AWSXRay.endSegment();
14 }
```

`SchemaExport` runs automatically and uses an SQL client. Since the client is instrumented, Scorekeep must override the default implementation and provide a segment for the SDK to use when the client is invoked.

Instrumenting Scripts

You can also instrument code that isn't part of your application. When the X-Ray daemon is running, it will relay any segments that it receives to X-Ray, even if they are not generated by the X-Ray SDK. Scorekeep uses its own scripts to instrument the build that compiles the application during deployment.

Example https://github.com/awslabs/eb-java-scorekeep/tree/xray/bin/build.sh − Instrumented build script

```
1 SEGMENT=$(python bin/xray_start.py)
2 gradle build --quiet --stacktrace &> /var/log/gradle.log; GRADLE_RETURN=$?
3 if (( GRADLE_RETURN != 0 )); then
4   echo "Gradle failed with exit status $GRADLE_RETURN" >&2
5   python bin/xray_error.py "$SEGMENT" "$(cat /var/log/gradle.log)"
6   exit 1
7 fi
8 python bin/xray_success.py "$SEGMENT"
```

https://github.com/awslabs/eb-java-scorekeep/tree/xray/bin/xray_start.py, https://github.com/awslabs/eb-java-scorekeep/tree/xray/bin/xray_error.py and https://github.com/awslabs/eb-java-scorekeep/tree/xray/bin/xray_success.py are simple Python scripts that construct segment objects, convert them to JSON documents, and send them to the daemon over UDP. If the Gradle build fails, you can find the error message by clicking on the **scorekeep-build** node in the X-Ray console service map.

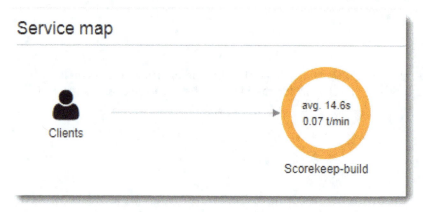

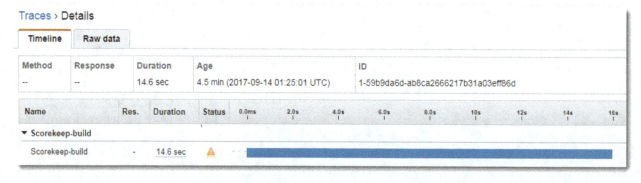

Segment - Scorekeep-build

| Overview | Resources | Annotations | Metadata | **Exceptions** |

Working directory   /var/app/current
Paths   /var/app/current/src/main/java/scorekeep/

Cause

/var/app/staging/src/main/java/scorekeep/RdsWebConfig.java:89: error: cannot find symbol
   AWSXRayRecorderBuilder builder = AWSXRayRecorderBuilder.standard().withPlugin(new EC2Plugin()).withPlugin(new ElasticBeanstalkPlugin());
                                        ^

 symbol: class ElasticBeanstalkPlugin
 location: class RdsWebConfig
1 error

FAILURE: Build failed with an exception.

Close

Instrumenting a Web App Client

In the https://github.com/awslabs/eb-java-scorekeep/tree/xray-cognito branch, Scorekeep uses Amazon Cognito to enable users to create an account and sign in with it to retrieve their user information from an Amazon Cognito user pool. When a user signs in, Scorekeep uses an Amazon Cognito identity pool to get temporary AWS credentials for use with the AWS SDK for JavaScript.

The identity pool is configured to let signed-in users write trace data to AWS X-Ray. The web app uses these credentials to record the signed-in user's ID, the browser path, and the client's view of calls to the Scorekeep API.

Most of the work is done in a service class named **xray**. This service class provides methods for generating the required identifiers, creating in-progress segments, finalizing segments, and sending segment documents to the X-Ray API.

Example https://github.com/awslabs/eb-java-scorekeep/tree/xray-cognito/public/app/xray.js – Record and upload segments

```
1  ...
2    service.beginSegment = function() {
3      var segment = {};
4      var traceId = '1-' + service.getHexTime() + '-' + service.getHexId(24);
5
6      var id = service.getHexId(16);
7      var startTime = service.getEpochTime();
8
9      segment.trace_id = traceId;
10     segment.id = id;
11     segment.start_time = startTime;
12     segment.name = 'Scorekeep-client';
13     segment.in_progress = true;
14     segment.user = sessionStorage['userid'];
15     segment.http = {
16       request: {
17         url: window.location.href
18       }
19     };
20
21     var documents = [];
22     documents[0] = JSON.stringify(segment);
23     service.putDocuments(documents);
24     return segment;
25   }
26
27   service.endSegment = function(segment) {
28     var endTime = service.getEpochTime();
29     segment.end_time = endTime;
30     segment.in_progress = false;
31     var documents = [];
32     documents[0] = JSON.stringify(segment);
33     service.putDocuments(documents);
34   }
35
36   service.putDocuments = function(documents) {
37     var xray = new AWS.XRay();
38     var params = {
```

```
39        TraceSegmentDocuments: documents
40    };
41    xray.putTraceSegments(params, function(err, data) {
42      if (err) {
43        console.log(err, err.stack);
44      } else {
45        console.log(data);
46      }
47    })
48  }
```

These methods are called in header and `transformResponse` functions in the resource services that the web app uses to call the Scorekeep API. To include the client segment in the same trace as the segment that the API generates, the web app must include the trace ID and segment ID in a tracing header (`X-Amzn-Trace-Id`) that the X-Ray SDK can read. When the instrumented Java application receives a request with this header, the X-Ray SDK for Java uses the same trace ID and makes the segment from the web app client the parent of its segment.

Example   https://github.com/awslabs/eb-java-scorekeep/tree/xray/public/app/services.js   —
Recording segments for Angular resource calls and writing tracing headers

```
1  var module = angular.module('scorekeep');
2  module.factory('SessionService', function($resource, api, XRay) {
3    return $resource(api + 'session/:id', { id: '@_id' }, {
4      segment: {},
5      get: {
6        method: 'GET',
7        headers: {
8          'X-Amzn-Trace-Id': function(config) {
9            segment = XRay.beginSegment();
10           return XRay.getTraceHeader(segment);
11         }
12       },
13       transformResponse: function(data) {
14         XRay.endSegment(segment);
15         return angular.fromJson(data);
16       },
17     },
18  ...
```

The resulting service map includes a node for the web app client.

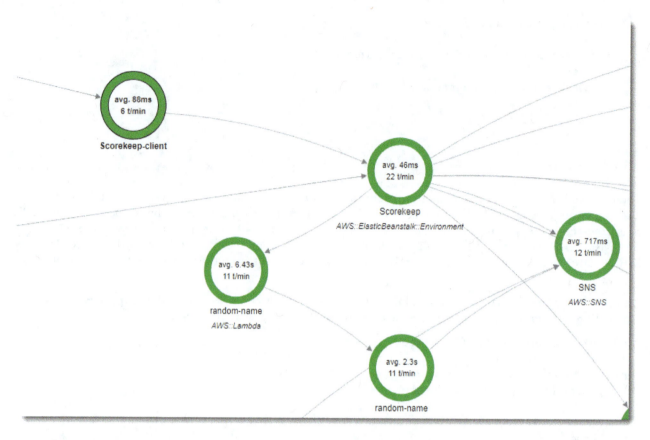

Traces that include segments from the web app show the URL that the user sees in the browser (paths starting with /#/). Without client instrumentation, you only get the URL of the API resource that the web app calls (paths starting with /api/).

Trace overview

Group by: URL ▼

URL	Avg response time ▼
http://scorekeep.elasticbeanstalk.com/#/	86.2 ms
http://scorekeep.elasticbeanstalk.com/#/session/4ORP7OB5/47H4SETD	58.5 ms
http://scorekeep.elasticbeanstalk.com/#/game/4ORP7OB5/A94SAFFD/47H4SETD	255 ms

Using Instrumented Clients in Worker Threads

Scorekeep uses a worker thread to publish a notification to Amazon SNS when a user wins a game. Publishing the notification takes longer than the rest of the request operations combined, and doesn't affect the client or user. Therefore, performing the task asynchronously is a good way to improve response time.

However, the X-Ray SDK for Java doesn't know which segment was active when the thread is created. As a result, when you try to use the instrumented AWS SDK for Java client within the thread, it throws a `SegmentNotFoundException`, crashing the thread.

Example web-1.error.log

```
1 Exception in thread "Thread-2" com.amazonaws.xray.exceptions.SegmentNotFoundException: Failed to
     begin subsegment named 'AmazonSNS': segment cannot be found.
2       at sun.reflect.NativeConstructorAccessorImpl.newInstance0(Native Method)
3       at sun.reflect.NativeConstructorAccessorImpl.newInstance(NativeConstructorAccessorImpl.
         java:62)
4       at sun.reflect.DelegatingConstructorAccessorImpl.newInstance(
         DelegatingConstructorAccessorImpl.java:45)
5 ...
```

To fix this, the application uses `GetTraceEntity` to get a reference to the segment in the main thread, and `SetTraceEntity` to pass the segment back to the recorder in the worker thread.

Example   https://github.com/awslabs/eb-java-scorekeep/tree/xray/src/main/java/scorekeep/ MoveFactory.java#L70 – Passing trace context to a worker thread

```
1 import [com\.amazonaws\.xray\.AWSXRay](http://docs.aws.amazon.com/xray-sdk-for-java/latest/
     javadoc/com/amazonaws/xray/AWSXRay.html);
2 import [com\.amazonaws\.xray\.AWSXRayRecorder](http://docs.aws.amazon.com/xray-sdk-for-java/
     latest/javadoc/com/amazonaws/xray/AWSXRayRecorder.html);
3 import [com\.amazonaws\.xray\.entities\.Entity](http://docs.aws.amazon.com/xray-sdk-for-java/
     latest/javadoc/com/amazonaws/xray/entities/Entity.html);
4 import [com\.amazonaws\.xray\.entities\.Segment](http://docs.aws.amazon.com/xray-sdk-for-java/
     latest/javadoc/com/amazonaws/xray/entities/Segment.html);
5 import [com\.amazonaws\.xray\.entities\.Subsegment](http://docs.aws.amazon.com/xray-sdk-for-java
     /latest/javadoc/com/amazonaws/xray/entities/Subsegment.html);
6 ...
7       Entity segment = recorder.getTraceEntity();
8       Thread comm = new Thread() {
9         public void run() {
10          recorder.setTraceEntity(segment);
11          Subsegment subsegment = AWSXRay.beginSubsegment("## Send notification");
12          Sns.sendNotification("Scorekeep game completed", "Winner: " + userId);
13          AWSXRay.endSubsegment();
14        }
```

Because the request is now resolved before the call to Amazon SNS, the application creates a separate subsegment for the thread. This prevents the X-Ray SDK from closing the segment before it records the response from Amazon SNS. If no subsegment is open when Scorekeep resolved the request, the response from Amazon SNS could be lost.

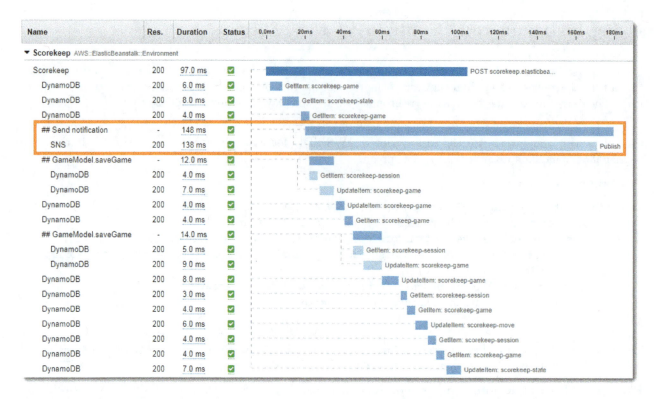

Name	Res.	Duration	Status										
				0.0ms	20ms	40ms	60ms	80ms	100ms	120ms	140ms	160ms	180ms
▼ **Scorekeep** AWS::ElasticBeanstalk::Environment													
Scorekeep	200	97.0 ms	✅							POST scorekeep.elasticbea...			
DynamoDB	200	6.0 ms	✅		GetItem: scorekeep-game								
DynamoDB	200	8.0 ms	✅			GetItem: scorekeep-state							
DynamoDB	200	4.0 ms	✅			GetItem: scorekeep-game							
## Send notification	-	148 ms	✅										
SNS	200	138 ms	✅										Publish
## GameModel.saveGame	-	12.0 ms	✅										
DynamoDB	200	4.0 ms	✅			GetItem: scorekeep-session							
DynamoDB	200	7.0 ms	✅				UpdateItem: scorekeep-game						
DynamoDB	200	4.0 ms	✅				UpdateItem: scorekeep-game						
DynamoDB	200	4.0 ms	✅				GetItem: scorekeep-game						
## GameModel.saveGame	-	14.0 ms	✅										
DynamoDB	200	5.0 ms	✅				GetItem: scorekeep-session						
DynamoDB	200	9.0 ms	✅				UpdateItem: scorekeep-game						
DynamoDB	200	8.0 ms	✅				UpdateItem: scorekeep-game						
DynamoDB	200	3.0 ms	✅				GetItem: scorekeep-session						
DynamoDB	200	4.0 ms	✅				GetItem: scorekeep-game						
DynamoDB	200	6.0 ms	✅				UpdateItem: scorekeep-move						
DynamoDB	200	4.0 ms	✅				GetItem: scorekeep-session						
DynamoDB	200	4.0 ms	✅				GetItem: scorekeep-game						
DynamoDB	200	7.0 ms	✅				UpdateItem: scorekeep-state						

See Passing Segment Context between Threads in a Multithreaded Application for more information about multithreading.

Deep Linking to the X-Ray Console

The session and game pages of the Scorekeep web app use deep linking to link to filtered trace lists and service maps.

Example https://github.com/awslabs/eb-java-scorekeep/tree/xray/public/game.html – deep links

```
1 <div id="xray-link">
2   <p><a href="https://console.aws.amazon.com/xray/home#/traces?filter=http.url%20CONTAINS
        %20%22{{ gameid }}%22&timeRange=PT1H" target="blank">View traces for this game</a></p>
3   <p><a href="https://console.aws.amazon.com/xray/home#/service-map&timeRange=PT1H" target="
        blank">View service map</a></p>
4 </div>
```

See Deep Linking for details on how to construct deep links.

AWS X-Ray Daemon

The AWS X-Ray daemon is a software application that listens for traffic on UDP port 2000, gathers raw segment data, and relays it to the AWS X-Ray API. The daemon works in conjunction with the AWS X-Ray SDKs and must be running so that data sent by the SDKs can reach the X-Ray service.

Note
The X-Ray daemon is an open source project. You can follow the project and submit issues and pull requests on GitHub: github.com/aws/aws-xray-daemon

On AWS Lambda and AWS Elastic Beanstalk, use those services' integration with X-Ray to run the daemon. Lambda runs the daemon automatically any time a function is invoked for a sampled request. On Elastic Beanstalk, use the `XRayEnabled` configuration option to run the daemon on the instances in your environment.

To run the X-Ray daemon locally, on-premises, or on other AWS services, download it from Amazon S3, run it, and then give it permission to upload segment documents to X-Ray.

Downloading the Daemon

You can download the daemon from Amazon S3 to run it locally, or to install it on an Amazon EC2 instance on launch.

X-Ray daemon installers and executables

- **Linux (executable)** – https://s3.dualstack.us-east-2.amazonaws.com/aws-xray-assets.us-east-2/xray-daemon/aws-xray-daemon-linux-2.x.zip (sig)
- **Linux (RPM installer)** – https://s3.dualstack.us-east-2.amazonaws.com/aws-xray-assets.us-east-2/xray-daemon/aws-xray-daemon-2.x.rpm
- **Linux (DEB installer)** – https://s3.dualstack.us-east-2.amazonaws.com/aws-xray-assets.us-east-2/xray-daemon/aws-xray-daemon-2.x.deb
- **OS X (executable)** – https://s3.dualstack.us-east-2.amazonaws.com/aws-xray-assets.us-east-2/xray-daemon/aws-xray-daemon-macos-2.x.zip (sig)
- **Windows (executable)** – https://s3.dualstack.us-east-2.amazonaws.com/aws-xray-assets.us-east-2/xray-daemon/aws-xray-daemon-windows-process-2.x.zip (sig)
- ****Windows (service) **** – https://s3.dualstack.us-east-2.amazonaws.com/aws-xray-assets.us-east-2/xray-daemon/aws-xray-daemon-windows-service-2.x.zip (sig)

These links always point to the latest v2 release of the daemon. To download a specific release, replace `2.x` with the version number. For example, `2.1.0`.

X-Ray assets are replicated to buckets in every supported region. To use the bucket closest to you or your AWS resources, replace the region in the above links with your region.

```
1 https://s3.dualstack.us-west-2.amazonaws.com/aws-xray-assets.us-west-2/xray-daemon/aws-xray-
      daemon-2.x.rpm
```

Verifying the Daemon Archive's Signature

GPG signature files are included for daemon assets compressed in ZIP archives. The public key is here: https://s3.dualstack.us-east-2.amazonaws.com/aws-xray-assets.us-east-2/xray-daemon/aws-xray.gpg.

You can use the public key to verify that the daemon's ZIP archive is original and unmodified. First, import the public key with GnuPG.

To import the public key

1. Download the public key.

```
1 $ BUCKETURL=https://s3.dualstack.us-east-2.amazonaws.com/aws-xray-assets.us-east-2
2 $ wget $BUCKETURL/xray-daemon/aws-xray.gpg
```

2. Import the public key into your keyring.

```
1 $ gpg --import aws-xray.gpg
2 gpg: /Users/me/.gnupg/trustdb.gpg: trustdb created
3 gpg: key 7BFE036BFE6157D3: public key "AWS X-Ray <aws-xray@amazon.com>" imported
4 gpg: Total number processed: 1
5 gpg:                imported: 1
```

Use the imported key to verify the signature of the daemon's ZIP archive.

To verify an archive's signature

1. Download the archive and signature file.

```
1 $ BUCKETURL=https://s3.dualstack.us-east-2.amazonaws.com/aws-xray-assets.us-east-2
2 $ wget $BUCKETURL/xray-daemon/aws-xray-daemon-linux-2.0.0.zip
3 $ wget $BUCKETURL/xray-daemon/aws-xray-daemon-linux-2.0.0.zip.sig
```

2. Run gpg --verify to verify the signature.

```
1 $ gpg --verify aws-xray-daemon-linux-2.0.0.zip.sig aws-xray-daemon-linux-2.0.0.zip
2 gpg: Signature made Wed 19 Apr 2017 05:06:31 AM UTC using RSA key ID FE6157D3
3 gpg: Good signature from "AWS X-Ray <aws-xray@amazon.com>"
4 gpg: WARNING: This key is not certified with a trusted signature!
5 gpg:          There is no indication that the signature belongs to the owner.
6 Primary key fingerprint: EA6D 9271 FBF3 6990 277F  4B87 7BFE 036B FE61 57D3
```

Note the warning about trust. A key is only trusted if you or someone you trust has signed it. This does not mean that the signature is invalid, only that you have not verified the public key.

Running the Daemon

Run the daemon locally from the command line. Use the -o option to run in local mode, and -n to set the region.

```
1 ~/Downloads$ ./xray -o -n us-east-2
```

For detailed platform-specific instructions, see the following topics:

- **Linux (local)** – Running the X-Ray Daemon on Linux
- **Windows (local)** – Running the X-Ray Daemon on Windows
- **Elastic Beanstalk** – Running the X-Ray Daemon on AWS Elastic Beanstalk
- **Amazon EC2** – Running the X-Ray Daemon on Amazon EC2
- **Amazon ECS** – Running the X-Ray Daemon on Amazon ECS

You can customize the daemon's behavior further by using command line options or a configuration file. See Configuring the AWS X-Ray Daemon for details.

Giving the Daemon Permission to Send Data to X-Ray

The X-Ray daemon uses the AWS SDK to upload trace data to X-Ray, and it needs AWS credentials with permission to do that.

On Amazon EC2, the daemon uses the instance's instance profile role automatically. Locally, save your access keys to a file named `credentials` in your user directory under a folder named `.aws`.

```
```

Example ~/.aws/credentials

```
1 [default]
2 aws_access_key_id = AKIAIOSFODNN7EXAMPLE
3 aws_secret_access_key = wJalrXUtnFEMI/K7MDENG/bPxRfiCYEXAMPLEKEY
```

If you specify credentials in more than one location (credentials file, instance profile, or environment variables), the SDK provider chain determines which credentials are used. For more information about providing credentials to the SDK, see Specifying Credentials in the *AWS SDK for Go Developer Guide*.

The IAM role or user that the daemon's credentials belong to must have permission to write data to the service on your behalf.

- To use the daemon on Amazon EC2, create a new instance profile role or add the managed policy to an existing one.
- To use the daemon on Elastic Beanstalk, add the managed policy to the Elastic Beanstalk default instance profile role.
- To run the daemon locally, create an IAM user and save its access keys on your computer.

For more information, see AWS X-Ray Permissions.

X-Ray Daemon Logs

The daemon outputs information about its current configuration and segments that it sends to AWS X-Ray.

```
1 2016-11-24T06:07:06Z [Info] Initializing AWS X-Ray daemon 2.1.0
2 2016-11-24T06:07:06Z [Info] Using memory limit of 49 MB
3 2016-11-24T06:07:06Z [Info] 313 segment buffers allocated
4 2016-11-24T06:07:08Z [Info] Successfully sent batch of 1 segments (0.123 seconds)
5 2016-11-24T06:07:09Z [Info] Successfully sent batch of 1 segments (0.006 seconds)
```

By default, the daemon outputs logs to STDOUT. If you run the daemon in the background, use the `--log-file` command line option or a configuration file to set the log file path. You can also set the log level and disable log rotation. See Configuring the AWS X-Ray Daemon for instructions.

On Elastic Beanstalk, the platform sets the location of the daemon logs. See Running the X-Ray Daemon on AWS Elastic Beanstalk for details.

Configuring the AWS X-Ray Daemon

You can use command line options or a configuration file to customize the X-Ray daemon's behavior. Most options are available using both methods, but some are only available in configuration files and some only at the command line.

To get started, the only option that you need to know is `-n` or `--region`, which you use to set the region that the daemon uses to send trace data to X-Ray.

```
1 ~/xray-daemon$ ./xray -n us-east-2
```

If you are running the daemon locally, that is, not on Amazon EC2, you can add the `-o` option to skip checking for instance profile credentials so the daemon will become ready more quickly.

```
1 ~/xray-daemon$ ./xray -o -n us-east-2
```

The rest of the command line options let you configure logging, listen on a different port, limit the amount of memory that the daemon can use, or assume a role to send trace data to a different account.

You can pass a configuration file to the daemon to access advanced configuration options and do things like limit the number of concurrent calls to X-Ray, disable log rotation, and send traffic to a proxy.

Topics

- Using Command Line Options
- Using a Configuration File

Using Command Line Options

Pass these options to the daemon when you run it locally or with a user data script.

Command Line Options

- `-b, --bind` – Bind the daemon to a different port.

```
1 --bind "127.0.0.1:3000"
```

  Default – 2000.

- `-c, --config` – Load a configuration file from the specified path.

```
1 --config "/home/ec2-user/xray-daemon.yaml"
```

- `-f, --log-file` – Output logs to the specified file path.

```
1 --log-file "/var/log/xray-daemon.log"
```

- `-l, --log-level` – Log level, from most verbose to least: dev, debug, info, warn, error, prod.

```
1 --log-level warn
```

  Default – prod

- `-m, --buffer-memory` – Change the amount of memory in MB that buffers can use (minimum 3).

```
1 --buffer-memory 50
```

  Default – 1% of available memory.

- `-o, --local-mode` – Don't check for EC2 instance metadata.

- `-r, --role-arn` – Assume the specified IAM role to upload segments to a different account.

119

```
1 --role-arn "arn:aws:iam::123456789012:role/xray-cross-account"
```

- `-a`, `--resource-arn` – Amazon Resource Name (ARN) of the AWS resource running the daemon.
- `-n`, `--region` – Send segments to X-Ray service in a specific region.
- `-v`, `--version` – Show AWS X-Ray daemon version.
- `-h`, `--help` – Show the help screen.

Using a Configuration File

You can also use a YAML format file to configure the daemon. Pass the configuration file to the daemon by using the `-c` option.

```
1 ~$ ./xray -c ~/xray-daemon.yaml
```

Configuration file options

- `TotalBufferSizeMB` – Maximum buffer size in MB (minimum 3). Choose 0 to use 1% of host memory.
- `Concurrency` – Maximum number of concurrent calls to AWS X-Ray to upload segment documents.
- `Region` – Send segments to AWS X-Ray service in a specific region.
- `Socket` – Configure the daemon's binding.
  - `UDPAddress` – Change the port on which the daemon listens.
- `Logging` – Configure logging behavior.
  - `LogRotation` – Set to `false` to disable log rotation.
  - `LogLevel` – Change the log level, from most verbose to least: `dev`, `debug`, `info`, `warn`, `error`, `prod` (default).
  - `LogPath` – Output logs to the specified file path.
- `LocalMode` – Set to `true` to skip checking for EC2 instance metadata.
- `ResourceARN` – Amazon Resource Name (ARN) of the AWS resource running the daemon.
- `RoleARN` – Assume the specified IAM role to upload segments to a different account.
- `ProxyAddress` – Upload segments to AWS X-Ray through a proxy.
- `Endpoint` – Change the X-Ray service endpoint to which the daemon sends segment documents.
- `NoVerifySSL` – Disable TLS certificate verification.
- `Version` – Daemon configuration file format version.

Example xray-daemon.yaml
This configuration file changes the daemon's listening port to 3000, turns off checks for instance metadata, sets a role to use for uploading segments, and changes region and logging options.

```
1 Socket:
2   UDPAddress: "127.0.0.1:3000"
3 Region: "us-west-2"
4 Logging:
5   LogLevel: "warn"
6   LogPath: "/var/log/xray-daemon.log"
7 LocalMode: true
8 RoleARN: "arn:aws:iam::123456789012:role/xray-cross-account"
9 Version: 1
```

Running the X-Ray Daemon Locally

You can run the AWS X-Ray daemon locally on Linux, MacOS, Windows, or in a Docker container. Run the daemon to relay trace date to X-Ray when you are developing and testing your instrumented application. Download and extract the daemon by using the instructions here.

When running locally, the daemon can read credentials from an AWS SDK credentials file (.aws/credentials in your user directory) or from environment variables. For more information, see Giving the Daemon Permission to Send Data to X-Ray.

The daemon listens for UDP data on port 2000. You can change the port and other options by using a configuration file and command line options. For more information, see Configuring the AWS X-Ray Daemon.

Running the X-Ray Daemon on Linux

You can run the daemon executable from the command line. Use the -o option to run in local mode, and -n to set the region.

```
1 ~/xray-daemon$ ./xray -o -n us-east-2
```

To run the daemon in the background, use &.

```
1 ~/xray-daemon$ ./xray -o -n us-east-2 &
```

Terminate a daemon process running in the background with pkill.

```
1 ~$ pkill xray
```

Running the X-Ray Daemon in a Docker Container

To run the daemon locally in a Docker container, save the following text to a file named Dockerfile.

Example Dockerfile – Amazon Linux

```
1 FROM amazonlinux
2 RUN yum install -y unzip
3 RUN curl -o daemon.zip https://s3.dualstack.us-east-2.amazonaws.com/aws-xray-assets.us-east-2/
    xray-daemon/aws-xray-daemon-linux-2.x.zip
4 RUN unzip daemon.zip && cp xray /usr/bin/xray
5 ENTRYPOINT ["/usr/bin/xray", "-b", "0.0.0.0:2000"]
6 EXPOSE 2000/udp
```

Build the container image with docker build.

```
1 ~/xray-daemon$ docker build -t xray-daemon .
```

Run the image in a container with docker run.

```
1 ~/xray-daemon$ docker run \
2       --attach STDOUT \
3       -v ~/.aws/:/root/.aws/:ro \
4       --net=host \
5       -e AWS_REGION=us-east-2 \
6       --name xray-daemon \
7       -p 2000:2000/udp \
8       xray-daemon -o
```

This command uses the following options:

- --attach STDOUT – View output from the daemon in the terminal.
- -v ~/.aws/:/root/.aws/:ro – Give the container read-only access to the .aws directory to let it read your AWS SDK credentials.
- AWS_REGION=us-east-2 – Set the AWS_REGION environment variable to tell the daemon which region to use.
- --net=host – Attach the container to the host network. Containers on the host network can communicate with each other without publishing ports.
- -p 2000:2000/udp – Map UDP port 2000 on your machine to the same port on the container. This is not required for containers on the same network to communicate, but it does let you send segments to the daemon from the command line or from an application not running in Docker.
- --name xray-daemon – Name the container xray-daemon instead of generating a random name.
- -o (after the image name) – Append the -o option to the entry point that runs the daemon within the container. This option tells the daemon to run in local mode to prevent it from trying to read Amazon EC2 instance metadata.

To stop the daemon, use docker stop. If you make changes to the Dockerfile and build a new image, you need to delete the existing container before you can create another one with the same name. Use docker rm to delete the container.

```
1 $ docker stop xray-daemon
2 $ docker rm xray-daemon
```

The Scorekeep sample application shows how to use the X-Ray daemon in a local Docker container. See Instrumenting Amazon ECS Applications for details.

Running the X-Ray Daemon on Windows

You can run the daemon executable from the command line. Use the -o option to run in local mode, and -n to set the region.

```
1 > .\xray_windows.exe -o -n us-east-2
```

Use a PowerShell script to create and run a service for the daemon.

Example PowerShell Script - Windows

```
1 if ( Get-Service "AWSXRayDaemon" -ErrorAction SilentlyContinue ){
2     sc.exe stop AWSXRayDaemon
3     sc.exe delete AWSXRayDaemon
4 }
5 if ( Get-Item -path aws-xray-daemon -ErrorAction SilentlyContinue ) {
6     Remove-Item -Recurse -Force aws-xray-daemon
7 }
8
9 $currentLocation = Get-Location
10 $zipFileName = "aws-xray-daemon-windows-service-2.x.zip"
11 $zipPath = "$currentLocation\$zipFileName"
12 $destPath = "$currentLocation\aws-xray-daemon"
13 $daemonPath = "$destPath\xray.exe"
14 $daemonLogPath = "C:\inetpub\wwwroot\xray-daemon.log"
15 $url = "https://s3.dualstack.us-west-2.amazonaws.com/aws-xray-assets.us-west-2/xray-daemon/aws-xray-daemon-windows-service-2.x.zip"
16
17 Invoke-WebRequest -Uri $url -OutFile $zipPath
18 Add-Type -Assembly "System.IO.Compression.Filesystem"
```

```
19 [io.compression.zipfile]::ExtractToDirectory($zipPath, $destPath)
20
21 sc.exe create AWSXRayDaemon binPath= "$daemonPath -f $daemonLogPath"
22 sc.exe start AWSXRayDaemon
```

Running the X-Ray Daemon on OS X

You can run the daemon executable from the command line. Use the -o option to run in local mode, and -n to set the region.

```
1 ~/xray-daemon$ ./xray_mac -o -n us-east-2
```

To run the daemon in the background, use &.

```
1 ~/xray-daemon$ ./xray_mac -o -n us-east-2 &
```

Use nohup to prevent the daemon from terminating when the terminal is closed.

```
1 ~/xray-daemon$ nohup ./xray_mac &
```

Running the X-Ray Daemon on AWS Elastic Beanstalk

To relay trace data from your application to AWS X-Ray, you can run the X-Ray daemon on your Elastic Beanstalk environment's Amazon EC2 instances. For a list of supported platforms, see Configuring AWS X-Ray Debugging in the *AWS Elastic Beanstalk Developer Guide*.

Note
The daemon uses your environment's instance profile for permissions. For instructions about adding permissions to the Elastic Beanstalk instance profile, see Giving the Daemon Permission to Send Data to X-Ray.

Elastic Beanstalk platforms provide a configuration option that you can set to run the daemon automatically. You can enable the daemon in a configuration file in your source code or by choosing an option in the Elastic Beanstalk console. When you enable the configuration option, the daemon is installed on the instance and runs as a service.

The version included on Elastic Beanstalk platforms might not be the latest version. See the Supported Platforms topic to find out the version of the daemon that is available for your platform configuration.

Elastic Beanstalk does not provide the X-Ray daemon on the Multicontainer Docker (Amazon ECS) platform. The Scorekeep sample application shows how to use the X-Ray daemon on Amazon ECS with Elastic Beanstalk. See Instrumenting Amazon ECS Applications for details.

Using the Elastic Beanstalk X-Ray Integration to Run the X-Ray Daemon

Use the console to turn on X-Ray integration, or configure it in your application source code with a configuration file.

To enable the X-Ray daemon in the Elastic Beanstalk console

1. Open the Elastic Beanstalk console.

2. Navigate to the management console for your environment.

3. Choose **Configuration**.

4. Choose **Software Settings**.

5. For **X-Ray daemon**, choose **Enabled**.

6. Choose **Apply**.

You can include a configuration file in your source code to make your configuration portable between environments.

Example .ebextensions/xray-daemon.config

```
1 option_settings:
2   aws:elasticbeanstalk:xray:
3     XRayEnabled: true
```

Elastic Beanstalk passes a configuration file to the daemon and outputs logs to a standard location.

On Windows Server Platforms

- **Configuration file** – `C:\Progam Files\Amazon\XRay\cfg.yaml`
- **Logs** – `c:\Program Files\Amazon\XRay\logs\xray-service.log`

On Linux Platforms

- **Configuration file** – `/etc/amazon/xray/cfg.yaml`
- **Logs** – `/var/log/xray/xray.log`

Elastic Beanstalk provides tools for pulling instance logs from the AWS Management Console or command line. You can tell Elastic Beanstalk to include the X-Ray daemon logs by adding a task with a configuration file.

Example .ebextensions/xray-logs.config - Linux

```
1 files:
2   "/opt/elasticbeanstalk/tasks/taillogs.d/xray-daemon.conf" :
3     mode: "000644"
4     owner: root
5     group: root
6     content: |
7       /var/log/xray/xray.log
```

Example .ebextensions/xray-logs.config - Windows Server

```
1 files:
2   "c:/Program Files/Amazon/ElasticBeanstalk/config/taillogs.d/xray-daemon.conf" :
3     mode: "000644"
4     owner: root
5     group: root
6     content: |
7       c:\Progam Files\Amazon\XRay\logs\xray-service.log
```

See Viewing Logs from Your Elastic Beanstalk Environment's Amazon EC2 Instances in the *AWS Elastic Beanstalk Developer Guide* for more information.

Downloading and Running the X-Ray Daemon Manually (Advanced)

If the X-Ray daemon isn't available for your platform configuration, you can download it from Amazon S3 and run it with a configuration file.

Use an Elastic Beanstalk configuration file to download and run the daemon.

Example .ebextensions/xray.config - Linux

```
1  commands:
2    01-stop-tracing:
3      command: yum remove -y xray
4      ignoreErrors: true
5    02-copy-tracing:
6      command: curl https://s3.dualstack.us-east-2.amazonaws.com/aws-xray-assets.us-east-2/xray-
           daemon/aws-xray-daemon-2.x.rpm -o /home/ec2-user/xray.rpm
7    03-start-tracing:
8      command: yum install -y /home/ec2-user/xray.rpm
9
10 files:
11   "/opt/elasticbeanstalk/tasks/taillogs.d/xray-daemon.conf" :
12     mode: "000644"
13     owner: root
14     group: root
15     content: |
16       /var/log/xray/xray.log
17   "/etc/amazon/xray/cfg.yaml" :
18     mode: "000644"
19     owner: root
20     group: root
21     content: |
```

```
22      Logging:
23        LogLevel: "debug"
```

Example .ebextensions/xray.config - Windows Server

```
1  container_commands:
2    01-execute-config-script:
3      command: Powershell.exe -ExecutionPolicy Bypass -File c:\\temp\\installDaemon.ps1
4      waitAfterCompletion: 0
5
6  files:
7    "c:/temp/installDaemon.ps1":
8      content: |
9        if ( Get-Service "AWSXRayDaemon" -ErrorAction SilentlyContinue ) {
10           sc.exe stop AWSXRayDaemon
11           sc.exe delete AWSXRayDaemon
12        }
13
14        $targetLocation = "C:\Program Files\Amazon\XRay"
15        if ((Test-Path $targetLocation) -eq 0) {
16           mkdir $targetLocation
17        }
18
19        $zipFileName = "aws-xray-daemon-windows-service-2.x.zip"
20        $zipPath = "$targetLocation\$zipFileName"
21        $destPath = "$targetLocation\aws-xray-daemon"
22        if ((Test-Path $destPath) -eq 1) {
23           Remove-Item -Recurse -Force $destPath
24        }
25
26        $daemonPath = "$destPath\xray.exe"
27        $daemonLogPath = "$targetLocation\xray-daemon.log"
28        $url = "https://s3.dualstack.us-west-2.amazonaws.com/aws-xray-assets.us-west-2/xray-daemon
             /aws-xray-daemon-windows-service-2.x.zip"
29
30        Invoke-WebRequest -Uri $url -OutFile $zipPath
31        Add-Type -Assembly "System.IO.Compression.Filesystem"
32        [io.compression.zipfile]::ExtractToDirectory($zipPath, $destPath)
33
34        New-Service -Name "AWSXRayDaemon" -StartupType Automatic -BinaryPathName "`"$daemonPath`"
             -f `"$daemonLogPath`""
35        sc.exe start AWSXRayDaemon
36      encoding: plain
37    "c:/Program Files/Amazon/ElasticBeanstalk/config/taillogs.d/xray-daemon.conf" :
38      mode: "000644"
39      owner: root
40      group: root
41      content: |
42        C:\Program Files\Amazon\XRay\xray-daemon.log
```

These examples also add the daemon's log file to the Elastic Beanstalk tail logs task, so that it's included when you request logs with the console or Elastic Beanstalk Command Line Interface (EB CLI).

Running the X-Ray Daemon on Amazon EC2

You can run the X-Ray daemon on the following operating systems on Amazon EC2:

- Amazon Linux
- Ubuntu
- Windows Server (2012 R2 and newer)

Use an instance profile to grant the daemon permission to upload trace data to X-Ray. For more information, see Giving the Daemon Permission to Send Data to X-Ray.

Use a user data script to run the daemon automatically when you launch the instance.

Example User Data Script - Linux

```
#!/bin/bash
curl https://s3.dualstack.us-east-2.amazonaws.com/aws-xray-assets.us-east-2/xray-daemon/aws-xray
    -daemon-2.x.rpm -o /home/ec2-user/xray.rpm
yum install -y /home/ec2-user/xray.rpm
```

Example User Data Script - Windows Server

```
<powershell>
if ( Get-Service "AWSXRayDaemon" -ErrorAction SilentlyContinue ) {
    sc.exe stop AWSXRayDaemon
    sc.exe delete AWSXRayDaemon
}

$targetLocation = "C:\Program Files\Amazon\XRay"
if ((Test-Path $targetLocation) -eq 0) {
    mkdir $targetLocation
}

$zipFileName = "aws-xray-daemon-windows-service-2.x.zip"
$zipPath = "$targetLocation\$zipFileName"
$destPath = "$targetLocation\aws-xray-daemon"
if ((Test-Path $destPath) -eq 1) {
    Remove-Item -Recurse -Force $destPath
}

$daemonPath = "$destPath\xray.exe"
$daemonLogPath = "$targetLocation\xray-daemon.log"
$url = "https://s3.dualstack.us-west-2.amazonaws.com/aws-xray-assets.us-west-2/xray-daemon/aws-
    xray-daemon-windows-service-2.x.zip"

Invoke-WebRequest -Uri $url -OutFile $zipPath
Add-Type -Assembly "System.IO.Compression.Filesystem"
[io.compression.zipfile]::ExtractToDirectory($zipPath, $destPath)

New-Service -Name "AWSXRayDaemon" -StartupType Automatic -BinaryPathName "`"$daemonPath`" -f `"
    $daemonLogPath`""
sc.exe start AWSXRayDaemon
</powershell>
```

Running the X-Ray Daemon on Amazon ECS

On Amazon ECS, create a Docker image that runs the X-Ray daemon, upload it to a Docker image repository, and then deploy it to your Amazon ECS cluster. You can use port mappings and network mode settings in your task definition file to allow your application to communicate with the daemon container.

Note
The Scorekeep sample application shows how to use the X-Ray daemon on Amazon ECS. See Instrumenting Amazon ECS Applications for details.

Add managed policies to your task role to grant the daemon permission to upload trace data to X-Ray. For more information, see Giving the Daemon Permission to Send Data to X-Ray.

Use one of the following Dockerfiles to create an image that runs the daemon.

Example Dockerfile – Amazon Linux

```
1  FROM amazonlinux
2  RUN yum install -y unzip
3  RUN curl -o daemon.zip https://s3.dualstack.us-east-2.amazonaws.com/aws-xray-assets.us-east-2/
       xray-daemon/aws-xray-daemon-linux-2.x.zip
4  RUN unzip daemon.zip && cp xray /usr/bin/xray
5  ENTRYPOINT ["/usr/bin/xray", "-b", "0.0.0.0:2000"]
6  EXPOSE 2000/udp
```

Example Dockerfile – Ubuntu

For Debian derivatives, you also need to install certificate authority (CA) certificates to avoid issues when downloading the installer.

```
1  FROM ubuntu:16.04
2  RUN apt-get update && apt-get install -y --force-yes --no-install-recommends apt-transport-https
       curl ca-certificates wget && apt-get clean && apt-get autoremove && rm -rf /var/lib/apt/
       lists/*
3  RUN wget https://s3.dualstack.us-east-2.amazonaws.com/aws-xray-assets.us-east-2/xray-daemon/aws-
       xray-daemon-2.x.deb
4  RUN dpkg -i aws-xray-daemon-2.x.deb
5  CMD ["/usr/bin/xray", "--bind=0.0.0.0:2000"]
6  EXPOSE 2000/udp
```

In your task definition, the configuration depends on the networking mode that you use. Bridge networking is the default and can be used in your default VPC. In a bridge network, publish UDP port 2000, and create a link from your application container to the daemon container. Use the `AWS_XRAY_DAEMON_ADDRESS` environment variable to tell the X-Ray SDK where to send traces.

Example Task definition

```
1   {
2     "name": "xray-daemon",
3     "image": "123456789012.dkr.ecr.us-east-2.amazonaws.com/xray-daemon",
4     "cpu": 32,
5     "memoryReservation": 256,
6     "portMappings" : [
7        {
8            "hostPort": 2000,
9            "containerPort": 2000,
10           "protocol": "udp"
11       }
12     ],
```

```
13        },
14        {
15            "name": "scorekeep-api",
16            "image": "123456789012.dkr.ecr.us-east-2.amazonaws.com/scorekeep-api",
17            "cpu": 192,
18            "memoryReservation": 512,
19            "environment": [
20                { "name" : "AWS_REGION", "value" : "us-east-2" },
21                { "name" : "NOTIFICATION_TOPIC", "value" : "arn:aws:sns:us-east-2:123456789012:
                      scorekeep-notifications" },
22                { "name" : "AWS_XRAY_DAEMON_ADDRESS", "value" : "xray-daemon:2000" }
23            ],
24            "portMappings" : [
25                {
26                    "hostPort": 5000,
27                    "containerPort": 5000
28                }
29            ],
30            "links": [
31                "xray-daemon"
32            ]
33        }
```

If you run your cluster in the private subnet of a VPC, you can use the `awsvpc` network mode to attach an elastic network interface (ENI) to your containers. This enables you to avoid using links. Omit the host port in the port mappings, the link, and the `AWS_XRAY_DAEMON_ADDRESS` environment variable.

Example VPC task definition

```
1  {
2      "family": "scorekeep",
3      "networkMode":"awsvpc",
4      "containerDefinitions": [
5          {
6              "name": "xray-daemon",
7              "image": "123456789012.dkr.ecr.us-east-2.amazonaws.com/xray-daemon",
8              "cpu": 32,
9              "memoryReservation": 256,
10             "portMappings" : [
11                 {
12                     "containerPort": 2000,
13                     "protocol": "udp"
14                 }
15             ]
16         }
17         {
18             "name": "scorekeep-api",
19             "image": "123456789012.dkr.ecr.us-east-2.amazonaws.com/scorekeep-api",
20             "cpu": 192,
21             "memoryReservation": 512,
22             "environment": [
23                 { "name" : "AWS_REGION", "value" : "us-east-2" },
24                 { "name" : "NOTIFICATION_TOPIC", "value" : "arn:aws:sns:us-east-2:123456789012:
                       scorekeep-notifications" }
25             ],
26             "portMappings" : [
```

```
27                   {
28                       "containerPort": 5000
29                   }
30               ]
31           }
32       ]
```

AWS X-Ray SDK for Java

The X-Ray SDK for Java is a set of libraries for Java web applications that provide classes and methods for generating and sending trace data to the X-Ray daemon. Trace data includes information about incoming HTTP requests served by the application, and calls that the application makes to downstream services using the AWS SDK, HTTP clients, or an SQL database connector. You can also create segments manually and add debug information in annotations and metadata.

Note
The X-Ray SDK for Java is an open source project. You can follow the project and submit issues and pull requests on GitHub: github.com/aws/aws-xray-sdk-java

Start by adding `AWSXRayServletFilter` as a servlet filter to trace incoming requests. A servlet filter creates a segment While the segment is open you can use the SDK client's methods to add information to the segment and create subsegments to trace downstream calls. The SDK also automatically records exceptions that your application throws while the segment is open.

Starting in release 1.3, you can now instrument your application using aspect-oriented programming (AOP) in Spring. What this means is that you can instrument your application, while it is running on AWS, without adding any code to your application's runtime.

Next, use the X-Ray SDK for Java to instrument your AWS SDK for Java clients by including the SDK Instrumentor submodule in your build configuration. Whenever you make a call to a downstream AWS service or resource with an instrumented client, the SDK records information about the call in a subsegment. AWS services and the resources that you access within the services appear as downstream nodes on the service map to help you identify errors and throttling issues on individual connections.

If you don't want to instrument all downstream calls to AWS services, you can leave out the Instrumentor submodule and choose which clients to instrument. Instrument individual clients by adding a `TracingHandler` to an AWS SDK service client.

Other X-Ray SDK for Java submodules provide instrumentation for downstream calls to HTTP web APIs and SQL databases. You can use the X-Ray SDK for Java's versions of `HTTPClient` and `HTTPClientBuilder` in the Apache HTTP submodule to instrument Apache HTTP clients. To instrument SQL queries, add the SDK's interceptor to your data source.

Once you get going with the SDK, customize its behavior by configuring the recorder and servlet filter. You can add plugins to record data about the compute resources running your application, customize sampling behavior by defining sampling rules, and set the log level to see more or less information from the SDK in your application logs.

Record additional information about requests and the work that your application does in annotations and metadata. Annotations are simple key-value pairs that are indexed for use with filter expressions, so that you can search for traces that contain specific data. Metadata entries are less restrictive and can record entire objects and arrays — anything that can be serialized into JSON.

Annotations and Metadata
Annotations and metadata are arbitrary text that you add to segments with the X-Ray SDK. Annotations are indexed for use with filter expressions. Metadata are not indexed, but can be viewed in the raw segment with the X-Ray console or API. Anyone that you grant read access to X-Ray can view this data.

When you have a lot of instrumented clients in your code, a single request segment can contain a large number of subsegments, one for each call made with an instrumented client. You can organize and group subsegments by wrapping client calls in custom subsegments. You can create a custom subsegment for an entire function or any section of code, and record metadata and annotations on the subsegment instead of writing everything on the parent segment.

You can download the X-Ray SDK for Java from Maven. The X-Ray SDK for Java is split into submodules by use case, with a bill of materials for version management:

- https://mvnrepository.com/artifact/com.amazonaws/aws-xray-recorder-sdk-core (required) – Basic functionality for creating segments and transmitting segments. Includes `AWSXRayServletFilter` for instrumenting incoming requests.
- https://mvnrepository.com/artifact/com.amazonaws/aws-xray-recorder-sdk-aws-sdk – Instruments calls to AWS services made with AWS SDK for Java clients by adding a tracing client as a request handler.
- https://mvnrepository.com/artifact/com.amazonaws/aws-xray-recorder-sdk-aws-sdk-instrumentor – With `aws-xray-recorder-sdk-aws-sdk`, instruments all AWS SDK for Java clients automatically.
- https://mvnrepository.com/artifact/com.amazonaws/aws-xray-recorder-sdk-apache-http – Instruments outbound HTTP calls made with Apache HTTP clients.
- `aws-xray-recorder-sdk-spring` – Provides interceptors for Spring AOP Framework applications.
- https://mvnrepository.com/artifact/com.amazonaws/aws-xray-recorder-sdk-sql-postgres – Instruments outbound calls to a PostgreSQL database made with JDBC.
- https://mvnrepository.com/artifact/com.amazonaws/aws-xray-recorder-sdk-sql-mysql – Instruments outbound calls to a MySQL database made with JDBC.
- https://mvnrepository.com/artifact/com.amazonaws/aws-xray-recorder-sdk-bom – Provides a bill of materials that you can use to specify the version to use for all submodules.

If you use Maven or Gradle to build your application, add the X-Ray SDK for Java to your build configuration.

For reference documentation for of the SDK's classes and methods, see AWS X-Ray SDK for Java API Reference.

Requirements

The X-Ray SDK for Java requires Java 8 or later, Servlet API 3, the AWS SDK, and Jackson.

The SDK depends on the following libraries at compile and runtime:

- AWS SDK for Java version 1.11.106 or later
- Servlet API 3.1.0

These dependencies are declared in the SDK's `pom.xml` file and are included automatically if you build using Maven or Gradle.

If you use a library that is included in the X-Ray SDK for Java, you must use the included version. For example, if you already depend on Jackson at runtime and include JARs in your deployment for that dependency, you must remove those JARs because the SDK JAR includes its own versions of Jackson libraries.

Dependency Management

The X-Ray SDK for Java is available from Maven:

- **Group** – `com.amazonaws`
- **Bill of Materials** – `aws-xray-recorder-sdk-bom`
- **Version** – `1.3.1`

If you use Maven to build your application, add the SDK as a dependency in your `pom.xml` file.

Example pom.xml - dependencies

```
1  <dependencyManagement>
2    <dependencies>
3      <dependency>
4        <groupId>com.amazonaws</groupId>
5        <artifactId>aws-xray-recorder-sdk-bom</artifactId>
6        <version>1.3.1</version>
7        <type>pom</type>
8        <scope>import</scope>
9      </dependency>
```

```
10    </dependencies>
11  </dependencyManagement>
12  <dependencies>
13    <dependency>
14      <groupId>com.amazonaws</groupId>
15      <artifactId>aws-xray-recorder-sdk-core</artifactId>
16    </dependency>
17    <dependency>
18      <groupId>com.amazonaws</groupId>
19      <artifactId>aws-xray-recorder-sdk-apache-http</artifactId>
20    </dependency>
21    <dependency>
22      <groupId>com.amazonaws</groupId>
23      <artifactId>aws-xray-recorder-sdk-aws-sdk</artifactId>
24    </dependency>
25    <dependency>
26      <groupId>com.amazonaws</groupId>
27      <artifactId>aws-xray-recorder-sdk-aws-sdk-instrumentor</artifactId>
28    </dependency>
29    <dependency>
30      <groupId>com.amazonaws</groupId>
31      <artifactId>aws-xray-recorder-sdk-sql-postgres</artifactId>
32    </dependency>
33    <dependency>
34      <groupId>com.amazonaws</groupId>
35      <artifactId>aws-xray-recorder-sdk-sql-mysql</artifactId>
36    </dependency>
37  </dependencies>
```

For Gradle, add the SDK as a compile-time dependency in your build.gradle file.

Example build.gradle - dependencies

```
1  dependencies {
2    compile("org.springframework.boot:spring-boot-starter-web")
3    testCompile("org.springframework.boot:spring-boot-starter-test")
4    compile("com.amazonaws:aws-java-sdk-dynamodb")
5    compile("com.amazonaws:aws-xray-recorder-sdk-core")
6    compile("com.amazonaws:aws-xray-recorder-sdk-aws-sdk")
7    compile("com.amazonaws:aws-xray-recorder-sdk-aws-sdk-instrumentor")
8    compile("com.amazonaws:aws-xray-recorder-sdk-apache-http")
9    compile("com.amazonaws:aws-xray-recorder-sdk-sql-postgres")
10   compile("com.amazonaws:aws-xray-recorder-sdk-sql-mysql")
11   testCompile("junit:junit:4.11")
12 }
13 dependencyManagement {
14     imports {
15         mavenBom('com.amazonaws:aws-java-sdk-bom:1.11.39')
16         mavenBom('com.amazonaws:aws-xray-recorder-sdk-bom:1.3.1')
17     }
18 }
```

If you use Elastic Beanstalk to deploy your application, you can use Maven or Gradle to build on-instance each time you deploy, instead of building and uploading a large archive that includes all of your dependencies. See the sample application for an example that uses Gradle.

Configuring the X-Ray SDK for Java

The X-Ray SDK for Java provides a class named `AWSXRay` that provides the global recorder, a `TracingHandler` that you can use to instrument your code. You can configure the global recorder to customize the `AWSXRayServletFilter` that creates segments for incoming HTTP calls.

Topics

- Service Plugins
- Sampling Rules
- Logging
- Environment Variables
- System Properties

Service Plugins

Use `plugins` to record information about the service hosting your application.

Plugins

- Amazon EC2 – `EC2Plugin` adds the instance ID and Availability Zone.
- Elastic Beanstalk – `ElasticBeanstalkPlugin` adds the environment name, version label, and deployment ID.
- Amazon ECS – `ECSPlugin` adds the container ID.

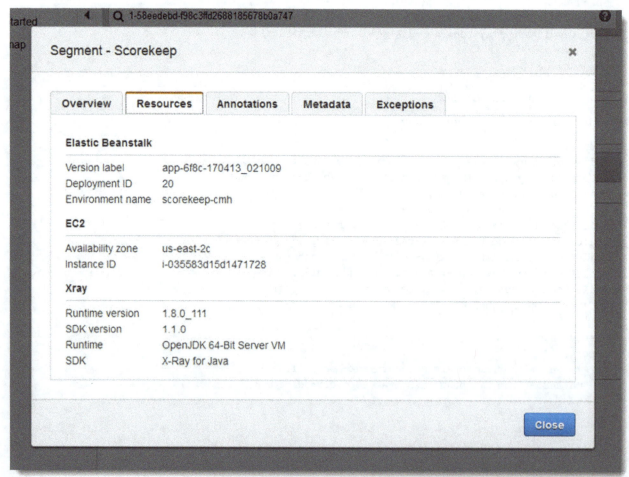

To use a plugin, call `withPlugin` on your `AWSXRayRecorderBuilder`.

Example src/main/java/scorekeep/WebConfig.java - Recorder

```
1  import [com\.amazonaws\.xray\.AWSXRay](http://docs.aws.amazon.com/xray-sdk-for-java/latest/
       javadoc/com/amazonaws/xray/AWSXRay.html);
2  import [com\.amazonaws\.xray\.AWSXRayRecorderBuilder](http://docs.aws.amazon.com/xray-sdk-for-
       java/latest/javadoc/com/amazonaws/xray/AWSXRayRecorderBuilder.html);
3  import [com\.amazonaws\.xray\.plugins\.EC2Plugin](http://docs.aws.amazon.com/xray-sdk-for-java/
       latest/javadoc/com/amazonaws/xray/plugins/EC2Plugin.html);
4  import [com\.amazonaws\.xray\.plugins\.ElasticBeanstalkPlugin](http://docs.aws.amazon.com/xray-
       sdk-for-java/latest/javadoc/com/amazonaws/xray/plugins/ElasticBeanstalkPlugin.html);
5  import [com\.amazonaws\.xray\.strategy\.sampling\.LocalizedSamplingStrategy](http://docs.aws.
       amazon.com/xray-sdk-for-java/latest/javadoc/com/amazonaws/xray/strategy/sampling/
       LocalizedSamplingStrategy.html);
6
7  @Configuration
8  public class WebConfig {
9  ...
10   static {
11     AWSXRayRecorderBuilder builder = AWSXRayRecorderBuilder.standard().withPlugin(new EC2Plugin
           ()).withPlugin(new ElasticBeanstalkPlugin());
12
13     URL ruleFile = WebConfig.class.getResource("/sampling-rules.json");
14     builder.withSamplingStrategy(new LocalizedSamplingStrategy(ruleFile));
15
16     AWSXRay.setGlobalRecorder(builder.build());
17   }
18 }
```

The SDK also uses plugin settings to set the `origin` field on the segment. This indicates the type of AWS resource that runs your application. The resource type appears under your application's name in the service map. For example, `AWS::ElasticBeanstalk::Environment`.

When you use multiple plugins, the SDK uses the plugin that was loaded last to determine the origin.

Sampling Rules

The SDK has a default sampling strategy that determines which requests get traced. By default, the SDK traces the first request each second, and five percent of any additional requests. You can customize the SDK's sampling behavior by applying rules you define in a local file.

Example sampling-rules.json

```
1  {
2    "version": 1,
3    "rules": [
4      {
5        "description": "Player moves.",
6        "service_name": "*",
7        "http_method": "*",
8        "url_path": "/api/move/*",
9        "fixed_target": 0,
10       "rate": 0.05
11     }
12   ],
13   "default": {
14     "fixed_target": 1,
15     "rate": 0.1
16   }
17 }
```

This example defines one custom rule and a default rule. The custom rule applies a five-percent sampling rate with no minimum number of requests to trace for paths under /api/move/. The default rule traces the first request each second and 10 percent of additional requests.

The SDK applies custom rules in the order in which they are defined. If a request matches multiple custom rules, the SDK applies only the first rule.

On Lambda, you cannot modify the sampling rate. If your function is called by an instrumented service, calls generated requests that were sampled by that service will be recorded by Lambda. If active tracing is enabled and no tracing header is present, Lambda makes the sampling decision.

For Spring, configure the global recorder in a configuration class.

Example src/main/java/myapp/WebConfig.java - Recorder Configuration

```
1  import [com\.amazonaws\.xray\.AWSXRay](http://docs.aws.amazon.com/xray-sdk-for-java/latest/
      javadoc/com/amazonaws/xray/AWSXRay.html);
2  import [com\.amazonaws\.xray\.AWSXRayRecorderBuilder](http://docs.aws.amazon.com/xray-sdk-for-
      java/latest/javadoc/com/amazonaws/xray/AWSXRayRecorderBuilder.html);
3  import [com\.amazonaws\.xray\.javax\.servlet\.AWSXRayServletFilter](http://docs.aws.amazon.com/
      xray-sdk-for-java/latest/javadoc/com/amazonaws/xray/javax/servlet/AWSXRayServletFilter.html)
      ;
4  import [com\.amazonaws\.xray\.plugins\.EC2Plugin](http://docs.aws.amazon.com/xray-sdk-for-java/
      latest/javadoc/com/amazonaws/xray/plugins/EC2Plugin.html);
5  import [com\.amazonaws\.xray\.strategy\.sampling\.LocalizedSamplingStrategy](http://docs.aws.
      amazon.com/xray-sdk-for-java/latest/javadoc/com/amazonaws/xray/strategy/sampling/
      LocalizedSamplingStrategy.html);
6
7  @Configuration
8  public class WebConfig {
9
10   static {
11   AWSXRayRecorderBuilder builder = AWSXRayRecorderBuilder.standard().withPlugin(new EC2Plugin())
        ;
12
13   URL ruleFile = WebConfig.class.getResource("file://sampling-rules.json");
```

```
14    builder.withSamplingStrategy(new LocalizedSamplingStrategy(ruleFile));
15
16    AWSXRay.setGlobalRecorder(builder.build());
17  }
```

For Tomcat, add a listener that extends `ServletContextListener`.

Example src/com/myapp/web/Startup.java

```
1  import [com\.amazonaws\.xray\.AWSXRay](http://docs.aws.amazon.com/xray-sdk-for-java/latest/
       javadoc/com/amazonaws/xray/AWSXRay.html);
2  import [com\.amazonaws\.xray\.AWSXRayRecorderBuilder](http://docs.aws.amazon.com/xray-sdk-for-
       java/latest/javadoc/com/amazonaws/xray/AWSXRayRecorderBuilder.html);
3  import [com\.amazonaws\.xray\.plugins\.EC2Plugin](http://docs.aws.amazon.com/xray-sdk-for-java/
       latest/javadoc/com/amazonaws/xray/plugins/EC2Plugin.html);
4  import [com\.amazonaws\.xray\.strategy\.sampling\.LocalizedSamplingStrategy](http://docs.aws.
       amazon.com/xray-sdk-for-java/latest/javadoc/com/amazonaws/xray/strategy/sampling/
       LocalizedSamplingStrategy.html);
5
6  import java.net.URL;
7  import javax.servlet.ServletContextEvent;
8  import javax.servlet.ServletContextListener;
9
10 public class Startup implements ServletContextListener {
11
12     @Override
13     public void contextInitialized(ServletContextEvent event) {
14         AWSXRayRecorderBuilder builder = AWSXRayRecorderBuilder.standard().withPlugin(new
               EC2Plugin());
15
16         URL ruleFile = Startup.class.getResource("/sampling-rules.json");
17         builder.withSamplingStrategy(new LocalizedSamplingStrategy(ruleFile));
18
19         AWSXRay.setGlobalRecorder(builder.build());
20     }
21
22     @Override
23     public void contextDestroyed(ServletContextEvent event) { }
24 }
```

Register the listener in the deployment descriptor.

Example WEB-INF/web.xml

```
1  ...
2  <listener>
3    <listener-class>com.myapp.web.Startup</listener-class>
4  </listener>
```

Logging

By default, the SDK outputs SEVERE level and ERROR level messages to your application logs. You can enable debug-level logging on the SDK to output more detailed logs to your application log file.

Example application.properties
Set the logging level with the `logging.level.com.amazonaws.xray` property.

```
1  logging.level.com.amazonaws.xray = DEBUG
```

Use debug logs to identify issues, such as unclosed subsegments, when you generate subsegments manually.

Environment Variables

You can use environment variables to configure the X-Ray SDK for Java. The SDK supports the following variables.

- AWS_XRAY_TRACING_NAME – Set a service name that the SDK uses for segments. Overrides the service name that you set on the servlet filter's segment naming strategy.
- AWS_XRAY_DAEMON_ADDRESS – Set the host and port of the X-Ray daemon listener. By default, the SDK sends trace data to 127.0.0.1:2000. Use this variable if you have configured the daemon to listen on a different port or if it is running on a different host.
- AWS_XRAY_CONTEXT_MISSING – Set to LOG_ERROR to avoid throwing exceptions when your instrumented code attempts to record data when no segment is open.

Valid Values

- RUNTIME_ERROR – Throw a runtime exception (default).
- LOG_ERROR – Log an error and continue.

Errors related to missing segments or subsegments can occur when you attempt to use an instrumented client in startup code that runs when no request is open, or in code that spawns a new thread.

Environment variables override equivalent system properties and values set in code.

System Properties

You can use system properties as a JVM-specific alternative to environment variables. The SDK supports the following properties.

- com.amazonaws.xray.strategy.tracingName – Equivalent to AWS_XRAY_TRACING_NAME.
- com.amazonaws.xray.emitters.daemonAddress – Equivalent to AWS_XRAY_DAEMON_ADDRESS.
- com.amazonaws.xray.strategy.contextMissingStrategy – Equivalent to AWS_XRAY_CONTEXT_MISSING.

If both a system property and the equivalent environment variable are set, the environment variable values is used. Either method overrides values set in code.

Tracing Incoming Requests with the X-Ray SDK for Java

You can use the X-Ray SDK to trace incoming HTTP requests that your application serves on an EC2 instance in Amazon EC2, AWS Elastic Beanstalk, or Amazon ECS.

Use a `Filter` to instrument incoming HTTP requests. When you add the X-Ray servlet filter to your application, the X-Ray SDK for Java creates a segment for each sampled request. This segment includes timing, method, and disposition of the HTTP request. Additional instrumentation creates subsegments on this segment.

Note
For AWS Lambda functions, Lambda creates a segment for each sampled request. See AWS Lambda and AWS X-Ray for more information.

Each segment has a name that identifies your application in the service map. The segment can be named statically, or you can configure the SDK to name it dynamically based on the host header in the incoming request. Dynamic naming lets you group traces based on the domain name in the request, and apply a default name if the name doesn't match an expected pattern (for example, if the host header is forged).

Forwarded Requests
If a load balancer or other intermediary forwards a request to your application, X-Ray takes the client IP from the `X-Forwarded-For` header in the request instead of from the source IP in the IP packet. The client IP that is recorded for a forwarded request can be forged, so it should not be trusted.

When a request is forwarded, the SDK sets an additional field in the segment to indicate this. If the segment contains the field `x_forwarded_for` set to `true`, the client IP was taken from the `X-Forwarded-For` header in the HTTP request.

The message handler creates a segment for each incoming request with an `http` block that contains the following information:

- **HTTP method** – GET, POST, PUT, DELETE, etc.
- **Client address** – The IP address of the client that sent the request.
- **Response code** – The HTTP response code for the completed request.
- **Timing** – The start time (when the request was received) and end time (when the response was sent).
- **User agent** — The `user-agent` from the request.
- **Content length** — The `content-length` from the response.

Topics

- Adding a Tracing Filter to your Application (Tomcat)
- Adding a Tracing Filter to your Application (Spring)
- Configuring a Segment Naming Strategy

Adding a Tracing Filter to your Application (Tomcat)

For Tomcat, add a `<filter>` to your project's `web.xml` file. Use the `fixedName` parameter to specify a service name to apply to segments created for incoming requests.

Example WEB-INF/web.xml - Tomcat

```
1 <filter>
2   <filter-name>AWSXRayServletFilter</filter-name>
3   <filter-class>com.amazonaws.xray.javax.servlet.AWSXRayServletFilter</filter-class>
4   <init-param>
5     <param-name>fixedName</param-name>
6     <param-value>MyApp</param-value>
7   </init-param>
8 </filter>
9 <filter-mapping>
```

```
10    <filter-name>AWSXRayServletFilter</filter-name>
11    <url-pattern>*</url-pattern>
12  </filter-mapping>
```

Adding a Tracing Filter to your Application (Spring)

For Spring, add a `Filter` to your `WebConfig` class. Pass the segment name to the http://docs.aws.amazon.com/xray-sdk-for-java/latest/javadoc/com/amazonaws/xray/javax/servlet/AWSXRayServletFilter.html constructor as a string.

Example src/main/java/myapp/WebConfig.java - Spring

```
1 package myapp;
2 import org.springframework.context.annotation.Configuration;
3 import org.springframework.context.annotation.Bean;
4 import javax.servlet.Filter;
5 import [com\.amazonaws\.xray\.javax\.servlet\.AWSXRayServletFilter](http://docs.aws.amazon.com/
      xray-sdk-for-java/latest/javadoc/com/amazonaws/xray/javax/servlet/AWSXRayServletFilter.html)
      ;
6
7 @Configuration
8 public class WebConfig {
9
10   @Bean
11   public Filter TracingFilter() {
12     return new AWSXRayServletFilter("Scorekeep");
13   }
14 }
```

Configuring a Segment Naming Strategy

AWS X-Ray uses a *service name* to identify your application and distinguish it from the other applications, databases, external APIs, and AWS resources that your application uses. When the X-Ray SDK generates segments for incoming requests, it records your application's service name in the segment's name field.

The X-Ray SDK can name segments after the hostname in the HTTP request header. However, this header can be forged, which could result in unexpected nodes in your service map. To prevent the SDK from naming segments incorrectly due to requests with forged host headers, you must specify a default name for incoming requests.

If your application serves requests for multiple domains, you can configure the SDK to use a dynamic naming strategy to reflect this in segment names. A dynamic naming strategy allows the SDK to use the hostname for requests that match an expected pattern, and apply the default name to requests that don't.

For example, you might have a single application serving requests to three subdomains– www.example.com, api.example.com, and static.example.com. You can use a dynamic naming strategy with the pattern *.example.com to identify segments for each subdomain with a different name, resulting in three service nodes on the service map. If your application receives requests with a hostname that doesn't match the pattern, you will see a fourth node on the service map with a fallback name that you specify.

To use the same name for all request segments, specify the name of your application when you initialize the servlet filter, as shown in the previous section. This has the same effect as creating a FixedSegmentNamingStrategy and passing it to http://docs.aws.amazon.com/xray-sdk-for-java/latest/javadoc/com/amazonaws/xray/javax/servlet/AWSXRayServletFilter.html constructor.

Note

You can override the default service name that you define in code with the `AWS_XRAY_TRACING_NAME` environment variable.

A dynamic naming strategy defines a pattern that hostnames should match, and a default name to use if the hostname in the HTTP request does not match the pattern. To name segments dynamically in Tomcat, use the `dynamicNamingRecognizedHosts` and `dynamicNamingFallbackName` to define the pattern and default name, respectively.

Example WEB-INF/web.xml - Servlet Filter with Dynamic Naming

```
1  <filter>
2    <filter-name>AWSXRayServletFilter</filter-name>
3    <filter-class>com.amazonaws.xray.javax.servlet.AWSXRayServletFilter</filter-class>
4    <init-param>
5      <param-name>dynamicNamingRecognizedHosts</param-name>
6      <param-value>*.example.com</param-value>
7    </init-param>
8    <init-param>
9      <param-name>dynamicNamingFallbackName</param-name>
10     <param-value>MyApp</param-value>
11   </init-param>
12 </filter>
13 <filter-mapping>
14   <filter-name>AWSXRayServletFilter</filter-name>
15   <url-pattern>*</url-pattern>
16 </filter-mapping>
```

For Spring, create a DynamicSegmentNamingStrategy and pass it to the `AWSXRayServletFilter` constructor.

Example src/main/java/myapp/WebConfig.java - Servlet Filter with Dynamic Naming

```
1  package myapp;
2  import org.springframework.context.annotation.Configuration;
3  import org.springframework.context.annotation.Bean;
4  import javax.servlet.Filter;
5  import [com\.amazonaws\.xray\.javax\.servlet\.AWSXRayServletFilter](http://docs.aws.amazon.com/
       xray-sdk-for-java/latest/javadoc/com/amazonaws/xray/javax/servlet/AWSXRayServletFilter.html)
       ;
6  import [com\.amazonaws\.xray\.strategy\.DynamicSegmentNamingStrategy](http://docs.aws.amazon.com
       /xray-sdk-for-java/latest/javadoc/com/amazonaws/xray/strategy/DynamicSegmentNamingStrategy.
       html);
7
8  @Configuration
9  public class WebConfig {
10
11   @Bean
12   public Filter TracingFilter() {
13     return new AWSXRayServletFilter(new DynamicSegmentNamingStrategy("MyApp", "*.example.com"));
14   }
15 }
```

Tracing AWS SDK Calls with the X-Ray SDK for Java

When your application makes calls to AWS services to store data, write to a queue, or send notifications, the X-Ray SDK for Java tracks the calls downstream in subsegments. Traced AWS services and resources that you access within those services (for example, an Amazon S3 bucket or Amazon SQS queue), appear as downstream nodes on the service map in the X-Ray console.

The X-Ray SDK for Java automatically instruments all AWS SDK clients when you include the `aws-sdk` and `aws-sdk-instrumentor` submodules in your build. If you don't include the Instrumentor submodule, you can choose to instrument some clients while excluding others.

To instrument individual clients, remove the `aws-sdk-instrumentor` submodule from your build and add an `XRayClient` as a `TracingHandler` on your AWS SDK client using the service's client builder.

For example, to instrument an `AmazonDynamoDB` client, pass a tracing handler to `AmazonDynamoDBClientBuilder`.

Example MyModel.java - DynamoDB Client

```
1 import [com\.amazonaws\.xray\.AWSXRay](http://docs.aws.amazon.com/xray-sdk-for-java/latest/
      javadoc/com/amazonaws/xray/AWSXRay.html);
2 import [com\.amazonaws\.xray\.handlers\.TracingHandler](http://docs.aws.amazon.com/xray-sdk-for-
      java/latest/javadoc/com/amazonaws/xray/handlers/TracingHandler.html);
3
4 ...
5 public class MyModel {
6   private AmazonDynamoDB client = AmazonDynamoDBClientBuilder.standard()
7       .withRegion(Regions.fromName(System.getenv("AWS_REGION")))
8       .withRequestHandlers(new TracingHandler(AWSXRay.getGlobalRecorder()))
9       .build();
10 ...
```

For all services, you can see the name of the API called in the X-Ray console. For a subset of services, the X-Ray SDK adds information to the segment to provide more granularity in the service map.

For example, when you make a call with an instrumented DynamoDB client, the SDK adds the table name to the segment for calls that target a table. In the console, each table appears as a separate node in the service map, with a generic DynamoDB node for calls that don't target a table.

Example Subsegment for a Call to DynamoDB to Save an Item

```
1 {
2   "id": "24756640c0d0978a",
3   "start_time": 1.480305974194E9,
4   "end_time": 1.4803059742E9,
5   "name": "DynamoDB",
6   "namespace": "aws",
7   "http": {
8     "response": {
9       "content_length": 60,
10      "status": 200
11    }
12  },
13  "aws": {
14    "table_name": "scorekeep-user",
15    "operation": "UpdateItem",
16    "request_id": "UBQNS05AEM8T4FDA4RQDEB940VTDRVV4K4HIRGVJF66Q9ASUAAJG",
17  }
18 }
```

When you access named resources, calls to the following services create additional nodes in the service map. Calls that don't target specific resources create a generic node for the service.

- **Amazon DynamoDB** – Table name
- **Amazon Simple Storage Service** – Bucket and key name
- **Amazon Simple Queue Service** – Queue name

Tracing Calls to Downstream HTTP Web Services with the X-Ray SDK for Java

When your application makes calls to microservices or public HTTP APIs, you can use the X-Ray SDK for Java's version of `HttpClient` to instrument those calls and add the API to the service graph as a downstream service.

The X-Ray SDK for Java includes `DefaultHttpClient` and `HttpClientBuilder` classes that can be used in place of the Apache HttpComponents equivalents to instrument outgoing HTTP calls.

- `com.amazonaws.xray.proxies.apache.http.DefaultHttpClient` - `org.apache.http.impl.client.DefaultHttpClient`
- `com.amazonaws.xray.proxies.apache.http.HttpClientBuilder` - `org.apache.http.impl.client.HttpClientBuilder`

These libraries are in the `aws-xray-recorder-sdk-apache-http` submodule.

You can replace your existing import statements with the X-Ray equivalent to instrument all clients, or use the fully qualified name when you initialize a client to instrument specific clients.

Example HttpClientBuilder

```
1  import com.fasterxml.jackson.databind.ObjectMapper;
2  import org.apache.http.HttpEntity;
3  import org.apache.http.client.methods.CloseableHttpResponse;
4  import org.apache.http.client.methods.HttpGet;
5  import org.apache.http.impl.client.CloseableHttpClient;
6  import org.apache.http.util.EntityUtils;
7  import [com\.amazonaws\.xray\.proxies\.apache\.http\.HttpClientBuilder](http://docs.aws.amazon.
       com/xray-sdk-for-java/latest/javadoc/com/amazonaws/xray/proxies/apache/http/
       HttpClientBuilder.html);
8  ...
9    public String randomName() throws IOException {
10     CloseableHttpClient httpclient = HttpClientBuilder.create().build();
11     HttpGet httpGet = new HttpGet("http://names.example.com/api/");
12     CloseableHttpResponse response = httpclient.execute(httpGet);
13     try {
14       HttpEntity entity = response.getEntity();
15       InputStream inputStream = entity.getContent();
16       ObjectMapper mapper = new ObjectMapper();
17       Map<String, String> jsonMap = mapper.readValue(inputStream, Map.class);
18       String name = jsonMap.get("name");
19       EntityUtils.consume(entity);
20       return name;
21     } finally {
22       response.close();
23     }
24   }
```

When you instrument a call to a downstream web api, the X-Ray SDK for Java records a subsegment with information about the HTTP request and response. X-Ray uses the subsegment to generate an inferred segment for the remote API.

Example Subsegment for a Downstream HTTP Call

```
1  {
2    "id": "004f72be19cddc2a",
3    "start_time": 1484786387.131,
```

```
 4     "end_time": 1484786387.501,
 5     "name": "names.example.com",
 6     "namespace": "remote",
 7     "http": {
 8       "request": {
 9         "method": "GET",
10         "url": "https://names.example.com/"
11       },
12       "response": {
13         "content_length": -1,
14         "status": 200
15       }
16     }
17 }
```

Example Inferred Segment for a Downstream HTTP Call

```
 1 {
 2     "id": "168416dc2ea97781",
 3     "name": "names.example.com",
 4     "trace_id": "1-5880168b-fd5153bb58284b67678aa78c",
 5     "start_time": 1484786387.131,
 6     "end_time": 1484786387.501,
 7     "parent_id": "004f72be19cddc2a",
 8     "http": {
 9       "request": {
10         "method": "GET",
11         "url": "https://names.example.com/"
12       },
13       "response": {
14         "content_length": -1,
15         "status": 200
16       }
17     },
18     "inferred": true
19 }
```

Tracing SQL Queries with the X-Ray SDK for Java

Instrument SQL database queries by adding the X-Ray SDK for Java JDBC interceptor to your data source configuration.

- **PostgreSQL** – com.amazonaws.xray.sql.postgres.TracingInterceptor
- **MySQL** – com.amazonaws.xray.sql.mysql.TracingInterceptor

These interceptors are in the aws-xray-recorder-sql-postgres and aws-xray-recorder-sql-mysql submodules, respectively. They implement org.apache.tomcat.jdbc.pool.JdbcInterceptor and are compatible with Tomcat connection pools.

For Spring, add the interceptor in a properties file and build the data source with Spring Boot's DataSourceBuilder.

Example src/main/java/resources/application.properties - PostgreSQL JDBC Interceptor

```
1  spring.datasource.continue-on-error=true
2  spring.jpa.show-sql=false
3  spring.jpa.hibernate.ddl-auto=create-drop
4  spring.datasource.jdbc-interceptors=com.amazonaws.xray.sql.postgres.TracingInterceptor
5  spring.jpa.database-platform=org.hibernate.dialect.PostgreSQL94Dialect
```

Example src/main/java/myapp/WebConfig.java - Data Source

```
1  import org.springframework.boot.autoconfigure.EnableAutoConfiguration;
2  import org.springframework.boot.autoconfigure.jdbc.DataSourceBuilder;
3  import org.springframework.boot.context.properties.ConfigurationProperties;
4  import org.springframework.context.annotation.Bean;
5  import org.springframework.context.annotation.Configuration;
6  import org.springframework.data.jpa.repository.config.EnableJpaRepositories;
7
8  import javax.servlet.Filter;
9  import javax.sql.DataSource;
10 import java.net.URL;
11
12 @Configuration
13 @EnableAutoConfiguration
14 @EnableJpaRepositories("myapp")
15 public class RdsWebConfig {
16
17   @Bean
18   @ConfigurationProperties(prefix = "spring.datasource")
19   public DataSource dataSource() {
20       logger.info("Initializing PostgreSQL datasource");
21       return DataSourceBuilder.create()
22               .driverClassName("org.postgresql.Driver")
23               .url("jdbc:postgresql://" + System.getenv("RDS_HOSTNAME") + ":" + System.getenv("
                   RDS_PORT") + "/ebdb")
24               .username(System.getenv("RDS_USERNAME"))
25               .password(System.getenv("RDS_PASSWORD"))
26               .build();
27   }
28 ...
29 }
```

For Tomcat, call `setJdbcInterceptors` on the JDBC data source with a reference to the X-Ray SDK for Java class.

Example `src/main/myapp/model.java` - Data Source

```
1 import org.apache.tomcat.jdbc.pool.DataSource;
2 ...
3 DataSource source = new DataSource();
4 source.setUrl(url);
5 source.setUsername(user);
6 source.setPassword(password);
7 source.setDriverClassName("com.mysql.jdbc.Driver");
8 source.setJdbcInterceptors("com.amazonaws.xray.sql.mysql.TracingInterceptor;");
```

The Tomcat JDBC Data Source library is included in the X-Ray SDK for Java, but you can declare it as a provided dependency to document that you use it.

Example `pom.xml` - JDBC Data Source

```
1 <dependency>
2   <groupId>org.apache.tomcat</groupId>
3   <artifactId>tomcat-jdbc</artifactId>
4   <version>8.0.36</version>
5   <scope>provided</scope>
6 </dependency>
```

Generating Custom Subsegments with the X-Ray SDK for Java

Subsegments extend a trace's segment with details about work done in order to serve a request. Each time you make a call with an instrumented client, the X-Ray SDK records the information generated in a subsegment. You can create additional subsegments to group other subsegments, to measure the performance of a section of code, or to record annotations and metadata.

To manage subsegments, use the `beginSubsegment` and `endSubsegment` methods.

Example GameModel.java - Custom Subsegment

```
1 import [com\.amazonaws\.xray\.AWSXRay](http://docs.aws.amazon.com/xray-sdk-for-java/latest/
    javadoc/com/amazonaws/xray/AWSXRay.html);
2 ...
3   public void saveGame(Game game) throws SessionNotFoundException {
4     // wrap in subsegment
5     Subsegment subsegment = AWSXRay.beginSubsegment("Save Game");
6     try {
7       // check session
8       String sessionId = game.getSession();
9       if (sessionModel.loadSession(sessionId) == null ) {
10        throw new SessionNotFoundException(sessionId);
11      }
12      mapper.save(game);
13    } catch (Exception e) {
14      subsegment.addException(e);
15      throw e;
16    } finally {
17      AWSXRay.endSubsegment();
18    }
19  }
```

In this example, the code within the subsegment loads the game's session from DynamoDB with a method on the session model, and uses the AWS SDK for Java's DynamoDB mapper to save the game. Wrapping this code in a subsegment makes the calls DynamoDB children of the `Save Game` subsegment in the trace view in the console.

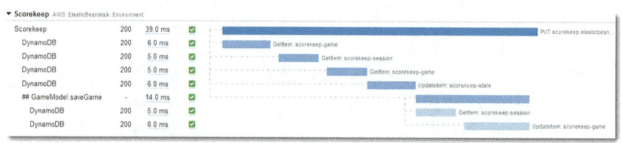

If the code in your subsegment throws checked exceptions, wrap it in a `try` block and call `AWSXRay.endSubsegment` `()` in a `finally` block to ensure that the subsegment is always closed. If a subsegment is not closed, the parent segment cannot be completed and won't be sent to X-Ray.

For code that doesn't throw checked exceptions, you can pass the code to `AWSXRay.CreateSubsegment` as a Lambda function.

Example Subsegment Lambda Function

```
1 import [com\.amazonaws\.xray\.AWSXRay](http://docs.aws.amazon.com/xray-sdk-for-java/latest/
    javadoc/com/amazonaws/xray/AWSXRay.html);
2
```

```
3 AWSXRay.createSubsegment("getMovies", (subsegment) -> {
4     // function code
5 });
```

When you create a subsegment within a segment or another subsegment, the X-Ray SDK for Java generates an ID for it and records the start time and end time.

Example Subsegment with Metadata

```
1 "subsegments": [{
2   "id": "6f1605cd8a07cb70",
3   "start_time": 1.480305974194E9,
4   "end_time": 1.4803059742E9,
5   "name": "Custom subsegment for UserModel.saveUser function",
6   "metadata": {
7     "debug": {
8       "test": "Metadata string from UserModel.saveUser"
9     }
10   },
```

Add Annotations and Metadata to Segments with the X-Ray SDK for Java

You can record additional information about requests, the environment, or your application with annotations and metadata. You can add annotations and metadata to the segments that the X-Ray SDK creates, or to custom subsegments that you create.

Annotations are key-value pairs with string, number, or Boolean values. Annotations are indexed for use with filter expressions. Use annotations to record data that you want to use to group traces in the console, or when calling the http://docs.aws.amazon.com/xray/latest/api/API_GetTraceSummaries.html API.

Metadata are key-value pairs that can have values of any type, including objects and lists, but are not indexed for use with filter expressions. Use metadata to record additional data that you want stored in the trace but don't need to use with search.

In addition to annotations and metadata, you can also record user ID strings on segments. User IDs are recorded in a separate field on segments and are indexed for use with search.

Topics

- Recording Annotations with the X-Ray SDK for Java
- Recording Metadata with the X-Ray SDK for Java
- Recording User IDs with the X-Ray SDK for Java

Recording Annotations with the X-Ray SDK for Java

Use annotations to record information on segments or subsegments that you want indexed for search.

Annotation Requirements

- **Keys** – Up to 500 alphanumeric characters. No spaces or symbols except underscores.
- **Values** – Up to 1,000 Unicode characters.
- **Entries** – Up to 50 annotations per trace.

To record annotations

1. Get a reference to the current segment or subsegment from `AWSXRay`.

```
1 import [com\.amazonaws\.xray\.AWSXRay](http://docs.aws.amazon.com/xray-sdk-for-java/latest/
     javadoc/com/amazonaws/xray/AWSXRay.html);
2 import [com\.amazonaws\.xray\.entities\.Segment](http://docs.aws.amazon.com/xray-sdk-for-
     java/latest/javadoc/com/amazonaws/xray/entities/Segment.html);
3 ...
4 Segment document = AWSXRay.getCurrentSegment();
```

   or

```
1 import [com\.amazonaws\.xray\.AWSXRay](http://docs.aws.amazon.com/xray-sdk-for-java/latest/
     javadoc/com/amazonaws/xray/AWSXRay.html);
2 import [com\.amazonaws\.xray\.entities\.Subsegment](http://docs.aws.amazon.com/xray-sdk-for
     -java/latest/javadoc/com/amazonaws/xray/entities/Subsegment.html);
3 ...
4 Subsegment document = AWSXRay.getCurrentSubsegment();
```

2. Call `putAnnotation` with a String key, and a Boolean, Number, or String value.

```
1 document.putAnnotation("mykey", "my value");
```

The SDK records annotations as key-value pairs in an `annotations` object in the segment document. Calling `putAnnotation` twice with the same key overwrites previously recorded values on the same segment or subsegment.

To find traces that have annotations with specific values, use the `annotations.key` keyword in a filter expression.

Example   https://github.com/awslabs/eb-java-scorekeep/tree/xray/src/main/java/scorekeep/
GameModel.java – Annotations and Metadata

```
1 import [com\.amazonaws\.xray\.AWSXRay](http://docs.aws.amazon.com/xray-sdk-for-java/latest/
      javadoc/com/amazonaws/xray/AWSXRay.html);
2 import [com\.amazonaws\.xray\.entities\.Segment](http://docs.aws.amazon.com/xray-sdk-for-java/
      latest/javadoc/com/amazonaws/xray/entities/Segment.html);
3 import [com\.amazonaws\.xray\.entities\.Subsegment](http://docs.aws.amazon.com/xray-sdk-for-java
      /latest/javadoc/com/amazonaws/xray/entities/Subsegment.html);
4 ...
5   public void saveGame(Game game) throws SessionNotFoundException {
6     // wrap in subsegment
7     Subsegment subsegment = AWSXRay.beginSubsegment("## GameModel.saveGame");
8     try {
9       // check session
10      String sessionId = game.getSession();
11      if (sessionModel.loadSession(sessionId) == null ) {
12        throw new SessionNotFoundException(sessionId);
13      }
14      Segment segment = AWSXRay.getCurrentSegment();
15      subsegment.putMetadata("resources", "game", game);
16      segment.putAnnotation("gameid", game.getId());
17      mapper.save(game);
18    } catch (Exception e) {
19      subsegment.addException(e);
20      throw e;
21    } finally {
22      AWSXRay.endSubsegment();
23    }
24  }
```

Recording Metadata with the X-Ray SDK for Java

Use metadata to record information on segments or subsegments that you don't need indexed for search. Metadata values can be strings, numbers, Booleans, or any object that can be serialized into a JSON object or array.

To record metadata

1. Get a reference to the current segment or subsegment from `AWSXRay`.

```
1 import [com\.amazonaws\.xray\.AWSXRay](http://docs.aws.amazon.com/xray-sdk-for-java/latest/
      javadoc/com/amazonaws/xray/AWSXRay.html);
2 import [com\.amazonaws\.xray\.entities\.Segment](http://docs.aws.amazon.com/xray-sdk-for-
      java/latest/javadoc/com/amazonaws/xray/entities/Segment.html);
3 ...
4 Segment document = AWSXRay.getCurrentSegment();
```

   or

```
1 import [com\.amazonaws\.xray\.AWSXRay](http://docs.aws.amazon.com/xray-sdk-for-java/latest/
      javadoc/com/amazonaws/xray/AWSXRay.html);
```

```
 2 import [com\.amazonaws\.xray\.entities\.Subsegment](http://docs.aws.amazon.com/xray-sdk-for
     -java/latest/javadoc/com/amazonaws/xray/entities/Subsegment.html);
 3 ...
 4 Subsegment document = AWSXRay.getCurrentSubsegment();
```

2. Call `putMetadata` with a String namespace, String key, and a Boolean, Number, String, or Object value.

```
 1 document.putMetadata("my namespace", "my key", "my value");
```

or

Call `putMetadata` with just a key and value.

```
 1 document.putMetadata("my key", "my value");
```

If you don't specify a namespace, the SDK uses `default`. Calling `putMetadata` twice with the same key overwrites previously recorded values on the same segment or subsegment.

Example   https://github.com/awslabs/eb-java-scorekeep/tree/xray/src/main/java/scorekeep/ GameModel.java – Annotations and Metadata

```
 1 import [com\.amazonaws\.xray\.AWSXRay](http://docs.aws.amazon.com/xray-sdk-for-java/latest/
     javadoc/com/amazonaws/xray/AWSXRay.html);
 2 import [com\.amazonaws\.xray\.entities\.Segment](http://docs.aws.amazon.com/xray-sdk-for-java/
     latest/javadoc/com/amazonaws/xray/entities/Segment.html);
 3 import [com\.amazonaws\.xray\.entities\.Subsegment](http://docs.aws.amazon.com/xray-sdk-for-java
     /latest/javadoc/com/amazonaws/xray/entities/Subsegment.html);
 4 ...
 5 public void saveGame(Game game) throws SessionNotFoundException {
 6   // wrap in subsegment
 7   Subsegment subsegment = AWSXRay.beginSubsegment("## GameModel.saveGame");
 8   try {
 9     // check session
10     String sessionId = game.getSession();
11     if (sessionModel.loadSession(sessionId) == null ) {
12       throw new SessionNotFoundException(sessionId);
13     }
14     Segment segment = AWSXRay.getCurrentSegment();
15     subsegment.putMetadata("resources", "game", game);
16     segment.putAnnotation("gameid", game.getId());
17     mapper.save(game);
18   } catch (Exception e) {
19     subsegment.addException(e);
20     throw e;
21   } finally {
22     AWSXRay.endSubsegment();
23   }
24 }
```

Recording User IDs with the X-Ray SDK for Java

Record user IDs on request segments to identify the user who sent the request.

To record user IDs

1. Get a reference to the current segment from `AWSXRay`.

```
1 import [com\.amazonaws\.xray\.AWSXRay](http://docs.aws.amazon.com/xray-sdk-for-java/latest/
    javadoc/com/amazonaws/xray/AWSXRay.html);
2 import [com\.amazonaws\.xray\.entities\.Segment](http://docs.aws.amazon.com/xray-sdk-for-
    java/latest/javadoc/com/amazonaws/xray/entities/Segment.html);
3 ...
4 Segment document = AWSXRay.getCurrentSegment();
```

2. Call setUser with a String ID of the user who sent the request.

```
1 document.setUser("U12345");
```

You can call setUser in your controllers to record the user ID as soon as your application starts processing a request. If you will only use the segment to set the user ID, you can chain the calls in a single line.

Example src/main/java/scorekeep/MoveController.java – User ID

```
1 import [com\.amazonaws\.xray\.AWSXRay](http://docs.aws.amazon.com/xray-sdk-for-java/latest/
    javadoc/com/amazonaws/xray/AWSXRay.html);
2 ...
3 @RequestMapping(value="/{userId}", method=RequestMethod.POST)
4 public Move newMove(@PathVariable String sessionId, @PathVariable String gameId, @PathVariable
      String userId, @RequestBody String move) throws SessionNotFoundException,
    GameNotFoundException, StateNotFoundException, RulesException {
5   AWSXRay.getCurrentSegment().setUser(userId);
6   return moveFactory.newMove(sessionId, gameId, userId, move);
7 }
```

To find traces for a user ID, use the **user** keyword in a filter expression.

Passing Segment Context between Threads in a Multithreaded Application

When you create a new thread in your application, the `AWSXRayRecorder` doesn't maintain a reference to the current segment or subsegment Entity. If you use an instrumented client in the new thread, the SDK tries to write to a segment that doesn't exist, causing a SegmentNotFoundException.

To avoid throwing exceptions during development, you can configure the recorder with a ContextMissingStrategy that tells it to log an error instead. You can configure the strategy in code with SetContextMissingStrategy, or configure equivalent options with an environment variable or system property.

One way to address the error is to use a new segment by calling beginSegment when you start the thread and endSegment when you close it. This works if you are instrumenting code that doesn't run in response to an HTTP request, like code that runs when your application starts.

If you use multiple threads to handle incoming requests, you can pass the current segment or subsegment to the new thread and provide it to the global recorder. This ensures that the information recorded within the new thread is associated with the same segment as the rest of the information recorded about that request.

To pass trace context between threads, call GetTraceEntity on the global recorder to get a reference to the current entity (segment or subsegment). Pass the entity to the new thread, and then call SetTraceEntity to configure the global recorder to use it to record trace data within the thread.

See Using Instrumented Clients in Worker Threads for an example.

AOP with Spring and the X-Ray SDK for Java

This topic describes how to use the X-Ray SDK and the Spring Framework to instrument your application without changing its core logic. This means that there is now a non-invasive way to instrument your applications running remotely in AWS.

You must perform three tasks to enable this feature.

To enable AOP in Spring

1. Configure Spring

2. Annotate your code or implement an interface

3. Activate X-Ray in your application

Configuring Spring

You can use Maven or Gradle to configure Spring to use AOP to instrument you application.

If you use Maven to build your application, add the the following dependency in your `pom.xml` file.

```
1 <dependency>
2     <groupId>com.amazonaws</groupId>
3     <artifactId>aws-xray-recorder-sdk-spring</artifactId>
4     <version>1.3.1</version>
5 </dependency>
```

For Gradle, add the following dependency in your `build.gradle` file.

```
1 compile 'com.amazonaws:aws-xray-recorder-sdk-spring:1.3.1'
```

Annotating Your Code or Implementing an Interface

Your classes must either be annotated with the `@XRayEnabled` annotation, or implement the `XRayTraced` interface. This tells the AOP system to wrap the functions of the affected class for X-Ray instrumentation.

Activating X-Ray in Your Application

To activate X-Ray tracing in your application, your code must extend the abstract class `AbstractXRayInterceptor` by overriding the following methods.

- `generateMetadata`—This function allows customization of the metadata attached to the current function's trace. By default, the class name of the executing function is recorded in the metadata. You can add more data if you need additional insights.

- `xrayEnabledClasses`—This function is empty, and should remain so. It serves as the host for a pointcut instructing the interceptor about which methods to wrap. Define the pointcut by specifying which of the classes that are annotated with `@XRayEnabled` to trace. The following pointcut statement tells the interceptor to wrap all controller beans annotated with the `@XRayEnabled` annotation.

```
1 @Pointcut"(@within(com.amazonaws.xray.spring.aop.XRayEnabled) && bean(*Controller)")
```

Example

The following code extends the abstract class `AbstractXRayInterceptor`.

```
1 @Aspect
2 @Component
3 public class XRayInspector extends AbstractXRayInterceptor {
4     @Override
5     protected Map<String, Map<String, Object>> generateMetadata(ProceedingJoinPoint
           proceedingJoinPoint, Subsegment subsegment) throws Exception {
6         return super.generateMetadata(proceedingJoinPoint, subsegment);
7     }
8
9   @Override
10  @Pointcut("@within(com.amazonaws.xray.spring.aop.XRayEnabled) && bean(*Controller)")
11  public void xrayEnabledClasses() {}
12
13 }
```

The following code is a class that will be instrumented by X-Ray.

```
1 @Service
2 @XRayEnabled
3 public class MyServiceImpl implements MyService {
4     private final MyEntityRepository myEntityRepository;
5
6     @Autowired
7     public MyServiceImpl(MyEntityRepository myEntityRepository) {
8         this.myEntityRepository = myEntityRepository;
9     }
10
11    @Transactional(readOnly = true)
12    public List<MyEntity> getMyEntities(){
13        try(Stream<MyEntity> entityStream = this.myEntityRepository.streamAll()){
14            return entityStream.sorted().collect(Collectors.toList());
15        }
16    }
17 }
```

If you've configured your application correctly, you should see the complete call stack of the application, from the controller down through the service calls, as shown in the following screen shot of the console.

Traces › Details

| Timeline | Raw data |

Method	Response	Duration	Age	ID
GET	200	20.0 ms	1.0 day (2017-12-14 16:55:56 UTC)	1-5a32ad1c-56e2c75fffcf01a767b26e4a

Name	Res.	Duration	Status
▼ **metering-server** AWS::ElasticBeanstalk::Environment			
metering-server	200	20.0 ms	☑
limitFullReport	-	18.0 ms	☑
limitReport	-	13.0 ms	☑
findOne	-	2.0 ms	☑
metering@null	-	0.0 ms	☑
findAllByTenantId	-	2.0 ms	☑
metering@null	-	1.0 ms	☑
findPeriodMeasureTotal	-	2.0 ms	☑
metering@null	-	0.0 ms	☑
findOne	-	6.0 ms	☑
metering@null	-	1.0 ms	☑
▶ **metering@null** Database::SQL (Client Response)			

AWS X-Ray SDK for Go

The X-Ray SDK for Go is a set of libraries for Go applications that provide classes and methods for generating and sending trace data to the X-Ray daemon. Trace data includes information about incoming HTTP requests served by the application, and calls that the application makes to downstream services using the AWS SDK, HTTP clients, or an SQL database connector. You can also create segments manually and add debug information in annotations and metadata.

Download the SDK from its GitHub repository with go `get`:

```
1 $ go get -u github.com/aws/aws-xray-sdk-go
```

For web applications, start by using the `xray.Handler` function to trace incoming requests. The message handler creates a segment for each traced request, and completes the segment when the response is sent. While the segment is open you can use the SDK client's methods to add information to the segment and create subsegments to trace downstream calls. The SDK also automatically records exceptions that your application throws while the segment is open.

For Lambda functions called by an instrumented application or service, Lambda reads the tracing header and traces sampled requests automatically. For other functions, you can configure Lambda to sample and trace incoming requests. In either case, Lambda creates the segment and provides it to the X-Ray SDK.

Note
On Lambda, the X-Ray SDK is optional. If you don't use it in your function, your service map will still include a node for the Lambda service, and one for each Lambda function. By adding the SDK, you can instrument your function code to add subsegments to the function segment recorded by Lambda. See AWS Lambda and AWS X-Ray for more information.

Next, wrap your client with a call to the `AWS` function. This step ensures that X-Ray instruments calls to any client methods. You can also instrument calls to SQL databases.

Once you get going with the SDK, customize its behavior by configuring the recorder and middleware. You can add plugins to record data about the compute resources running your application, customize sampling behavior by defining sampling rules, and set the log level to see more or less information from the SDK in your application logs.

Record additional information about requests and the work that your application does in annotations and metadata. Annotations are simple key-value pairs that are indexed for use with filter expressions, so that you can search for traces that contain specific data. Metadata entries are less restrictive and can record entire objects and arrays — anything that can be serialized into JSON.

Annotations and Metadata
Annotations and metadata are arbitrary text that you add to segments with the X-Ray SDK. Annotations are indexed for use with filter expressions. Metadata are not indexed, but can be viewed in the raw segment with the X-Ray console or API. Anyone that you grant read access to X-Ray can view this data.

When you have a lot of instrumented clients in your code, a single request segment can contain a large number of subsegments, one for each call made with an instrumented client. You can organize and group subsegments by wrapping client calls in custom subsegments. You can create a custom subsegment for an entire function or any section of code, and record metadata and annotations on the subsegment instead of writing everything on the parent segment.

Requirements

The X-Ray SDK for Go requires Go 1.7 or later.

The SDK depends on the following libraries at compile and runtime:

- AWS SDK for Go version 1.10.0 or newer

These dependencies are declared in the SDK's `README.md` file.

Reference Documentation

Once you have downloaded the SDK, build and host the documentation locally to view it in a web browser.

To view the reference documentation

1. Navigating to the `$GOPATH/src/github.com/aws/aws-xray-sdk-go` (Linux or Mac) directory or the `%GOPATH%\src\github.com\aws\aws-xray-sdk-go` (Windows) folder

2. Run the `godoc` command.

```
1  $ godoc -http=:6060
```

3. Opening a browser at `http://localhost:6060/pkg/github.com/aws/aws-xray-sdk-go/`.

Configuring the X-Ray SDK for Go

You can specify the configuration for for X-Ray SDK for Go through environment variables, by calling `Configure` with a `Config` object, or by assuming default values. Environment variables take precedence over `Config` values, which take precedence over any default value.

Topics

- Service Plugins
- Sampling Rules
- Logging
- Environment Variables
- Using Configure

Service Plugins

Use `plugins` to record information about the service hosting your application.

Plugins

- Amazon EC2 – `EC2Plugin` adds the instance ID and Availability Zone.
- Elastic Beanstalk – `ElasticBeanstalkPlugin` adds the environment name, version label, and deployment ID.
- Amazon ECS – `ECSPlugin` adds the container ID.

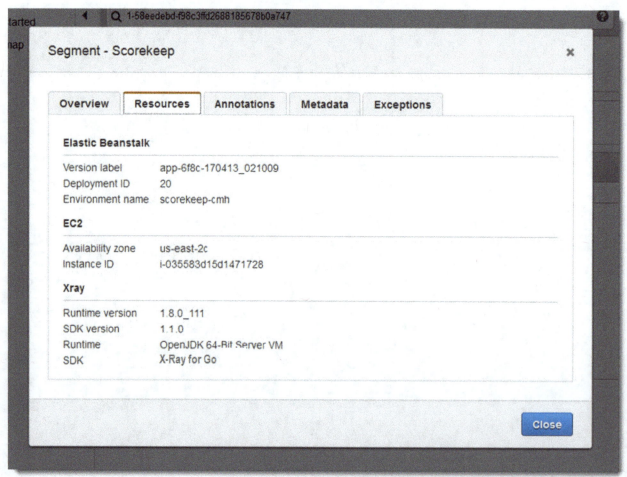

To use a plugin, import one of the following packages.

```
1 _ "github.com/aws/aws-xray-sdk-go/plugins/ec2"
2 _ "github.com/aws/aws-xray-sdk-go/plugins/ecs"
3 _ "github.com/aws/aws-xray-sdk-go/plugins/beanstalk"
```

The SDK also uses plugin settings to set the `origin` field on the segment. This indicates the type of AWS resource that runs your application. The resource type appears under your application's name in the service map. For example, `AWS::ElasticBeanstalk::Environment`.

When you use multiple plugins, the SDK uses the plugin that was loaded last to determine the origin.

Sampling Rules

The SDK has a default sampling strategy that determines which requests get traced. By default, the SDK traces the first request each second, and five percent of any additional requests. You can customize the SDK's sampling behavior by applying rules you define in a local file.

Example sampling-rules.json

```
1 {
2   "version": 1,
3   "rules": [
4     {
5       "description": "Player moves.",
6       "service_name": "*",
7       "http_method": "*",
8       "url_path": "/api/move/*",
9       "fixed_target": 0,
10      "rate": 0.05
11    }
12  ],
13  "default": {
14    "fixed_target": 1,
15    "rate": 0.1
16  }
17 }
```

This example defines one custom rule and a default rule. The custom rule applies a five-percent sampling rate with no minimum number of requests to trace for paths under `/api/move/`. The default rule traces the first request each second and 10 percent of additional requests.

The SDK applies custom rules in the order in which they are defined. If a request matches multiple custom rules, the SDK applies only the first rule.

On Lambda, you cannot modify the sampling rate. If your function is called by an instrumented service, calls generated requests that were sampled by that service will be recorded by Lambda. If active tracing is enabled and no tracing header is present, Lambda makes the sampling decision.

Once you've defined your rules, use `xray.Configure` to add them to your Go application.

Example main.go – sampling rule configuration

```
1 func init() {
2     ss, err := sampling.NewLocalizedStrategyFromFilePath("conf/sampling.json")
3
4     if err != nil {
5         panic(err)
6     }
7
8     xray.Configure(xray.Config{
9         SamplingStrategy: ss,
10     })
11 }
```

Logging

You can change the log level and format with `xray.Configure`.

Example main.go

```
1 func main() {
2   http.Handle("/", xray.Handler(xray.NewFixedSegmentNamer("MyApp"), http.HandlerFunc(func(w http
        .ResponseWriter, r *http.Request) {
3
4     xray.Configure(xray.Config{
5         LogLevel: "warn",
6         LogFormat: "[%Level] [%Time] %Msg%n"
7     })
8
9     w.Write([]byte("Hello!"))
10   })))
11
12   http.ListenAndServe(":8000", nil)
13 }
```

See Using Configure for more information.

Environment Variables

You can use environment variables to configure the X-Ray SDK for Go. The SDK supports the following variables.

- `AWS_XRAY_TRACING_NAME` – Set the service name that the SDK uses for segments.
- `AWS_XRAY_DAEMON_ADDRESS` – Set the host and port of the X-Ray daemon listener. By default, the SDK sends trace data to `127.0.0.1:2000`. Use this variable if you have configured the daemon to listen on a different port or if it is running on a different host.

Environment variables override equivalent values set in code.

Using Configure

You can also configure the X-Ray SDK for Go using the `Configure` method. `Configure` takes one argument, a `Config` object, with the following, optional fields.

DaemonAddr
This string specifies the host and port of the X-Ray daemon listener. If not specified, X-Ray uses the value of the `AWS_XRAY_DAEMON_ADDRESS` environment variable. If that value is not set, it uses "127.0.0.1:2000".

ServiceVersion
This string specifies the version of the service. If not specified, X-Ray uses the empty string ("").

SamplingStrategy
This `SamplingStrategy` object specifies which of your application calls are traced. If not specified, X-Ray uses a `LocalizedSamplingStrategy`, which takes the strategy as defined in `xray/resources/DefaultSamplingRules.json`.

StreamingStrategy
This `StreamingStrategy` object specifies whether to stream a segment when **RequiresStreaming** returns **true**. If not specified, X-Ray uses a `DefaultStreamingStrategy` that streams a sampled segment if the number of subsegments is greater than 20.

ExceptionFormattingStrategy
This `ExceptionFormattingStrategy` object specifies how you want to handle various exceptions. If not specified, X-Ray uses a `DefaultExceptionFormattingStrategy` with an `XrayError` of type `error`, the error message, and stack trace.

LogLevel
This string specifies the default logging level for your application. You can set this to "trace", "debug", "info", "warn" or "error". If not specified, X-Ray uses "info".

LogFormat
This string specifies the format of the log messages. If not specified, X-Ray uses "%Date(2006-01-02T15:04:05Z07:00) [%Level] %Msg%n".

Instrumenting Incoming HTTP Requests with the X-Ray SDK for Go

You can use the X-Ray SDK to trace incoming HTTP requests that your application serves on an EC2 instance in Amazon EC2, AWS Elastic Beanstalk, or Amazon ECS.

Use `xray.Handler` to instrument incoming HTTP requests. The X-Ray SDK for Go implements the standard Go library `http.Handler` interface in the `xay.Handler` class to intercept web requests. The `xay.Handler` class wraps the provided `http.Handler` with `xray.Capture` using the request's context, parsing the incoming headers, adding response headers if needed, and sets HTTP-specific trace fields.

When you use this class to handle HTTP requests and responses, the X-Ray SDK for Go creates a segment for each sampled request. This segment includes timing, method, and disposition of the HTTP request. Additional instrumentation creates subsegments on this segment.

Note
For AWS Lambda functions, Lambda creates a segment for each sampled request. See AWS Lambda and AWS X-Ray for more information.

The following example intercepts requests on port 8000 and returns "Hello!" as a response. It creates the segment `myApp` and instruments calls through any application.

Example main.go

```
1 func main() {
2   http.Handle("/", xray.Handler(xray.NewFixedSegmentNamer("MyApp"), http.HandlerFunc(func(w http
       .ResponseWriter, r *http.Request) {
3     w.Write([]byte("Hello!"))
4   })))
5
6   http.ListenAndServe(":8000", nil)
7 }
```

Each segment has a name that identifies your application in the service map. The segment can be named statically, or you can configure the SDK to name it dynamically based on the host header in the incoming request. Dynamic naming lets you group traces based on the domain name in the request, and apply a default name if the name doesn't match an expected pattern (for example, if the host header is forged).

Forwarded Requests
If a load balancer or other intermediary forwards a request to your application, X-Ray takes the client IP from the `X-Forwarded-For` header in the request instead of from the source IP in the IP packet. The client IP that is recorded for a forwarded request can be forged, so it should not be trusted.

When a request is forwarded, the SDK sets an additional field in the segment to indicate this. If the segment contains the field `x_forwarded_for` set to `true`, the client IP was taken from the `X-Forwarded-For` header in the HTTP request.

The handler creates a segment for each incoming request with an `http` block that contains the following information:

- **HTTP method** – GET, POST, PUT, DELETE, etc.
- **Client address** – The IP address of the client that sent the request.
- **Response code** – The HTTP response code for the completed request.
- **Timing** – The start time (when the request was received) and end time (when the response was sent).
- **User agent** — The `user-agent` from the request.
- **Content length** — The `content-length` from the response.

Configuring a Segment Naming Strategy

AWS X-Ray uses a *service name* to identify your application and distinguish it from the other applications, databases, external APIs, and AWS resources that your application uses. When the X-Ray SDK generates segments for incoming requests, it records your application's service name in the segment's name field.

The X-Ray SDK can name segments after the hostname in the HTTP request header. However, this header can be forged, which could result in unexpected nodes in your service map. To prevent the SDK from naming segments incorrectly due to requests with forged host headers, you must specify a default name for incoming requests.

If your application serves requests for multiple domains, you can configure the SDK to use a dynamic naming strategy to reflect this in segment names. A dynamic naming strategy allows the SDK to use the hostname for requests that match an expected pattern, and apply the default name to requests that don't.

For example, you might have a single application serving requests to three subdomains– www.example.com, api.example.com, and static.example.com. You can use a dynamic naming strategy with the pattern *.example.com to identify segments for each subdomain with a different name, resulting in three service nodes on the service map. If your application receives requests with a hostname that doesn't match the pattern, you will see a fourth node on the service map with a fallback name that you specify.

To use the same name for all request segments, specify the name of your application when you create the handler, as shown in the previous section.

Note
You can override the default service name that you define in code with the AWS_XRAY_TRACING_NAME environment variable.

A dynamic naming strategy defines a pattern that hostnames should match, and a default name to use if the hostname in the HTTP request doesn't match the pattern. To name segments dynamically, use NewDynamicSegmentNamer to configure the default name and pattern to match.

Example main.go
If the hostname in the request matches the pattern *.example.com, use the hostname. Otherwise, use MyApp.

```
1 func main() {
2   http.Handle("/", xray.Handler(xray.NewDynamicSegmentNamer("MyApp", "*.example.com"), http.
        HandlerFunc(func(w http.ResponseWriter, r *http.Request) {
3     w.Write([]byte("Hello!"))
4   })))
5
6   http.ListenAndServe(":8000", nil)
7 }
```

Tracing AWS SDK Calls with the X-Ray SDK for Go

When your application makes calls to AWS services to store data, write to a queue, or send notifications, the X-Ray SDK for Go tracks the calls downstream in subsegments. Traced AWS services and resources that you access within those services (for example, an Amazon S3 bucket or Amazon SQS queue), appear as downstream nodes on the service map in the X-Ray console.

To trace AWS SDK clients, wrap the client object with the `xray.AWS()` call as shown in the following example.

Example main.go

```
1 var dynamo *dynamodb.DynamoDB
2 func main() {
3   dynamo = dynamodb.New(session.Must(session.NewSession()))
4   xray.AWS(dynamo.Client)
5 }
```

Then, when you use the AWS SDK client, use the `withContext` version of the call method, and pass it the `context` from the `http.Request` object passed to the handler.

Example main.go – AWS SDK call

```
1 func listTablesWithContext(ctx context.Context) {
2   output := dynamo.ListTablesWithContext(ctx, &dynamodb.ListTablesInput{})
3   doSomething(output)
4 }
```

For all services, you can see the name of the API called in the X-Ray console. For a subset of services, the X-Ray SDK adds information to the segment to provide more granularity in the service map.

For example, when you make a call with an instrumented DynamoDB client, the SDK adds the table name to the segment for calls that target a table. In the console, each table appears as a separate node in the service map, with a generic DynamoDB node for calls that don't target a table.

Example Subsegment for a Call to DynamoDB to Save an Item

```
1  {
2    "id": "24756640c0d0978a",
3    "start_time": 1.480305974194E9,
4    "end_time": 1.4803059742E9,
5    "name": "DynamoDB",
6    "namespace": "aws",
7    "http": {
8      "response": {
9        "content_length": 60,
10        "status": 200
11     }
12   },
13   "aws": {
14     "table_name": "scorekeep-user",
15     "operation": "UpdateItem",
16     "request_id": "UBQNSO5AEM8T4FDA4RQDEB94O VTDRVV4K4HIRGVJF66Q9ASUAAJG",
17   }
18 }
```

When you access named resources, calls to the following services create additional nodes in the service map. Calls that don't target specific resources create a generic node for the service.

- **Amazon DynamoDB** – Table name

- **Amazon Simple Storage Service** – Bucket and key name
- **Amazon Simple Queue Service** – Queue name

Tracing Calls to Downstream HTTP Web Services with the X-Ray SDK for Go

When your application makes calls to microservices or public HTTP APIs, you can use the `xray.Client` to instrument those calls as subsegments of your Go application, as shown in the following example, where *http-client* is an HTTP client.

Client creates a shallow copy of the provided http client, defaulting to `http.DefaultClient`, with roundtripper wrapped with `xray.RoundTripper`.

Example main.go – HTTP client

```
1 myClient := xray.Client(http-client)
```

Tracing SQL Queries with the X-Ray SDK for Go

To trace SQL calls to PostgreSQL or MySQL, replacing `sql.Open` calls to `xray.SQL`, as shown in the following example. Use URLs instead of configuration strings if possible.

Example main.go

```go
func main() {
  db := xray.SQL("postgres", "postgres://user:password@host:port/db")
  row, _ := db.QueryRow("SELECT 1") // Use as normal
}
```

Generating Custom Subsegments with the X-Ray SDK for Go

Subsegments extend a trace's segment with details about work done in order to serve a request. Each time you make a call with an instrumented client, the X-Ray SDK records the information generated in a subsegment. You can create additional subsegments to group other subsegments, to measure the performance of a section of code, or to record annotations and metadata.

Use the `Capture` method to create a subsegment around a function.

Example main.go – custom subsegment

```
1  func criticalSection(ctx context.Context) {
2    //this is an example of a subsegment
3    xray.Capture(ctx, "GameModel.saveGame", func(ctx1 context.Context) error {
4      var err error
5
6      section.Lock()
7      result := someLockedResource.Go()
8      section.Unlock()
9
10     xray.AddMetadata(ctx1, "ResourceResult", result)
11   })
```

The following screenshot shows an example of how the `saveGame` subsegment might appear in traces for the application Scorekeep.

Add Annotations and Metadata to Segments with the X-Ray SDK for Go

You can record additional information about requests, the environment, or your application with annotations and metadata. You can add annotations and metadata to the segments that the X-Ray SDK creates, or to custom subsegments that you create.

Annotations are key-value pairs with string, number, or Boolean values. Annotations are indexed for use with filter expressions. Use annotations to record data that you want to use to group traces in the console, or when calling the http://docs.aws.amazon.com/xray/latest/api/API_GetTraceSummaries.html API.

Metadata are key-value pairs that can have values of any type, including objects and lists, but are not indexed for use with filter expressions. Use metadata to record additional data that you want stored in the trace but don't need to use with search.

In addition to annotations and metadata, you can also record user ID strings on segments. User IDs are recorded in a separate field on segments and are indexed for use with search.

Topics

- Recording Annotations with the X-Ray SDK for Go
- Recording Metadata with the X-Ray SDK for Go
- Recording User IDs with the X-Ray SDK for Go

Recording Annotations with the X-Ray SDK for Go

Use annotations to record information on segments that you want indexed for search.

Annotation Requirements

- **Keys** – Up to 500 alphanumeric characters. No spaces or symbols except underscores.
- **Values** – Up to 1,000 Unicode characters.
- **Entries** – Up to 50 annotations per trace.

To record annotations, call `AddAnnotation` with a string containing the metadata you want to associate with the segment.

```
1 xray.AddAnnotation(context, "value", error)
```

The SDK records annotations as key-value pairs in an **annotations** object in the segment document. Calling `AddAnnotation` twice with the same key overwrites previously recorded values on the same segment.

To find traces that have annotations with specific values, use the **annotations.key** keyword in a filter expression.

Recording Metadata with the X-Ray SDK for Go

Use metadata to record information on segments that you don't need indexed for search.

To record metadata, call `AddMetadata` with a string containing the metadata you want to associate with the segment.

```
1 xray.AddMetadata(context, "value", error)
```

Recording User IDs with the X-Ray SDK for Go

Record user IDs on request segments to identify the user who sent the request.

To record user IDs

1. Get a reference to the current segment from `AWSXRay`.

```
1 import (
2   "context"
3   "github.com/aws/aws-xray-sdk-go/xray"
4 )
5
6 mySegment := xray.GetSegment(context)
```

2. Call **setUser** with a String ID of the user who sent the request.

```
1 mySegment.User = "U12345"
```

To find traces for a user ID, use the **user** keyword in a filter expression.

The X-Ray SDK for Node.js

The X-Ray SDK for Node.js is a library for Express web applications and Node.js Lambda functions that provides classes and methods for generating and sending trace data to the X-Ray daemon. Trace data includes information about incoming HTTP requests served by the application, and calls that the application makes to downstream services using the AWS SDK or HTTP clients.

Note
The X-Ray SDK for Node.js is an open source project. You can follow the project and submit issues and pull requests on GitHub: github.com/aws/aws-xray-sdk-node

If you use Express, start by adding the SDK as middleware on your application server to trace incoming requests. The middleware creates a segment for each traced request, and completes the segment when the response is sent. While the segment is open you can use the SDK client's methods to add information to the segment and create subsegments to trace downstream calls. The SDK also automatically records exceptions that your application throws while the segment is open.

For Lambda functions called by an instrumented application or service, Lambda reads the tracing header and traces sampled requests automatically. For other functions, you can configure Lambda to sample and trace incoming requests. In either case, Lambda creates the segment and provides it to the X-Ray SDK.

Note
On Lambda, the X-Ray SDK is optional. If you don't use it in your function, your service map will still include a node for the Lambda service, and one for each Lambda function. By adding the SDK, you can instrument your function code to add subsegments to the function segment recorded by Lambda. See AWS Lambda and AWS X-Ray for more information.

Next, use the X-Ray SDK for Node.js to instrument your AWS SDK for JavaScript in Node.js clients. Whenever you make a call to a downstream AWS service or resource with an instrumented client, the SDK records information about the call in a subsegment. AWS services and the resources that you access within the services appear as downstream nodes on the service map to help you identify errors and throttling issues on individual connections.

The X-Ray SDK for Node.js also provides instrumentation for downstream calls to HTTP web APIs and SQL queries. Wrap your HTTP client in the SDK's capture method to record information about outgoing HTTP calls. For SQL clients, use the capture method for your database type.

The middleware applies sampling rules to incoming requests to determine which requests to trace. You can configure the X-Ray SDK for Node.js to adjust the sampling behavior or to record information about the AWS compute resources on which your application runs.

Record additional information about requests and the work that your application does in annotations and metadata. Annotations are simple key-value pairs that are indexed for use with filter expressions, so that you can search for traces that contain specific data. Metadata entries are less restrictive and can record entire objects and arrays — anything that can be serialized into JSON.

Annotations and Metadata
Annotations and metadata are arbitrary text that you add to segments with the X-Ray SDK. Annotations are indexed for use with filter expressions. Metadata are not indexed, but can be viewed in the raw segment with the X-Ray console or API. Anyone that you grant read access to X-Ray can view this data.

When you have a lot of instrumented clients in your code, a single request segment can contain a large number of subsegments, one for each call made with an instrumented client. You can organize and group subsegments by wrapping client calls in custom subsegments. You can create a custom subsegment for an entire function or any section of code, and record metadata and annotations on the subsegment instead of writing everything on the parent segment.

For reference documentation about the SDK's classes and methods, see the AWS X-Ray SDK for Node.js API Reference.

Requirements

The X-Ray SDK for Node.js requires Node.js and the following libraries:

- `cls` – 0.1.5
- `continuation-local-storage` – 3.2.0
- `pkginfo` – 0.4.0
- `underscore` – 1.8.3

The SDK pulls these libraries in when you install it with NPM.

To trace AWS SDK clients, the X-Ray SDK for Node.js requires a minimum version of the AWS SDK for JavaScript in Node.js.

- `aws-sdk` – 2.7.15

Dependency Management

The X-Ray SDK for Node.js is available from NPM.

- **Package** – https://www.npmjs.com/package/aws-xray-sdk

For local development, install the SDK in your project directory with npm.

```
1  ~/nodejs-xray$ npm install aws-xray-sdk
2  nodejs-xray@0.0.0 ~/nodejs-xray
3   aws-xray-sdk@1.2.0
4     continuation-local-storage@3.2.0
5      async-listener@0.6.3
6       shimmer@1.0.0
7      emitter-listener@1.0.1
8     moment@2.17.1
9     pkginfo@0.4.0
10    semver@5.3.0
11    underscore@1.8.3
12    winston@2.3.1
13      async@1.0.0
14      colors@1.0.3
15      cycle@1.0.3
16      eyes@0.1.8
17      isstream@0.1.2
18      stack-trace@0.0.9
```

Use the `--save` option to save the SDK as a dependency in your application's `package.json`.

```
1  ~/nodejs-xray$ npm install aws-xray-sdk --save
2  nodejs-xray@0.0.0 ~/nodejs-xray
3   aws-xray-sdk@1.2.0
```

Configuring the X-Ray SDK for Node.js

You can configure the X-Ray SDK for Node.js with plugins to include information about the service that your application runs on, modify the default sampling behavior, or add sampling rules that apply to requests to specific paths.

Topics

- Service Plugins
- Sampling Rules
- Logging
- X-Ray Daemon Address
- Environment Variables

Service Plugins

Use `plugins` to record information about the service hosting your application.

Plugins

- Amazon EC2 – `EC2Plugin` adds the instance ID and Availability Zone.
- Elastic Beanstalk – `ElasticBeanstalkPlugin` adds the environment name, version label, and deployment ID.
- Amazon ECS – `ECSPlugin` adds the container ID.

To use a plugin, configure the X-Ray SDK for Node.js client by using the `config` method.

Example app.js - Plugins

```
1 var AWSXRay = require('aws-xray-sdk');
2 AWSXRay.config([AWSXRay.plugins.EC2Plugin,AWSXRay.plugins.ElasticBeanstalkPlugin]);
```

The SDK also uses plugin settings to set the `origin` field on the segment. This indicates the type of AWS resource that runs your application. The resource type appears under your application's name in the service map. For example, `AWS::ElasticBeanstalk::Environment`.

When you use multiple plugins, the SDK uses the plugin that was loaded last to determine the origin.

Sampling Rules

The SDK has a default sampling strategy that determines which requests get traced. By default, the SDK traces the first request each second, and five percent of any additional requests. You can customize the SDK's sampling behavior by applying rules you define in a local file.

Example sampling-rules.json

```
 1 {
 2   "version": 1,
 3   "rules": [
 4     {
 5       "description": "Player moves.",
 6       "service_name": "*",
 7       "http_method": "*",
 8       "url_path": "/api/move/*",
 9       "fixed_target": 0,
10       "rate": 0.05
11     }
12   ],
13   "default": {
14     "fixed_target": 1,
15     "rate": 0.1
16   }
17 }
```

This example defines one custom rule and a default rule. The custom rule applies a five-percent sampling rate with no minimum number of requests to trace for paths under /api/move/. The default rule traces the first request each second and 10 percent of additional requests.

The SDK applies custom rules in the order in which they are defined. If a request matches multiple custom rules, the SDK applies only the first rule.

On Lambda, you cannot modify the sampling rate. If your function is called by an instrumented service, calls generated requests that were sampled by that service will be recorded by Lambda. If active tracing is enabled and no tracing header is present, Lambda makes the sampling decision.

Tell the X-Ray SDK for Node.js to load sampling rules from a file with `setSamplingRules`.

Example app.js - Sampling rules from a file

```
 1 var AWSXRay = require('aws-xray-sdk');
 2 AWSXRay.middleware.setSamplingRules('sampling-rules.json');
```

You can also define your rules in code and pass them to `setSamplingRules` as an object.

Example app.js - Sampling rules from an object

```
 1 var AWSXRay = require('aws-xray-sdk');
 2 var rules = {
 3   "rules": [ { "description": "Player moves.", "service_name": "*", "http_method": "*", "
         url_path": "/api/move/*", "fixed_target": 0, "rate": 0.05 } ],
 4   "default": { "fixed_target": 1, "rate": 0.1 },
 5   "version": 1
 6 }
 7
 8 AWSXRay.middleware.setSamplingRules(rules);
```

Logging

To log output from the SDK, call `AWSXRay.setLogger(logger)`, where `logger` is an object that provides standard logging methods (`warn`, `info`, etc.).

Example app.js - Logging with Winston

```
1 var AWSXRay = require('aws-xray-sdk');
2 var logger = require('winston');
3 AWSXRay.setLogger(logger);
4 AWSXRay.config([AWSXRay.plugins.EC2Plugin]);
```

Call `setLogger` before you run other configuration methods to ensure that you capture output from those operations.

To configure the SDK to output logs to the console without using a logging library, use the `AWS_XRAY_DEBUG_MODE` environment variable.

X-Ray Daemon Address

If the X-Ray daemon listens on a port or host other than `127.0.0.1:2000`, you can configure the X-Ray SDK for Node.js to send trace data to a different UDP address.

```
1 AWSXRay.setDaemonAddress('host:port');
```

You can specify the host by name or by IPv4 address.

Example app.js - Daemon address

```
1 var AWSXRay = require('aws-xray-sdk');
2 AWSXRay.setDaemonAddress('daemonhost:8082');
```

You can also set the daemon address by using the `AWS_XRAY_DAEMON_ADDRESS` environment variable.

Environment Variables

You can use environment variables to configure the X-Ray SDK for Node.js. The SDK supports the following variables.

- `AWS_XRAY_TRACING_NAME` – Set a service name that the SDK uses for segments. Overrides the segment name that you set on the Express middleware.
- `AWS_XRAY_DAEMON_ADDRESS` – Set the host and port of the X-Ray daemon listener. By default, the SDK sends trace data to `127.0.0.1:2000`. Use this variable if you have configured the daemon to listen on a different port or if it is running on a different host.
- `AWS_XRAY_CONTEXT_MISSING` – Set to `LOG_ERROR` to avoid throwing exceptions when your instrumented code attempts to record data when no segment is open.

Valid Values

- `RUNTIME_ERROR` – Throw a runtime exception (default).
- `LOG_ERROR` – Log an error and continue.

Errors related to missing segments or subsegments can occur when you attempt to use an instrumented client in startup code that runs when no request is open, or in code that spawns a new thread.

- `AWS_XRAY_DEBUG_MODE` – Set to `TRUE` to configure the SDK to output logs to the console, instead of configuring a logger.

Tracing Incoming Requests with the X-Ray SDK for Node.js

You can use the X-Ray SDK for Node.js to trace incoming HTTP requests that your Express and Restify applications serve on an EC2 instance in Amazon EC2, AWS Elastic Beanstalk, or Amazon ECS.

The X-Ray SDK for Node.js provides middleware for applications that use the Express and Restify frameworks. When you add the X-Ray middleware to your application, the X-Ray SDK for Node.js creates a segment for each sampled request. This segment includes timing, method, and disposition of the HTTP request. Additional instrumentation creates subsegments on this segment.

Note
For AWS Lambda functions, Lambda creates a segment for each sampled request. See AWS Lambda and AWS X-Ray for more information.

Each segment has a name that identifies your application in the service map. The segment can be named statically, or you can configure the SDK to name it dynamically based on the host header in the incoming request. Dynamic naming lets you group traces based on the domain name in the request, and apply a default name if the name doesn't match an expected pattern (for example, if the host header is forged).

Forwarded Requests
If a load balancer or other intermediary forwards a request to your application, X-Ray takes the client IP from the `X-Forwarded-For` header in the request instead of from the source IP in the IP packet. The client IP that is recorded for a forwarded request can be forged, so it should not be trusted.

When a request is forwarded, the SDK sets an additional field in the segment to indicate this. If the segment contains the field `x_forwarded_for` set to `true`, the client IP was taken from the `X-Forwarded-For` header in the HTTP request.

The message handler creates a segment for each incoming request with an `http` block that contains the following information:

- **HTTP method** – GET, POST, PUT, DELETE, etc.
- **Client address** – The IP address of the client that sent the request.
- **Response code** – The HTTP response code for the completed request.
- **Timing** – The start time (when the request was received) and end time (when the response was sent).
- **User agent** — The `user-agent` from the request.
- **Content length** — The `content-length` from the response.

Topics

- Tracing Incoming Requests with Express
- Tracing Incoming Requests with Restify
- Configuring a Segment Naming Strategy

Tracing Incoming Requests with Express

To use the Express middleware, initialize the SDK client and use the middleware returned by the `express.openSegment` function before you define your routes.

Example app.js - Express

```
1 var app = express();
2
3 var AWSXRay = require('aws-xray-sdk');
4 app.use(AWSXRay.express.openSegment('MyApp'));
5
6 app.get('/', function (req, res) {
7   res.render('index');
8 });
```

```
 9
10 app.use(AWSXRay.express.closeSegment());
```

After you define your routes, use the output of `express.closeSegment` as shown to handle any errors returned by the X-Ray SDK for Node.js.

Tracing Incoming Requests with Restify

To use the Restify middleware, initialize the SDK client and run `enable`. Pass it your Restify server and segment name.

Example app.js - Restify

```
 1 var AWSXRay = require('aws-xray-sdk');
 2 var AWSXRayRestify = require('aws-xray-sdk-restify');
 3
 4 var restify = require('restify');
 5 var server = restify.createServer();
 6 AWSXRayRestify.enable(server, 'MyApp'));
 7
 8 server.get('/', function (req, res) {
 9   res.render('index');
10 });
```

Configuring a Segment Naming Strategy

AWS X-Ray uses a *service name* to identify your application and distinguish it from the other applications, databases, external APIs, and AWS resources that your application uses. When the X-Ray SDK generates segments for incoming requests, it records your application's service name in the segment's name field.

The X-Ray SDK can name segments after the hostname in the HTTP request header. However, this header can be forged, which could result in unexpected nodes in your service map. To prevent the SDK from naming segments incorrectly due to requests with forged host headers, you must specify a default name for incoming requests.

If your application serves requests for multiple domains, you can configure the SDK to use a dynamic naming strategy to reflect this in segment names. A dynamic naming strategy allows the SDK to use the hostname for requests that match an expected pattern, and apply the default name to requests that don't.

For example, you might have a single application serving requests to three subdomains– `www.example.com`, `api.example.com`, and `static.example.com`. You can use a dynamic naming strategy with the pattern `*. example.com` to identify segments for each subdomain with a different name, resulting in three service nodes on the service map. If your application receives requests with a hostname that doesn't match the pattern, you will see a fourth node on the service map with a fallback name that you specify.

To use the same name for all request segments, specify the name of your application when you initialize the middleware, as shown in the previous sections.

Note
You can override the default service name that you define in code with the `AWS_XRAY_TRACING_NAME` environment variable.

A dynamic naming strategy defines a pattern that hostnames should match, and a default name to use if the hostname in the HTTP request does not match the pattern. To name segments dynamically, use `AWSXRay. middleware.enableDynamicNaming`.

Example app.js - Dynamic Segment Names

If the hostname in the request matches the pattern `*.example.com`, use the hostname. Otherwise, use `MyApp`.

```
1  var app = express();
2
3  var AWSXRay = require('aws-xray-sdk');
4  app.use(AWSXRay.express.openSegment('MyApp'));
5  AWSXRay.middleware.enableDynamicNaming('*.example.com');
6
7  app.get('/', function (req, res) {
8    res.render('index');
9  });
10
11 app.use(AWSXRay.express.closeSegment());
```

Tracing AWS SDK Calls with the X-Ray SDK for Node.js

When your application makes calls to AWS services to store data, write to a queue, or send notifications, the X-Ray SDK for Node.js tracks the calls downstream in subsegments. Traced AWS services, and resources that you access within those services (for example, an Amazon S3 bucket or Amazon SQS queue), appear as downstream nodes on the service map in the X-Ray console.

You can instrument all AWS SDK clients by wrapping your `aws-sdk` require statement in a call to `AWSXRay.captureAWS`.

Example app.js - AWS SDK Instrumentation

```
1 var AWS = AWSXRay.captureAWS(require('aws-sdk'));
```

To instrument individual clients, wrap your AWS SDK client in a call to `AWSXRay.captureAWSClient`. For example, to instrument an `AmazonDynamoDB` client:

Example app.js - DynamoDB Client Instrumentation

```
1     var AWSXRay = require('aws-xray-sdk');
2 ...
3     var ddb = AWSXRay.captureAWSClient(new AWS.DynamoDB());
```

For all services, you can see the name of the API called in the X-Ray console. For a subset of services, the X-Ray SDK adds information to the segment to provide more granularity in the service map.

For example, when you make a call with an instrumented DynamoDB client, the SDK adds the table name to the segment for calls that target a table. In the console, each table appears as a separate node in the service map, with a generic DynamoDB node for calls that don't target a table.

Example Subsegment for a Call to DynamoDB to Save an Item

```
1  {
2    "id": "24756640c0d0978a",
3    "start_time": 1.480305974194E9,
4    "end_time": 1.4803059742E9,
5    "name": "DynamoDB",
6    "namespace": "aws",
7    "http": {
8      "response": {
9        "content_length": 60,
10       "status": 200
11     }
12   },
13   "aws": {
14     "table_name": "scorekeep-user",
15     "operation": "UpdateItem",
16     "request_id": "UBQNSO5AEM8T4FDA4RQDEB94OVTDRVV4K4HIRGVJF66Q9ASUAAJG",
17   }
18 }
```

When you access named resources, calls to the following services create additional nodes in the service map. Calls that don't target specific resources create a generic node for the service.

- **Amazon DynamoDB** – Table name
- **Amazon Simple Storage Service** – Bucket and key name
- **Amazon Simple Queue Service** – Queue name

Tracing Calls to Downstream HTTP Web Services Using the X-Ray SDK for Node.js

When your application makes calls to microservices or public HTTP APIs, you can use the X-Ray SDK for Node.js client to instrument those calls and add the API to the service graph as a downstream service.

Pass your `http` or `https` client to the X-Ray SDK for Node.js `captureHTTPs` method to trace outgoing calls.

Example app.js - HTTP Client

```
1 var AWSXRay = require('aws-xray-sdk');
2 var http = AWSXRay.captureHTTPs(require('http'));
```

To enable tracing on all HTTP clients, call `captureHTTPsGlobal` before you load `http`.

Example app.js - HTTP Client (Global)

```
1 var AWSXRay = require('aws-xray-sdk');
2 AWSXRay.captureHTTPsGlobal(require('http'));
3 var http = require('http');
```

When you instrument a call to a downstream web API, the X-Ray SDK for Node.js records a subsegment that contains information about the HTTP request and response. X-Ray uses the subsegment to generate an inferred segment for the remote API.

Example Subsegment for a Downstream HTTP Call

```
1  {
2    "id": "004f72be19cddc2a",
3    "start_time": 1484786387.131,
4    "end_time": 1484786387.501,
5    "name": "names.example.com",
6    "namespace": "remote",
7    "http": {
8      "request": {
9        "method": "GET",
10       "url": "https://names.example.com/"
11     },
12     "response": {
13       "content_length": -1,
14       "status": 200
15     }
16   }
17 }
```

Example Inferred Segment for a Downstream HTTP Call

```
1  {
2    "id": "168416dc2ea97781",
3    "name": "names.example.com",
4    "trace_id": "1-5880168b-fd5153bb58284b67678aa78c",
5    "start_time": 1484786387.131,
6    "end_time": 1484786387.501,
7    "parent_id": "004f72be19cddc2a",
8    "http": {
9      "request": {
10       "method": "GET",
11       "url": "https://names.example.com/"
```

```
12      },
13      "response": {
14        "content_length": -1,
15        "status": 200
16      }
17    },
18    "inferred": true
19  }
```

Tracing SQL Queries with the X-Ray SDK for Node.js

Instrument SQL database queries by wrapping your SQL client in the corresponding X-Ray SDK for Node.js client method.

- **PostgreSQL** – `AWSXRay.capturePostgres()`

```
1 var AWSXRay = require('aws-xray-sdk');
2 var pg = AWSXRay.capturePostgres(require('pg'));
3 var client = new pg.Client();
```

- **MySQL** – `AWSXRay.captureMySQL()`

```
1 var AWSXRay = require('aws-xray-sdk');
2 var mysql = AWSXRay.captureMySQL(require('mysql'));
3 ...
4 var connection = mysql.createConnection(config);
```

When you use an instrumented client to make SQL queries, the X-Ray SDK for Node.js records information about the connection and query in a subsegment.

Generating Custom Subsegments with the X-Ray SDK for Node.js

Subsegments extend a trace's segment with details about work done in order to serve a request. Each time you make a call with an instrumented client, the X-Ray SDK records the information generated in a subsegment. You can create additional subsegments to group other subsegments, to measure the performance of a section of code, or to record annotations and metadata.

To create a custom subsegment for a function that makes calls to downstream services, use the `captureAsyncFunc` function.

Example app.js - Custom Subsegments

```
 1 var AWSXRay = require('aws-xray-sdk');
 2
 3 app.use(AWSXRay.express.openSegment('MyApp'));
 4
 5 app.get('/', function (req, res) {
 6   var host = 'api.example.com';
 7
 8   AWSXRay.captureAsyncFunc('send', function(subsegment) {
 9     sendRequest(host, function() {
10       console.log('rendering!');
11       res.render('index');
12       subsegment.close();
13     });
14   });
15 });
16
17 app.use(AWSXRay.express.closeSegment());
18
19 function sendRequest(host, cb) {
20   var options = {
21     host: host,
22     path: '/',
23   };
24
25   var callback = function(response) {
26     var str = '';
27
28     response.on('data', function (chunk) {
29       str += chunk;
30     });
31
32     response.on('end', function () {
33       cb();
34     });
35   }
36
37   http.request(options, callback).end();
38 };
```

In this example, the application creates a custom subsegment named **send** for calls to the **sendRequest** function. **captureAsyncFunc** passes a subsegment that you must close within the callback function when the asynchronous calls that it makes are complete.

For synchronous functions, you can use the **captureFunc** function, which closes the subsegment automatically

185

as soon as the function block finishes executing.

When you create a subsegment within a segment or another subsegment, the X-Ray SDK for Node.js generates an ID for it and records the start time and end time.

Example Subsegment with Metadata

```
1  "subsegments": [{
2    "id": "6f1605cd8a07cb70",
3    "start_time": 1.480305974194E9,
4    "end_time": 1.4803059742E9,
5    "name": "Custom subsegment for UserModel.saveUser function",
6    "metadata": {
7      "debug": {
8        "test": "Metadata string from UserModel.saveUser"
9      }
10   },
```

Add Annotations and Metadata to Segments with the X-Ray SDK for Node.js

You can record additional information about requests, the environment, or your application with annotations and metadata. You can add annotations and metadata to the segments that the X-Ray SDK creates, or to custom subsegments that you create.

Annotations are key-value pairs with string, number, or Boolean values. Annotations are indexed for use with filter expressions. Use annotations to record data that you want to use to group traces in the console, or when calling the http://docs.aws.amazon.com/xray/latest/api/API_GetTraceSummaries.html API.

Metadata are key-value pairs that can have values of any type, including objects and lists, but are not indexed for use with filter expressions. Use metadata to record additional data that you want stored in the trace but don't need to use with search.

Topics

- Recording Annotations with the X-Ray SDK for Node.js
- Recording Metadata with the X-Ray SDK for Node.js

Recording Annotations with the X-Ray SDK for Node.js

Use annotations to record information on segments or subsegments that you want indexed for search.

Annotation Requirements

- **Keys** – Up to 500 alphanumeric characters. No spaces or symbols except underscores.
- **Values** – Up to 1,000 Unicode characters.
- **Entries** – Up to 50 annotations per trace.

To record annotations

1. Get a reference to the current segment or subsegment.

```
1 var AWSXRay = require('aws-xray-sdk');
2 ...
3 var document = AWSXRay.getSegment();
```

2. Call `addAnnotation` with a String key, and a Boolean, Number, or String value.

```
1 document.addAnnotation("mykey", "my value");
```

The SDK records annotations as key-value pairs in an `annotations` object in the segment document. Calling `addAnnotation` twice with the same key overwrites previously recorded values on the same segment or subsegment.

To find traces that have annotations with specific values, use the `annotations.key` keyword in a filter expression.

Example app.js - Annotations

```
1 var AWS = require('aws-sdk');
2 var AWSXRay = require('aws-xray-sdk');
3 var ddb = AWSXRay.captureAWSClient(new AWS.DynamoDB());
4 ...
5 app.post('/signup', function(req, res) {
6     var item = {
7         'email': {'S': req.body.email},
8         'name': {'S': req.body.name},
9         'preview': {'S': req.body.previewAccess},
10        'theme': {'S': req.body.theme}
```

```
11     };
12
13     var seg = AWSXRay.getSegment();
14     seg.addAnnotation('theme', req.body.theme);
15
16     ddb.putItem({
17       'TableName': ddbTable,
18       'Item': item,
19       'Expected': { email: { Exists: false } }
20   }, function(err, data) {
21 ...
```

Recording Metadata with the X-Ray SDK for Node.js

Use metadata to record information on segments or subsegments that you don't need indexed for search. Metadata values can be strings, numbers, Booleans, or any other object that can be serialized into a JSON object or array.

To record metadata

1. Get a reference to the current segment or subsegment.

```
1 var AWSXRay = require('aws-xray-sdk');
2 ...
3 var document = AWSXRay.getSegment();
```

2. Call addMetadata with a string key, a Boolean, number, string, or object value, and a string namespace.

```
1 document.addMetadata("my key", "my value", "my namespace");
```

   or

   Call addMetadata with just a key and value.

```
1 document.addMetadata("my key", "my value");
```

If you don't specify a namespace, the SDK uses default. Calling addMetadata twice with the same key overwrites previously recorded values on the same segment or subsegment.

AWS X-Ray SDK for Python

The X-Ray SDK for Python is a library for Python web applications that provides classes and methods for generating and sending trace data to the X-Ray daemon. Trace data includes information about incoming HTTP requests served by the application, and calls that the application makes to downstream services using the AWS SDK, HTTP clients, or an SQL database connector. You can also create segments manually and add debug information in annotations and metadata.

You can download the SDK with `pip`.

```
1 $ pip install aws-xray-sdk
```

Note

The X-Ray SDK for Python is an open source project. You can follow the project and submit issues and pull requests on GitHub: github.com/aws/aws-xray-sdk-python

If you use Django or Flask, start by adding the SDK middleware to your application to trace incoming requests. The middleware creates a segment for each traced request, and completes the segment when the response is sent. While the segment is open, you can use the SDK client's methods to add information to the segment and create subsegments to trace downstream calls. The SDK also automatically records exceptions that your application throws while the segment is open. For other applications, you can create segments manually.

For Lambda functions called by an instrumented application or service, Lambda reads the tracing header and traces sampled requests automatically. For other functions, you can configure Lambda to sample and trace incoming requests. In either case, Lambda creates the segment and provides it to the X-Ray SDK.

Note

On Lambda, the X-Ray SDK is optional. If you don't use it in your function, your service map will still include a node for the Lambda service, and one for each Lambda function. By adding the SDK, you can instrument your function code to add subsegments to the function segment recorded by Lambda. See AWS Lambda and AWS X-Ray for more information.

See Worker for a example Python function instrumented in Lambda.

Next, use the X-Ray SDK for Python to instrument downstream calls by patching your application's libraries. The SDK supports the following libraries.

Supported Libraries

- [botocore] (https://pypi.python.org/pypi/botocore), [boto3] (https://pypi.python.org/pypi/boto3) – Instrument AWS SDK for Python (Boto) clients.
- [pynamodb] (https://pypi.python.org/pypi/pynamodb/) – Instrument PynamoDB's version of the Amazon DynamoDB client.
- [aiobotocore] (https://pypi.python.org/pypi/aiobotocore), [aioboto3] (https://pypi.python.org/pypi/aioboto3) – Instrument asyncio-integrated versions of SDK for Python clients.
- [requests] (https://pypi.python.org/pypi/requests),   [aiohttp] (https://pypi.python.org/pypi/aiohttp) – Instrument high-level HTTP clients.
- [httplib] (https://docs.python.org/2/library/httplib.html), https://docs.python.org/3/library/http.client.html – Instrument low-level HTTP clients and the higher level libraries that use them.
- [sqlite3] (https://docs.python.org/3/library/sqlite3.html) – Instrument SQLite clients.
- [mysql\-connector\-python] (https://pypi.python.org/pypi/mysql-connector-python) – Instrument MySQL clients.

Whenever your application makes calls to AWS, an SQL database, or other HTTP services, the SDK records information about the call in a subsegment. AWS services and the resources that you access within the services appear as downstream nodes on the service map to help you identify errors and throttling issues on individual connections.

Once you get going with the SDK, customize its behavior by configuring the recorder and middleware. You can add plugins to record data about the compute resources running your application, customize sampling behavior by defining sampling rules, and set the log level to see more or less information from the SDK in your application logs.

Record additional information about requests and the work that your application does in annotations and metadata. Annotations are simple key-value pairs that are indexed for use with filter expressions, so that you can search for traces that contain specific data. Metadata entries are less restrictive and can record entire objects and arrays — anything that can be serialized into JSON.

Annotations and Metadata

Annotations and metadata are arbitrary text that you add to segments with the X-Ray SDK. Annotations are indexed for use with filter expressions. Metadata are not indexed, but can be viewed in the raw segment with the X-Ray console or API. Anyone that you grant read access to X-Ray can view this data.

When you have a lot of instrumented clients in your code, a single request segment can contain a large number of subsegments, one for each call made with an instrumented client. You can organize and group subsegments by wrapping client calls in custom subsegments. You can create a custom subsegment for an entire function or any section of code. You can then you can record metadata and annotations on the subsegment instead of writing everything on the parent segment.

For reference documentation for the SDK's classes and methods, see the AWS X-Ray SDK for Python API Reference.

Requirements

The X-Ray SDK for Python supports the following language and library versions.

- **Python** – 2.7, 3.4 and newer
- **Django** – 1.10 and newer
- **Flask** – 0.10 and newer
- **AWS SDK for Python (Boto)** – 1.4.0 and newer
- **botocore** – 1.5.0 and newer

Dependency Management

The X-Ray SDK for Python is available from `pip`.

- **Package** – `aws-xray-sdk`

Add the SDK as a dependency in your `requirements.txt` file.

Example requirements.txt

```
1 aws-xray-sdk==0.96
2 boto3==1.4.4
3 botocore==1.5.55
4 Django==1.11.3
```

If you use Elastic Beanstalk to deploy your application, Elastic Beanstalk installs all of the packages in `requirements.txt` automatically.

Configuring the X-Ray SDK for Python

The X-Ray SDK for Python has a class named `xray_recorder` that provides the global recorder. You can configure the global recorder to customize the middleware that creates segments for incoming HTTP calls.

Topics

- Service Plugins
- Sampling Rules
- Logging
- Recorder Configuration in Code
- Recorder Configuration with Django
- Environment Variables

Service Plugins

Use `plugins` to record information about the service hosting your application.

Plugins

- Amazon EC2 – `EC2Plugin` adds the instance ID and Availability Zone.
- Elastic Beanstalk – `ElasticBeanstalkPlugin` adds the environment name, version label, and deployment ID.
- Amazon ECS – `ECSPlugin` adds the container ID.

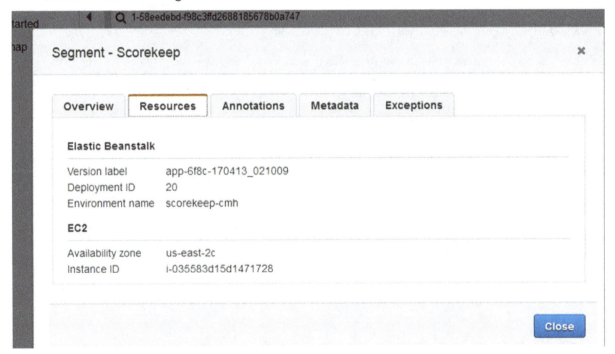

To use a plugin, call `configure` on the `xray_recorder`.

```
1 from aws_xray_sdk.core import xray_recorder
2 from aws_xray_sdk.core import patch_all
3
4 xray_recorder.configure(aws_xray_tracing_name='My app')
5 plugins = ('ElasticBeanstalkPlugin', 'EC2Plugin')
6 xray_recorder.configure(plugins=plugins)
7 patch_all()
```

You can also use environment variables, which take precedence over values set in code, to configure the recorder.

Configure plugins before patching libraries to record downstream calls.

The SDK also uses plugin settings to set the `origin` field on the segment. This indicates the type of AWS resource that runs your application. The resource type appears under your application's name in the service map. For example, `AWS::ElasticBeanstalk::Environment`.

When you use multiple plugins, the SDK uses the plugin that was loaded last to determine the origin.

Sampling Rules

The SDK has a default sampling strategy that determines which requests get traced. By default, the SDK traces the first request each second, and five percent of any additional requests. You can customize the SDK's sampling behavior by applying rules you define in a local file.

Example sampling-rules.json

```
1  {
2    "version": 1,
3    "rules": [
4      {
5        "description": "Player moves.",
6        "service_name": "*",
7        "http_method": "*",
8        "url_path": "/api/move/*",
9        "fixed_target": 0,
10       "rate": 0.05
11     }
12   ],
13   "default": {
14     "fixed_target": 1,
15     "rate": 0.1
16   }
17 }
```

This example defines one custom rule and a default rule. The custom rule applies a five-percent sampling rate with no minimum number of requests to trace for paths under **/api/move/**. The default rule traces the first request each second and 10 percent of additional requests.

The SDK applies custom rules in the order in which they are defined. If a request matches multiple custom rules, the SDK applies only the first rule.

On Lambda, you cannot modify the sampling rate. If your function is called by an instrumented service, calls generated requests that were sampled by that service will be recorded by Lambda. If active tracing is enabled and no tracing header is present, Lambda makes the sampling decision.

To configure sampling rules, call `xray_recorder.configure`, as shown in the following example, where *rules* is either a dictionary of rules or the absolute path to a JSON file containing sampling rules.

```
1 xray_recorder.configure(sampling_rules=rules)
```

You can also configure the global recorder to disable sampling and instrument all incoming requests.

Example main.py – disable sampling

```
1 xray_recorder.configure(sampling=False)
```

Logging

The SDK uses Python's built-in `logging` module. Get a reference to the logger for the `aws_xray_sdk` class and call `setLevel` on it to configure the different log level for the library and the rest of your application.

Example app.py – logging

```
1 logging.basicConfig(level='WARNING')
2 logging.getLogger('aws_xray_sdk').setLevel(logging.DEBUG)
```

Use debug logs to identify issues, such as unclosed subsegments, when you generate subsegments manually.

Recorder Configuration in Code

Additional settings are available from the `configure` method on `xray_recorder`.

- `context_missing` – Set to `LOG_ERROR` to avoid throwing exceptions when your instrumented code attempts to record data when no segment is open.
- `daemon_address` – Set the host and port of the X-Ray daemon listener.
- `service` – Set a service name that the SDK uses for segments.
- `plugins` – Record information about your application's AWS resources.
- `sampling` – Set to `False` to disable sampling.
- `sampling_rules` – Set the path of the JSON file containing your sampling rules.

Example main.py – disable context missing exceptions

```
1 from aws_xray_sdk.core import xray_recorder
2
3 xray_recorder.configure(context_missing='LOG_ERROR')
```

Recorder Configuration with Django

If you use the Django framework, you can use the Django `settings.py` file to configure options on the global recorder.

- `AUTO_INSTRUMENT` (Django only) – Record subsegments for built-in database and template rendering operations.
- `AWS_XRAY_CONTEXT_MISSING` – Set to `LOG_ERROR` to avoid throwing exceptions when your instrumented code attempts to record data when no segment is open.
- `AWS_XRAY_DAEMON_ADDRESS` – Set the host and port of the X-Ray daemon listener.
- `AWS_XRAY_TRACING_NAME` – Set a service name that the SDK uses for segments.

- `PLUGINS` – Record information about your application's AWS resources.
- `SAMPLING` – Set to `False` to disable sampling.
- `SAMPLING_RULES` – Set the path of the JSON file containing your sampling rules.

To enable recorder configuration in `settings.py`, add the Django middleware to the list of installed apps.

Example settings.py – installed apps

```
1 INSTALLED_APPS = [
2     ...
3     'django.contrib.sessions',
4     'aws_xray_sdk.ext.django',
5 ]
```

Configure the available settings in a list named `XRAY_RECORDER`.

Example settings.py – installed apps

```
1 XRAY_RECORDER = {
2     'AUTO_INSTRUMENT': True,
3     'AWS_XRAY_CONTEXT_MISSING': 'LOG_ERROR',
4     'AWS_XRAY_DAEMON_ADDRESS': '127.0.0.1:5000',
5     'AWS_XRAY_TRACING_NAME': 'My application',
6     'PLUGINS': ('ElasticBeanstalkPlugin', 'EC2Plugin', 'ECSPlugin'),
7     'SAMPLING': False,
8 }
```

Environment Variables

You can use environment variables to configure the X-Ray SDK for Python. The SDK supports the following variables:

- `AWS_XRAY_TRACING_NAME` – Set a service name that the SDK uses for segments. Overrides the service name that you set on the servlet filter's segment naming strategy.
- `AWS_XRAY_DAEMON_ADDRESS` – Set the host and port of the X-Ray daemon listener. By default, the SDK sends trace data to `127.0.0.1:2000`. Use this variable if you have configured the daemon to listen on a different port or if it is running on a different host.
- `AWS_XRAY_CONTEXT_MISSING` – Set to `LOG_ERROR` to avoid throwing exceptions when your instrumented code attempts to record data when no segment is open.

Valid Values

- `RUNTIME_ERROR` – Throw a runtime exception (default).
- `LOG_ERROR` – Log an error and continue.

Errors related to missing segments or subsegments can occur when you attempt to use an instrumented client in startup code that runs when no request is open, or in code that spawns a new thread.

Environment variables override values set in code.

Tracing Incoming Requests with the X-Ray SDK for Python Middleware

If you use Django or Flask, use the Django middleware or Flask middleware to instrument incoming HTTP requests. When you add the middleware to your application and configure a segment name, the X-Ray SDK for Python creates a segment for each sampled request. This segment includes timing, method, and disposition of the HTTP request. Additional instrumentation creates subsegments on this segment.

Note
For AWS Lambda functions, Lambda creates a segment for each sampled request. See AWS Lambda and AWS X-Ray for more information.

See Worker for a example Python function instrumented in Lambda.

For scripts or Python applications on other frameworks, you can create segments manually.

Each segment has a name that identifies your application in the service map. The segment can be named statically, or you can configure the SDK to name it dynamically based on the host header in the incoming request. Dynamic naming lets you group traces based on the domain name in the request, and apply a default name if the name doesn't match an expected pattern (for example, if the host header is forged).

Forwarded Requests
If a load balancer or other intermediary forwards a request to your application, X-Ray takes the client IP from the X-Forwarded-For header in the request instead of from the source IP in the IP packet. The client IP that is recorded for a forwarded request can be forged, so it should not be trusted.

When a request is forwarded, the SDK sets an additional field in the segment to indicate this. If the segment contains the field x_forwarded_for set to true, the client IP was taken from the X-Forwarded-For header in the HTTP request.

The middleware creates a segment for each incoming request with an http block that contains the following information:

- **HTTP method** – GET, POST, PUT, DELETE, etc.
- **Client address** – The IP address of the client that sent the request.
- **Response code** – The HTTP response code for the completed request.
- **Timing** – The start time (when the request was received) and end time (when the response was sent).
- **User agent** — The user-agent from the request.
- **Content length** — The content-length from the response.

Topics

- Adding the Middleware to Your Application (Django)
- Adding the Middleware to Your Application (Flask)
- Instrumenting Python Code Manually
- Configuring a Segment Naming Strategy

Adding the Middleware to Your Application (Django)

Add the middleware to the MIDDLEWARE list in your settings.py file. The X-Ray middleware should be the first line in your settings.py file to to ensure that requests that fail in other middleware are recorded.

Example settings.py - X-Ray SDK for Python middleware

```
1  MIDDLEWARE = [
2      'aws_xray_sdk.ext.django.middleware.XRayMiddleware',
3      'django.middleware.security.SecurityMiddleware',
4      'django.contrib.sessions.middleware.SessionMiddleware',
5      'django.middleware.common.CommonMiddleware',
```

```
6      'django.middleware.csrf.CsrfViewMiddleware',
7      'django.contrib.auth.middleware.AuthenticationMiddleware',
8      'django.contrib.messages.middleware.MessageMiddleware',
9      'django.middleware.clickjacking.XFrameOptionsMiddleware'
10 ]
```

Configure a segment name in your `settings.py` file.

Example settings.py – segment name

```
1 XRAY_RECORDER = {,
2     'AWS_XRAY_TRACING_NAME': 'My application',
3     'PLUGINS': ('EC2Plugin'),
4 }
```

This tells the X-Ray recorder to trace requests served by your Django application with the default sampling rate. You can configure the recorder your Django settings file to apply custom sampling rules or change other settings.

Adding the Middleware to Your Application (Flask)

To instrument your Flask application, first configure a segment name on the `xray_recorder`. Then, use the `XRayMiddleware` function to patch your Flask application in code.

Example app.py

```
1 from aws_xray_sdk.core import xray_recorder
2 from aws_xray_sdk.ext.flask.middleware import XRayMiddleware
3
4 app = Flask(__name__)
5
6 xray_recorder.configure(service='My application')
7 XRayMiddleware(app, xray_recorder)
```

This tells the X-Ray recorder to trace requests served by your Flask application with the default sampling rate. You can configure the recorder in code to apply custom sampling rules or change other settings.

Instrumenting Python Code Manually

If you don't use Django or Flask, you can create segments manually. You can create a segment for each incoming request, or create segments around patched HTTP or AWS SDK clients to provide context for the recorder to add subsegments.

Example main.rb – manual instrumentation

```
1 from aws_xray_sdk.core import xray_recorder
2
3 # Start a segment
4 segment = xray_recorder.begin_segment('segment_name')
5 # Start a subsegment
6 subsegment = xray_recorder.begin_subsegment('subsegment_name')
7
8 # Add metadata and annotations
9 segment.put_metadata('key', dict, 'namespace')
10 subsegment.put_annotation('key', 'value')
11
12 # Close the subsegment and segment
```

```
13 xray_recorder.end_subsegment()
14 xray_recorder.end_segment()
```

Configuring a Segment Naming Strategy

AWS X-Ray uses a *service name* to identify your application and distinguish it from the other applications, databases, external APIs, and AWS resources that your application uses. When the X-Ray SDK generates segments for incoming requests, it records your application's service name in the segment's name field.

The X-Ray SDK can name segments after the hostname in the HTTP request header. However, this header can be forged, which could result in unexpected nodes in your service map. To prevent the SDK from naming segments incorrectly due to requests with forged host headers, you must specify a default name for incoming requests.

If your application serves requests for multiple domains, you can configure the SDK to use a dynamic naming strategy to reflect this in segment names. A dynamic naming strategy allows the SDK to use the hostname for requests that match an expected pattern, and apply the default name to requests that don't.

For example, you might have a single application serving requests to three subdomains– www.example.com, api.example.com, and static.example.com. You can use a dynamic naming strategy with the pattern *.example.com to identify segments for each subdomain with a different name, resulting in three service nodes on the service map. If your application receives requests with a hostname that doesn't match the pattern, you will see a fourth node on the service map with a fallback name that you specify.

To use the same name for all request segments, specify the name of your application when you configure the recorder, as shown in the previous sections.

A dynamic naming strategy defines a pattern that hostnames should match, and a default name to use if the hostname in the HTTP request doesn't match the pattern. To name segments dynamically in Django, add the DYNAMIC_NAMING setting to your settings.py file.

Example settings.py – dynamic naming

```
1 XRAY_RECORDER = {
2     'AUTO_INSTRUMENT': True,
3     'AWS_XRAY_TRACING_NAME': 'My application',
4     'DYNAMIC_NAMING': '*.example.com',
5     'PLUGINS': ('ElasticBeanstalkPlugin', 'EC2Plugin'),
6 }
```

You can use '*' in the pattern to match any string, or '?' to match any single character. For Flask, configure the recorder in code.

Example main.py – segment name

```
1 from aws_xray_sdk.core import xray_recorder
2 xray_recorder.configure(service='My application')
3 xray_recorder.configure(dynamic_naming='*.example.com')
```

Note
You can override the default service name that you define in code with the AWS_XRAY_TRACING_NAME environment variable.

Patching Libraries to Instrument Downstream Calls

To instrument downstream calls, use the X-Ray SDK for Ruby to patch the libraries that your application uses. The X-Ray SDK for Ruby can patch the following libraries.

Supported Libraries

- [net/http](https://ruby-doc.org/stdlib-2.4.2/libdoc/net/http/rdoc/Net/HTTP.html) – Instrument HTTP clients.
- [aws\-sdk](https://aws.amazon.com/sdk-for-ruby) – Instrument AWS SDK for Ruby clients.

When you use a patched library, the X-Ray SDK for Ruby creates a subsegment for the call and records information from the request and response. A segment must be available for the SDK to create the subsegment, either from the SDK middleware or a call to XRay.recorder.begin_segment.

To patch libraries, specify them in the configuration object that you pass to the X-Ray recorder.

Example main.rb – patch libraries

```
1 require 'aws-xray-sdk'
2
3 config = {
4   name: 'my app',
5   patch: %I[net_http aws_sdk]
6 }
7
8 XRay.recorder.configure(config)
```

Tracing AWS SDK Calls with the X-Ray SDK for Python

When your application makes calls to AWS services to store data, write to a queue, or send notifications, the X-Ray SDK for Python tracks the calls downstream in subsegments. Traced AWS services and resources that you access within those services (for example, an Amazon S3 bucket or Amazon SQS queue), appear as downstream nodes on the service map in the X-Ray console.

The X-Ray SDK for Python automatically instruments all AWS SDK clients when you patch the `botocore` library. You cannot instrument individual clients.

For all services, you can see the name of the API called in the X-Ray console. For a subset of services, the X-Ray SDK adds information to the segment to provide more granularity in the service map.

For example, when you make a call with an instrumented DynamoDB client, the SDK adds the table name to the segment for calls that target a table. In the console, each table appears as a separate node in the service map, with a generic DynamoDB node for calls that don't target a table.

Example Subsegment for a Call to DynamoDB to Save an Item

```
1  {
2    "id": "24756640c0d0978a",
3    "start_time": 1.480305974194E9,
4    "end_time": 1.4803059742E9,
5    "name": "DynamoDB",
6    "namespace": "aws",
7    "http": {
8      "response": {
9        "content_length": 60,
10       "status": 200
11     }
12   },
13   "aws": {
14     "table_name": "scorekeep-user",
15     "operation": "UpdateItem",
16     "request_id": "UBQNS05AEM8T4FDA4RQDEB940VTDRVV4K4HIRGVJF66Q9ASUAAJG",
17   }
18 }
```

When you access named resources, calls to the following services create additional nodes in the service map. Calls that don't target specific resources create a generic node for the service.

- **Amazon DynamoDB** – Table name
- **Amazon Simple Storage Service** – Bucket and key name
- **Amazon Simple Queue Service** – Queue name

Tracing Calls to Downstream HTTP Web Services Using the X-Ray SDK for Python

When your application makes calls to microservices or public HTTP APIs, you can use the X-Ray SDK for Python client to instrument those calls and add the API to the service graph as a downstream service.

To instrument HTTP clients, patch the library that you use to make outgoing calls. If you use `requests` or Python's built in HTTP client, that's all you need to do. For `aiohttp`, also configure the recorder with an async context.

When you instrument a call to a downstream web API, the X-Ray SDK for Python records a subsegment that contains information about the HTTP request and response. X-Ray uses the subsegment to generate an inferred segment for the remote API.

Example Subsegment for a Downstream HTTP Call

```
1  {
2    "id": "004f72be19cddc2a",
3    "start_time": 1484786387.131,
4    "end_time": 1484786387.501,
5    "name": "names.example.com",
6    "namespace": "remote",
7    "http": {
8      "request": {
9        "method": "GET",
10       "url": "https://names.example.com/"
11     },
12     "response": {
13       "content_length": -1,
14       "status": 200
15     }
16   }
17 }
```

Example Inferred Segment for a Downstream HTTP Call

```
1  {
2    "id": "168416dc2ea97781",
3    "name": "names.example.com",
4    "trace_id": "1-5880168b-fd5153bb58284b67678aa78c",
5    "start_time": 1484786387.131,
6    "end_time": 1484786387.501,
7    "parent_id": "004f72be19cddc2a",
8    "http": {
9      "request": {
10       "method": "GET",
11       "url": "https://names.example.com/"
12     },
13     "response": {
14       "content_length": -1,
15       "status": 200
16     }
17   },
18   "inferred": true
19 }
```

Generating Custom Subsegments with the X-Ray SDK for Python

Subsegments extend a trace's segment with details about work done in order to serve a request. Each time you make a call with an instrumented client, the X-Ray SDK records the information generated in a subsegment. You can create additional subsegments to group other subsegments, to measure the performance of a section of code, or to record annotations and metadata.

To manage subsegments, use the `begin_subsegment` and `end_subsegment` methods.

Example main.py – custom subsegment

```
1 from aws_xray_sdk.core import xray_recorder
2
3 subsegment = xray_recorder.begin_subsegment('annotations')
4 subsegment.put_annotation('id', 12345)
5 xray_recorder.end_subsegment()
```

To create a subsegment for a synchronous function, use the `@xray_recorder.capture` decorator. You can pass a name for the subsegment to the capture function or leave it out to use the function name.

Example main.py – function subsegment

```
1 from aws_xray_sdk.core import xray_recorder
2
3 @xray_recorder.capture('## create_user')
4 def create_user():
5 ...
```

For an asynchronous function, use the `@xray_recorder.capture_async` decorator, and pass an async context to the recorder.

Example main.py – asynchronous function subsegment

```
1 from aws_xray_sdk.core.async_context import AsyncContext
2 from aws_xray_sdk.core import xray_recorder
3 xray_recorder.configure(service='my_service', context=AsyncContext())
4
5 @xray_recorder.capture_async('## create_user')
6 async def create_user():
7     ...
8
9 async def main():
10     await myfunc()
```

When you create a subsegment within a segment or another subsegment, the X-Ray SDK for Python generates an ID for it and records the start time and end time.

Example Subsegment with Metadata

```
1 "subsegments": [{
2   "id": "6f1605cd8a07cb70",
3   "start_time": 1.480305974194E9,
4   "end_time": 1.4803059742E9,
5   "name": "Custom subsegment for UserModel.saveUser function",
6   "metadata": {
7     "debug": {
8       "test": "Metadata string from UserModel.saveUser"
9     }
10   },
```

Add Annotations and Metadata to Segments with the X-Ray SDK for Python

You can record additional information about requests, the environment, or your application with annotations and metadata. You can add annotations and metadata to the segments that the X-Ray SDK creates, or to custom subsegments that you create.

Annotations are key-value pairs with string, number, or Boolean values. Annotations are indexed for use with filter expressions. Use annotations to record data that you want to use to group traces in the console, or when calling the http://docs.aws.amazon.com/xray/latest/api/API_GetTraceSummaries.html API.

Metadata are key-value pairs that can have values of any type, including objects and lists, but are not indexed for use with filter expressions. Use metadata to record additional data that you want stored in the trace but don't need to use with search.

In addition to annotations and metadata, you can also record user ID strings on segments. User IDs are recorded in a separate field on segments and are indexed for use with search.

Topics

- Recording Annotations with the X-Ray SDK for Python
- Recording Metadata with the X-Ray SDK for Python
- Recording User IDs with the X-Ray SDK for Python

Recording Annotations with the X-Ray SDK for Python

Use annotations to record information on segments or subsegments that you want indexed for search.

Annotation Requirements

- **Keys** – Up to 500 alphanumeric characters. No spaces or symbols except underscores.
- **Values** – Up to 1,000 Unicode characters.
- **Entries** – Up to 50 annotations per trace.

To record annotations

1. Get a reference to the current segment or subsegment from `xray_recorder`.

```
1 from aws_xray_sdk.core import xray_recorder
2 ...
3 document = xray_recorder.current_segment()
```

   or

```
1 from aws_xray_sdk.core import xray_recorder
2 ...
3 document = xray_recorder.current_subsegment()
```

2. Call `put_annotation` with a String key, and a Boolean, Number, or String value.

```
1 document.put_annotation("mykey", "my value");
```

The SDK records annotations as key-value pairs in an `annotations` object in the segment document. Calling `put_annotation` twice with the same key overwrites previously recorded values on the same segment or subsegment.

To find traces that have annotations with specific values, use the `annotations.key` keyword in a filter expression.

Recording Metadata with the X-Ray SDK for Python

Use metadata to record information on segments or subsegments that you don't need indexed for search. Metadata values can be strings, numbers, Booleans, or any object that can be serialized into a JSON object or array.

To record metadata

1. Get a reference to the current segment or subsegment from `xray_recorder`.

```
1 from aws_xray_sdk.core import xray_recorder
2 ...
3 document = xray_recorder.current_segment()
```

or

```
1 from aws_xray_sdk.core import xray_recorder
2 ...
3 document = xray_recorder.current_subsegment()
```

2. Call `put_metadata` with a String key; a Boolean, Number, String, or Object value; and a String namespace.

```
1 document.put_metadata("my key", "my value", "my namespace");
```

or

Call `put_metadata` with just a key and value.

```
1 document.put_metadata("my key", "my value");
```

If you don't specify a namespace, the SDK uses `default`. Calling `put_metadata` twice with the same key overwrites previously recorded values on the same segment or subsegment.

Recording User IDs with the X-Ray SDK for Python

Record user IDs on request segments to identify the user who sent the request.

To record user IDs

1. Get a reference to the current segment from `xray_recorder`.

```
1 from aws_xray_sdk.core import xray_recorder
2 ...
3 document = xray_recorder.current_segment()
```

2. Call `setUser` with a String ID of the user who sent the request.

```
1 document.set_user("U12345");
```

You can call `set_user` in your controllers to record the user ID as soon as your application starts processing a request.

To find traces for a user ID, use the `user` keyword in a filter expression.

AWS X-Ray SDK for Ruby

The X-Ray SDK is a library for Ruby web applications that provides classes and methods for generating and sending trace data to the X-Ray daemon. Trace data includes information about incoming HTTP requests served by the application, and calls that the application makes to downstream services using the AWS SDK, HTTP clients, or an active record client. You can also create segments manually and add debug information in annotations and metadata.

You can download the SDK by adding it to your gemfile and running `bundle install`.

Example Gemfile

```
1 gem 'aws-xray-sdk'
```

If you use Rails, start by adding the X-Ray SDK middleware to trace incoming requests. A request filter creates a segment. While the segment is open, you can use the SDK client's methods to add information to the segment and create subsegments to trace downstream calls. The SDK also automatically records exceptions that your application throws while the segment is open. For non-Rails applications, you can create segments manually.

Next, use the X-Ray SDK to instrument your AWS SDK for Ruby, HTTP, and SQL clients by configuring the recorder to patch the associated libraries. Whenever you make a call to a downstream AWS service or resource with an instrumented client, the SDK records information about the call in a subsegment. AWS services and the resources that you access within the services appear as downstream nodes on the service map to help you identify errors and throttling issues on individual connections.

Once you get going with the SDK, customize its behavior by configuring the recorder. You can add plugins to record data about the compute resources running your application, customize sampling behavior by defining sampling rules, and provide a logger to see more or less information from the SDK in your application logs.

Record additional information about requests and the work that your application does in annotations and metadata. Annotations are simple key-value pairs that are indexed for use with filter expressions, so that you can search for traces that contain specific data. Metadata entries are less restrictive and can record entire objects and arrays — anything that can be serialized into JSON.

Annotations and Metadata

Annotations and metadata are arbitrary text that you add to segments with the X-Ray SDK. Annotations are indexed for use with filter expressions. Metadata are not indexed, but can be viewed in the raw segment with the X-Ray console or API. Anyone that you grant read access to X-Ray can view this data.

When you have a lot of instrumented clients in your code, a single request segment can contain a large number of subsegments, one for each call made with an instrumented client. You can organize and group subsegments by wrapping client calls in custom subsegments. You can create a custom subsegment for an entire function or any section of code, and record metadata and annotations on the subsegment instead of writing everything on the parent segment.

For reference documentation for the SDK's classes and methods, see the AWS X-Ray SDK for Ruby API Reference.

Requirements

The X-Ray SDK requires Ruby 2.3 or later and is compatible with the following libraries:

- AWS SDK for Ruby version 3.0 or later
- Rails version 5.1 or later

Configuring the X-Ray SDK for Ruby

The X-Ray SDK for Ruby has a class named `XRay.recorder` that provides the global recorder. You can configure the global recorder to customize the middleware that creates segments for incoming HTTP calls.

Topics

- Service Plugins
- Sampling Rules
- Logging
- Recorder Configuration in Code
- Recorder Configuration with Rails
- Environment Variables

Service Plugins

Use `plugins` to record information about the service hosting your application.

Plugins

- Amazon EC2 – `ec2` adds the instance ID and Availability Zone.
- Elastic Beanstalk – `elastic_beanstalk` adds the environment name, version label, and deployment ID.
- Amazon ECS – `ecs` adds the container ID.

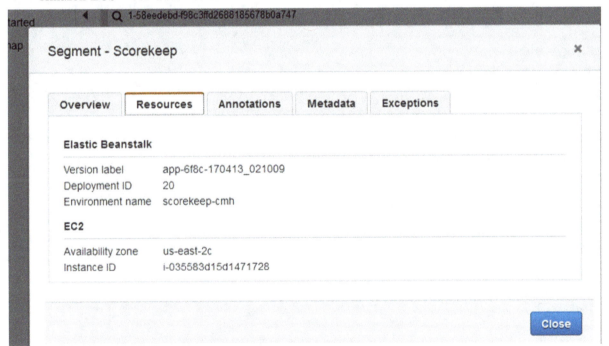

To use plugins, specify it in the configuration object that you pass to the recorder.

Example main.rb – plugin configuration

```
1 my_plugins = %I[ec2 elastic_beanstalk]
2
3 config = {
4   plugins: my_plugins,
5   name: 'my app',
6 }
7
```

```
8  XRay.recorder.configure(config)
```

You can also use environment variables, which take precedence over values set in code, to configure the recorder.

The SDK also uses plugin settings to set the `origin` field on the segment. This indicates the type of AWS resource that runs your application. The resource type appears under your application's name in the service map. For example, `AWS::ElasticBeanstalk::Environment`.

When you use multiple plugins, the SDK uses the plugin that was loaded last to determine the origin.

Sampling Rules

The SDK has a default sampling strategy that determines which requests get traced. By default, the SDK traces the first request each second, and five percent of any additional requests. You can customize the SDK's sampling behavior by applying rules you define in a local file.

Example sampling-rules.json

```
1  {
2    "version": 1,
3    "rules": [
4      {
5        "description": "Player moves.",
6        "service_name": "*",
7        "http_method": "*",
8        "url_path": "/api/move/*",
9        "fixed_target": 0,
10       "rate": 0.05
11     }
12   ],
13   "default": {
14     "fixed_target": 1,
15     "rate": 0.1
16   }
17 }
```

This example defines one custom rule and a default rule. The custom rule applies a five-percent sampling rate with no minimum number of requests to trace for paths under `/api/move/`. The default rule traces the first request each second and 10 percent of additional requests.

The SDK applies custom rules in the order in which they are defined. If a request matches multiple custom rules, the SDK applies only the first rule.

To configure sampling rules, define a hash for the document in the configuration object that you pass to the recorder.

Example main.rb – sampling rule configuration

```
1  require 'aws-xray-sdk'
2  my_sampling_rules = {
3    version: 1,
4    default: {
5      fixed_target: 1,
6      rate: 0.1
7    }
8  }
9  config = {
10   sampling_rules: my_sampling_rules,
11   name: 'my app',
12 }
13 XRay.recorder.configure(config)
```

To store the sampling rules independently, define the hash in a separate file and require the file to pull it into your application.

Example config/sampling-rules.rb

```
1  my_sampling_rules = {
2    version: 1,
3    default: {
4      fixed_target: 1,
5      rate: 0.1
6    }
7  }
```

Example main.rb – sampling rule from a file

```
1  require 'aws-xray-sdk'
2  require config/sampling-rules.rb
3
4  config = {
5    sampling_rules: my_sampling_rules,
6    name: 'my app',
7  }
8  XRay.recorder.configure(config)
```

You can also configure the global recorder to disable sampling and instrument all incoming requests.

Example main.rb – disable sampling

```
1  require 'aws-xray-sdk'
2  config = {
3    sampling: false,
4    name: 'my app',
5  }
6  XRay.recorder.configure(config)
```

Logging

By default, the recorder outputs info-level events to `$stdout`. You can customize logging by defining a logger in the configuration object that you pass to the recorder.

Example main.rb – logging

```
1 require 'aws-xray-sdk'
2 config = {
3   logger: my_logger,
4   name: 'my app',
5 }
6 XRay.recorder.configure(config)
```

Use debug logs to identify issues, such as unclosed subsegments, when you generate subsegments manually.

Recorder Configuration in Code

Additional settings are available from the `configure` method on `XRay.recorder`.

- `context_missing` – Set to `LOG_ERROR` to avoid throwing exceptions when your instrumented code attempts to record data when no segment is open.
- `daemon_address` – Set the host and port of the X-Ray daemon listener.
- `name` – Set a service name that the SDK uses for segments.
- `naming_pattern` – Set a domain name pattern to use dynamic naming.
- `plugins` – Record information about your application's AWS resources with plugins.
- `sampling` – Set to `false` to disable sampling.
- `sampling_rules` – Set the hash containing your sampling rules.

Example main.py – disable context missing exceptions

```
1 require 'aws-xray-sdk'
2 config = {
3   context_missing: LOG_ERROR
4 }
5
6 XRay.recorder.configure(config)
```

Recorder Configuration with Rails

If you use the Rails framework, you can configure options on the global recorder in a Ruby file under `app_root/initializers`. The X-Ray SDK supports an additional configuration key for use with Rails.

- `active_record` – Set to `true` to record subsegments for Active Record database transactions.

Configure the available settings in a configuration object named `Rails.application.config.xray`.

Example config/initializers/aws_xray.rb

```
1 Rails.application.config.xray = {
2   name: 'my app',
3   patch: %I[net_http aws_sdk],
4   active_record: true
5 }
```

Environment Variables

You can use environment variables to configure the X-Ray SDK for Ruby. The SDK supports the following variables:

- `AWS_XRAY_TRACING_NAME` – Set a service name that the SDK uses for segments. Overrides the service name that you set on the servlet filter's segment naming strategy.
- `AWS_XRAY_DAEMON_ADDRESS` – Set the host and port of the X-Ray daemon listener. By default, the SDK sends trace data to `127.0.0.1:2000`. Use this variable if you have configured the daemon to listen on a different port or if it is running on a different host.
- `AWS_XRAY_CONTEXT_MISSING` – Set to `LOG_ERROR` to avoid throwing exceptions when your instrumented code attempts to record data when no segment is open.

Valid Values

- `RUNTIME_ERROR` – Throw a runtime exception (default).
- `LOG_ERROR` – Log an error and continue.

Errors related to missing segments or subsegments can occur when you attempt to use an instrumented client in startup code that runs when no request is open, or in code that spawns a new thread.

Environment variables override values set in code.

Tracing Incoming Requests with the X-Ray SDK for Ruby Middleware

You can use the X-Ray SDK to trace incoming HTTP requests that your application serves on an EC2 instance in Amazon EC2, AWS Elastic Beanstalk, or Amazon ECS.

If you use Rails, use the Rails middleware to instrument incoming HTTP requests. When you add the middleware to your application and configure a segment name, the X-Ray SDK for Ruby creates a segment for each sampled request. Any segments created by additional instrumentation become subsegments of the request-level segment that provides information about the HTTP request and response. This information includes timing, method, and disposition of the request.

Each segment has a name that identifies your application in the service map. The segment can be named statically, or you can configure the SDK to name it dynamically based on the host header in the incoming request. Dynamic naming lets you group traces based on the domain name in the request, and apply a default name if the name doesn't match an expected pattern (for example, if the host header is forged).

Forwarded Requests

If a load balancer or other intermediary forwards a request to your application, X-Ray takes the client IP from the `X-Forwarded-For` header in the request instead of from the source IP in the IP packet. The client IP that is recorded for a forwarded request can be forged, so it should not be trusted.

When a request is forwarded, the SDK sets an additional field in the segment to indicate this. If the segment contains the field `x_forwarded_for` set to `true`, the client IP was taken from the `X-Forwarded-For` header in the HTTP request.

The middleware creates a segment for each incoming request with an `http` block that contains the following information:

- **HTTP method** – GET, POST, PUT, DELETE, etc.
- **Client address** – The IP address of the client that sent the request.
- **Response code** – The HTTP response code for the completed request.
- **Timing** – The start time (when the request was received) and end time (when the response was sent).
- **User agent** — The `user-agent` from the request.
- **Content length** — The `content-length` from the response.

Using the Rails Middleware

To use the middleware, update your gemfile to include the required railtie.

Example Gemfile - rails

```
1 gem 'aws-xray-sdk', require: ['aws-xray-sdk/facets/rails/railtie']
```

To use the middleware, you must also configure the recorder with a name that represents the application in the service map.

Example config/initializers/aws_xray.rb

```
1 Rails.application.config.xray = {
2   name: 'my app'
3 }
```

Instrumenting Code Manually

If you don't use Rails, create segments manually. You can create a segment for each incoming request, or create segments around patched HTTP or AWS SDK clients to provide context for the recorder to add subsegments.

210

```
 1 # Start a segment
 2 segment = XRay.recorder.begin_segment 'my_service'
 3 # Start a subsegment
 4 subsegment = XRay.recorder.begin_subsegment 'outbound_call', namespace: 'remote'
 5
 6 # Add metadata or annotation here if necessary
 7 my_annotations = {
 8   k1: 'v1',
 9   k2: 1024
10 }
11 segment.annotations.update my_annotations
12
13 # Add metadata to default namespace
14 subsegment.metadata[:k1] = 'v1'
15
16 # Set user for the segment (subsegment is not supported)
17 segment.user = 'my_name'
18
19 # End segment/subsegment
20 XRay.recorder.end_subsegment
21 XRay.recorder.end_segment
```

Configuring a Segment Naming Strategy

AWS X-Ray uses a *service name* to identify your application and distinguish it from the other applications, databases, external APIs, and AWS resources that your application uses. When the X-Ray SDK generates segments for incoming requests, it records your application's service name in the segment's name field.

The X-Ray SDK can name segments after the hostname in the HTTP request header. However, this header can be forged, which could result in unexpected nodes in your service map. To prevent the SDK from naming segments incorrectly due to requests with forged host headers, you must specify a default name for incoming requests.

If your application serves requests for multiple domains, you can configure the SDK to use a dynamic naming strategy to reflect this in segment names. A dynamic naming strategy allows the SDK to use the hostname for requests that match an expected pattern, and apply the default name to requests that don't.

For example, you might have a single application serving requests to three subdomains– www.example.com, api.example.com, and static.example.com. You can use a dynamic naming strategy with the pattern *. example.com to identify segments for each subdomain with a different name, resulting in three service nodes on the service map. If your application receives requests with a hostname that doesn't match the pattern, you will see a fourth node on the service map with a fallback name that you specify.

To use the same name for all request segments, specify the name of your application when you configure the recorder, as shown in the previous sections.

A dynamic naming strategy defines a pattern that hostnames should match, and a default name to use if the hostname in the HTTP request doesn't match the pattern. To name segments dynamically, specify a naming pattern in the config hash.

Example main.rb – dynamic naming

```
1 config = {
2   naming_pattern: '*mydomain*',
3   name: 'my app',
4 }
5
```

```
6   XRay.recorder.configure(config)
```

You can use '*' in the pattern to match any string, or '?' to match any single character.

Note
You can override the default service name that you define in code with the `AWS_XRAY_TRACING_NAME` environment variable.

Tracing AWS SDK Calls with the X-Ray SDK for Ruby

When your application makes calls to AWS services to store data, write to a queue, or send notifications, the X-Ray SDK for Ruby tracks the calls downstream in subsegments. Traced AWS services and resources that you access within those services (for example, an Amazon S3 bucket or Amazon SQS queue), appear as downstream nodes on the service map in the X-Ray console.

The X-Ray SDK for Ruby automatically instruments all AWS SDK clients when you patch the `aws-sdk` library. You cannot instrument individual clients.

For all services, you can see the name of the API called in the X-Ray console. For a subset of services, the X-Ray SDK adds information to the segment to provide more granularity in the service map.

For example, when you make a call with an instrumented DynamoDB client, the SDK adds the table name to the segment for calls that target a table. In the console, each table appears as a separate node in the service map, with a generic DynamoDB node for calls that don't target a table.

Example Subsegment for a Call to DynamoDB to Save an Item

```
1  {
2    "id": "24756640c0d0978a",
3    "start_time": 1.480305974194E9,
4    "end_time": 1.4803059742E9,
5    "name": "DynamoDB",
6    "namespace": "aws",
7    "http": {
8      "response": {
9        "content_length": 60,
10       "status": 200
11     }
12   },
13   "aws": {
14     "table_name": "scorekeep-user",
15     "operation": "UpdateItem",
16     "request_id": "UBQNSO5AEM8T4FDA4RQDEB94OVTDRVV4K4HIRGVJF66Q9ASUAAJG",
17   }
18 }
```

When you access named resources, calls to the following services create additional nodes in the service map. Calls that don't target specific resources create a generic node for the service.

- **Amazon DynamoDB** – Table name
- **Amazon Simple Storage Service** – Bucket and key name
- **Amazon Simple Queue Service** – Queue name

Generating Custom Subsegments with the X-Ray SDK

Subsegments extend a trace's segment with details about work done in order to serve a request. Each time you make a call with an instrumented client, the X-Ray SDK records the information generated in a subsegment. You can create additional subsegments to group other subsegments, to measure the performance of a section of code, or to record annotations and metadata.

To manage subsegments, use the `begin_subsegment` and `end_subsegment` methods.

```
1  subsegment = XRay.recorder.begin_subsegment name: 'annotations', namespace: 'remote'
2  my_annotations = { id: 12345 }
3  subsegment.annotations.update my_annotations
4  XRay.recorder.end_subsegment
```

To create a subsegment for a function, wrap it in a call to `XRay.recorder.capture`.

```
1  XRay.recorder.capture('name_for_subsegment') do |subsegment|
2    resp = myfunc() # myfunc is your function
3    subsegment.annotations.update k1: 'v1'
4    resp
5  end
```

When you create a subsegment within a segment or another subsegment, the X-Ray SDK generates an ID for it and records the start time and end time.

Example Subsegment with Metadata

```
1  "subsegments": [{
2    "id": "6f1605cd8a07cb70",
3    "start_time": 1.480305974194E9,
4    "end_time": 1.4803059742E9,
5    "name": "Custom subsegment for UserModel.saveUser function",
6    "metadata": {
7      "debug": {
8        "test": "Metadata string from UserModel.saveUser"
9      }
10   },
```

Add Annotations and Metadata to Segments with the X-Ray SDK for Ruby

You can record additional information about requests, the environment, or your application with annotations and metadata. You can add annotations and metadata to the segments that the X-Ray SDK creates, or to custom subsegments that you create.

Annotations are key-value pairs with string, number, or Boolean values. Annotations are indexed for use with filter expressions. Use annotations to record data that you want to use to group traces in the console, or when calling the http://docs.aws.amazon.com/xray/latest/api/API_GetTraceSummaries.html API.

Metadata are key-value pairs that can have values of any type, including objects and lists, but are not indexed for use with filter expressions. Use metadata to record additional data that you want stored in the trace but don't need to use with search.

In addition to annotations and metadata, you can also record user ID strings on segments. User IDs are recorded in a separate field on segments and are indexed for use with search.

Topics

- Recording Annotations with the X-Ray SDK for Ruby
- Recording Metadata with the X-Ray SDK for Ruby
- Recording User IDs with the X-Ray SDK for Ruby

Recording Annotations with the X-Ray SDK for Ruby

Use annotations to record information on segments or subsegments that you want indexed for search.

Annotation Requirements

- **Keys** – Up to 500 alphanumeric characters. No spaces or symbols except underscores.
- **Values** – Up to 1,000 Unicode characters.
- **Entries** – Up to 50 annotations per trace.

To record annotations

1. Get a reference to the current segment or subsegment from `xray_recorder`.

```
1 require 'aws-xray-sdk'
2 ...
3 document = XRay.recorder.current_segment
```

or

```
1 require 'aws-xray-sdk'
2 ...
3 document = XRay.recorder.current_subsegment
```

2. Call `update` with a hash value.

```
1 my_annotations = { id: 12345 }
2 document.annotations.update my_annotations
```

The SDK records annotations as key-value pairs in an **annotations** object in the segment document. Calling `add_annotations` twice with the same key overwrites previously recorded values on the same segment or subsegment.

To find traces that have annotations with specific values, use the **annotations.key** keyword in a filter expression.

Recording Metadata with the X-Ray SDK for Ruby

Use metadata to record information on segments or subsegments that you don't need indexed for search. Metadata values can be strings, numbers, Booleans, or any object that can be serialized into a JSON object or array.

To record metadata

1. Get a reference to the current segment or subsegment from `xray_recorder`.

```
1 require 'aws-xray-sdk'
2 ...
3 document = XRay.recorder.current_segment
```

or

```
1 require 'aws-xray-sdk'
2 ...
3 document = XRay.recorder.current_subsegment
```

2. Call `metadata` with a String key; a Boolean, Number, String, or Object value; and a String namespace.

```
1 my_metadata = {
2   my_namespace: {
3     key: 'value'
4   }
5 }
6 subsegment.metadata my_metadata
```

Calling `metadata` twice with the same key overwrites previously recorded values on the same segment or subsegment.

Recording User IDs with the X-Ray SDK for Ruby

Record user IDs on request segments to identify the user who sent the request.

To record user IDs

1. Get a reference to the current segment from `xray_recorder`.

```
1 require 'aws-xray-sdk'
2 ...
3 document = XRay.recorder.current_segment
```

2. Set the user field on the segment to a String ID of the user who sent the request.

```
1 segment.user = 'U12345'
```

You can set the user in your controllers to record the user ID as soon as your application starts processing a request.

To find traces for a user ID, use the `user` keyword in a filter expression.

AWS X-Ray SDK for .NET

The X-Ray SDK for .NET is a library for instrumenting C# .NET web applications, .NET Core web applications, and .NET Core functions on AWS Lambda. It provides classes and methods for generating and sending trace data to the X-Ray daemon. This includes information about incoming requests served by the application, and calls that the application makes to downstream AWS services, HTTP web APIs, and SQL databases.

Note
The X-Ray SDK for .NET is an open source project. You can follow the project and submit issues and pull requests on GitHub: github.com/aws/aws-xray-sdk-dotnet

For web applications, start by adding a message handler to your web configuration to trace incoming requests. The message handler creates a segment for each traced request, and completes the segment when the response is sent. While the segment is open you can use the SDK client's methods to add information to the segment and create subsegments to trace downstream calls. The SDK also automatically records exceptions that your application throws while the segment is open.

For Lambda functions called by an instrumented application or service, Lambda reads the tracing header and traces sampled requests automatically. For other functions, you can configure Lambda to sample and trace incoming requests. In either case, Lambda creates the segment and provides it to the X-Ray SDK.

Note
On Lambda, the X-Ray SDK is optional. If you don't use it in your function, your service map will still include a node for the Lambda service, and one for each Lambda function. By adding the SDK, you can instrument your function code to add subsegments to the function segment recorded by Lambda. See AWS Lambda and AWS X-Ray for more information.

Next, use the X-Ray SDK for .NET to instrument your AWS SDK for .NET clients. Whenever you make a call to a downstream AWS service or resource with an instrumented client, the SDK records information about the call in a subsegment. AWS services and the resources that you access within the services appear as downstream nodes on the service map to help you identify errors and throttling issues on individual connections.

The X-Ray SDK for .NET also provides instrumentation for downstream calls to HTTP web APIs and SQL databases. The `GetResponseTraced` extension method for `System.Net.HttpWebRequest` traces outgoing HTTP calls. You can use the X-Ray SDK for .NET's version of `SqlCommand` to instrument SQL queries.

Once you get going with the SDK, customize its behavior by configuring the recorder and message handler. You can add plugins to record data about the compute resources running your application, customize sampling behavior by defining sampling rules, and set the log level to see more or less information from the SDK in your application logs.

Record additional information about requests and the work that your application does in annotations and metadata. Annotations are simple key-value pairs that are indexed for use with filter expressions, so that you can search for traces that contain specific data. Metadata entries are less restrictive and can record entire objects and arrays — anything that can be serialized into JSON.

Annotations and Metadata
Annotations and metadata are arbitrary text that you add to segments with the X-Ray SDK. Annotations are indexed for use with filter expressions. Metadata are not indexed, but can be viewed in the raw segment with the X-Ray console or API. Anyone that you grant read access to X-Ray can view this data.

When you have many instrumented clients in your code, a single request segment can contain a large number of subsegments, one for each call made with an instrumented client. You can organize and group subsegments by wrapping client calls in custom subsegments. You can create a custom subsegment for an entire function or any section of code, and record metadata and annotations on the subsegment instead of writing everything on the parent segment.

For reference documentation about the SDK's classes and methods, see the following:

- AWS X-Ray SDK for .NET API Reference

- AWS X-Ray SDK for .NET Core API Reference

The same package supports both .NET and .NET Core, but the classes that are used vary. Examples in this chapter link to the .NET API reference unless the class is specific to .NET Core.

Requirements

The X-Ray SDK for .NET requires the .NET framework and AWS SDK for .NET.

For .NET Core applications and functions, the SDK requires .NET Core 2.0 or later.

Adding the X-Ray SDK for .NET to Your Application

Use NuGet to add the X-Ray SDK for .NET to your application.

To install the X-Ray SDK for .NET with NuGet Package Manager in Visual Studio

1. Choose **Tools**, **NuGet Package Manager**, **Manage NuGet Packages for Solution**.

2. Search for **AWSXRayRecorder**.

3. Choose the package, and then choose **Install**.

Configuring the X-Ray SDK for .NET

You can configure the X-Ray SDK for .NET with plugins to include information about the service that your application runs on, modify the default sampling behavior, or add sampling rules that apply to requests to specific paths.

For .NET web applications, add keys to the `appSettings` section of your `Web.config` file.

Example Web.config

```
1 <configuration>
2   <appSettings>
3     <add key="AWSXRayPlugins" value="EC2Plugin"/>
4     <add key="SamplingRuleManifest" value="sampling-rules.json"/>
5   </appSettings>
6 </configuration>
```

For .NET Core, create a file named `appsettings.json` with a top-level key named `XRay`.

Example appsettings.json

```
1 {
2   "XRay": {
3     "AWSXRayPlugins": "EC2Plugin",
4     "SamplingRuleManifest": "sampling-rules.json"
5   }
6 }
```

Then, in your application code, build a configuration object and use it to initialize the X-Ray recorder. Do this before you initialize the recorder.

Example Program.cs – .NET Core Configuration

```
1 using [Amazon\.XRay\.Recorder\.Core](http://docs.aws.amazon.com/xray-sdk-for-dotnet/latest/
    reference/html/N_Amazon_XRay_Recorder_Core.htm);
2 ...
3 AWSXRayRecorder.InitializeInstance(configuration);
```

If you are instrumenting a .NET Core web application, you can also pass the configuration object to the `UseXRay` method when you configure the message handler. For Lambda functions, use the `InitializeInstance` method as shown above.

For more information on the .NET Core configuration API, see Configure an ASP.NET Core App on docs.microsoft.com.

Topics

- Plugins
- Sampling Rules
- Logging (.NET)
- Logging (.NET Core)
- Environment Variables

Plugins

Use plugins to add data about the service that is hosting your application.

Plugins

- Amazon EC2 – `EC2Plugin` adds the instance ID and Availability Zone.
- Elastic Beanstalk – `ElasticBeanstalkPlugin` adds the environment name, version label, and deployment ID.
- Amazon ECS – `ECSPlugin` adds the container ID.

To use a plugin, configure the X-Ray SDK for .NET client by adding the `AWSXRayPlugins` setting. If multiple plugins apply to your application, specify all of them in the same setting, separated by commas.

Example Web.config - Plugins

```
1  <configuration>
2    <appSettings>
3      <add key="AWSXRayPlugins" value="EC2Plugin,ElasticBeanstalkPlugin"/>
4    </appSettings>
5  </configuration>
```

Example appsettings.json – Plugins

```
1  {
2    "XRay": {
3      "AWSXRayPlugins": "EC2Plugin,ElasticBeanstalkPlugin"
4    }
5  }
```

Sampling Rules

The SDK has a default sampling strategy that determines which requests get traced. By default, the SDK traces the first request each second, and five percent of any additional requests. You can customize the SDK's sampling behavior by applying rules you define in a local file.

Example sampling-rules.json

```
1  {
2    "version": 1,
3    "rules": [
4      {
5        "description": "Player moves.",
6        "service_name": "*",
7        "http_method": "*",
8        "url_path": "/api/move/*",
9        "fixed_target": 0,
10       "rate": 0.05
11     }
12   ],
13   "default": {
14     "fixed_target": 1,
15     "rate": 0.1
16   }
17 }
```

This example defines one custom rule and a default rule. The custom rule applies a five-percent sampling rate with no minimum number of requests to trace for paths under `/api/move/`. The default rule traces the first request each second and 10 percent of additional requests.

The SDK applies custom rules in the order in which they are defined. If a request matches multiple custom rules, the SDK applies only the first rule.

On Lambda, you cannot modify the sampling rate. If your function is called by an instrumented service, calls generated requests that were sampled by that service will be recorded by Lambda. If active tracing is enabled and no tracing header is present, Lambda makes the sampling decision.

Tell the X-Ray SDK for .NET to load sampling rules from a file with the `SamplingRuleManifest` setting.

Example Web.config - Sampling Rules

```
1  <configuration>
2    <appSettings>
3      <add key="SamplingRuleManifest" value="sampling-rules.json"/>
4    </appSettings>
5  </configuration>
```

Example appsettings.json – Sampling Rules

```
1  {
2    "XRay": {
3      "SamplingRuleManifest": "sampling-rules.json"
4    }
5  }
```

Logging (.NET)

The X-Ray SDK for .NET uses the same logging mechanism as the AWS SDK for .NET. If you already configured your application to log AWS SDK for .NET output, the same configuration applies to output from the X-Ray SDK for .NET.

To configure logging, add a configuration section named `aws` to your `App.config` file or `Web.config` file.

Example Web.config - Logging

```
1  ...
2  <configuration>
3    <configSections>
4      <section name="aws" type="Amazon.AWSSection, AWSSDK.Core"/>
5    </configSections>
6    <aws>
7      <logging logTo="Log4Net"/>
8    </aws>
9  </configuration>
```

For more information, see Configuring Your AWS SDK for .NET Application in the *AWS SDK for .NET Developer Guide*.

Logging (.NET Core)

For .NET Core applications, the X-Ray SDK supports the logging options in the AWS SDK for .NET LoggingOptions enum. To configure logging, pass one of these options to the `RegisterLogger` method.

```
1  AWSXRayRecorder.RegisterLogger(LoggingOptions.Console);
```

For example, to use log4net, create a configuration file that defines the logger, the output format, and the file location.

Example log4net.config

```
1  <?xml version="1.0" encoding="utf-8" ?>
2  <log4net>
3    <appender name="FileAppender" type="log4net.Appender.FileAppender,log4net">
4      <file value="c:\logs\sdk-log.txt" />
5      <layout type="log4net.Layout.PatternLayout">
6        <conversionPattern value="%date [%thread] %level %logger - %message%newline" />
7      </layout>
8    </appender>
9    <logger name="Amazon">
10     <level value="DEBUG" />
11     <appender-ref ref="FileAppender" />
12   </logger>
13 </log4net>
```

Then, create the logger and apply the configuration in your program code.

Example Program.cs – Logging

```
1  using log4net;
2  using [Amazon\.XRay\.Recorder\.Core](http://docs.aws.amazon.com/xray-sdk-for-dotnet/latest/
       reference/html/N_Amazon_XRay_Recorder_Core.htm);
3
4  class Program
5  {
6    private static ILog log;
7    static Program()
8    {
9      var logRepository = LogManager.GetRepository(Assembly.GetEntryAssembly());
10     XmlConfigurator.Configure(logRepository, new FileInfo("log4net.config"));
11     log = LogManager.GetLogger(typeof(Program));
12     AWSXRayRecorder.RegisterLogger(LoggingOptions.Log4Net);
13   }
14   static void Main(string[] args)
15   {
16     ...
17   }
18 }
```

For more information on configuring log4net, see Configuration on logging.apache.org.

Environment Variables

You can use environment variables to configure the X-Ray SDK for .NET. The SDK supports the following variables.

- AWS_XRAY_TRACING_NAME – Set a service name that the SDK uses for segments. Overrides the service name that you set on the servlet filter's segment naming strategy.
- AWS_XRAY_DAEMON_ADDRESS – Set the host and port of the X-Ray daemon listener. By default, the SDK sends trace data to 127.0.0.1:2000. Use this variable if you have configured the daemon to listen on a different port or if it is running on a different host.
- AWS_XRAY_CONTEXT_MISSING – Set to LOG_ERROR to avoid throwing exceptions when your instrumented code attempts to record data when no segment is open.

Valid Values

- RUNTIME_ERROR – Throw a runtime exception (default).

- `LOG_ERROR` – Log an error and continue.

Errors related to missing segments or subsegments can occur when you attempt to use an instrumented client in startup code that runs when no request is open, or in code that spawns a new thread.

Instrumenting Incoming HTTP Requests with the X-Ray SDK for .NET

You can use the X-Ray SDK to trace incoming HTTP requests that your application serves on an EC2 instance in Amazon EC2, AWS Elastic Beanstalk, or Amazon ECS.

Use a message handler to instrument incoming HTTP requests. When you add the X-Ray message handler to your application, the X-Ray SDK for .NET creates a segment for each sampled request. This segment includes timing, method, and disposition of the HTTP request. Additional instrumentation creates subsegments on this segment.

Note
For AWS Lambda functions, Lambda creates a segment for each sampled request. See AWS Lambda and AWS X-Ray for more information.

Each segment has a name that identifies your application in the service map. The segment can be named statically, or you can configure the SDK to name it dynamically based on the host header in the incoming request. Dynamic naming lets you group traces based on the domain name in the request, and apply a default name if the name doesn't match an expected pattern (for example, if the host header is forged).

Forwarded Requests
If a load balancer or other intermediary forwards a request to your application, X-Ray takes the client IP from the X-Forwarded-For header in the request instead of from the source IP in the IP packet. The client IP that is recorded for a forwarded request can be forged, so it should not be trusted.

The message handler creates a segment for each incoming request with an `http` block that contains the following information:

- **HTTP method** – GET, POST, PUT, DELETE, etc.
- **Client address** – The IP address of the client that sent the request.
- **Response code** – The HTTP response code for the completed request.
- **Timing** – The start time (when the request was received) and end time (when the response was sent).
- **User agent** — The `user-agent` from the request.
- **Content length** — The `content-length` from the response.

Topics

- Instrumenting Incoming Requests (.NET)
- Instrumenting Incoming Requests (.NET Core)
- Configuring a Segment Naming Strategy

Instrumenting Incoming Requests (.NET)

To instrument requests served by your application, call `RegisterXRay` in the `Init` method of your `global.asax` file.

Example global.asax - Message Handler

```
1 using System.Web.Http;
2 using [Amazon\.XRay\.Recorder\.Handlers\.AspNet](http://docs.aws.amazon.com/xray-sdk-for-dotnet/
      latest/reference/html/N_Amazon_XRay_Recorder_Handlers_AspNet.htm);
3
4 namespace SampleEBWebApplication
5 {
6   public class MvcApplication : System.Web.HttpApplication
7   {
8     public override void Init()
9     {
```

```
10        base.Init();
11        AWSXRayASPNET.RegisterXRay(this, "MyApp");
12    }
13  }
14 }
```

Instrumenting Incoming Requests (.NET Core)

To instrument requests served by your application, call the `UseExceptionHandler`, `UseXRay`, and `UseStaticFiles` methods in the `Configure` method of your `Startup` class.

Example Startup.cs

```
1 using Microsoft.AspNetCore.Builder;
2
3 public void Configure(IApplicationBuilder app, IHostingEnvironment env)
4   {
5     app.UseExceptionHandler("/Error");
6     app.UseXRay("MyApp");
7     app.UseStaticFiles();
8     app.UseMVC();
9   }
```

Always call `UseXRay` after `UseExceptionHandler` to record exceptions. If you use other middleware, enable it after you call `UseXRay`.

The `UseXRay` method can also take a configuration object as a second argument.

```
1 app.UseXRay("MyApp", configuration);
```

Configuring a Segment Naming Strategy

AWS X-Ray uses a *service name* to identify your application and distinguish it from the other applications, databases, external APIs, and AWS resources that your application uses. When the X-Ray SDK generates segments for incoming requests, it records your application's service name in the segment's name field.

The X-Ray SDK can name segments after the hostname in the HTTP request header. However, this header can be forged, which could result in unexpected nodes in your service map. To prevent the SDK from naming segments incorrectly due to requests with forged host headers, you must specify a default name for incoming requests.

If your application serves requests for multiple domains, you can configure the SDK to use a dynamic naming strategy to reflect this in segment names. A dynamic naming strategy allows the SDK to use the hostname for requests that match an expected pattern, and apply the default name to requests that don't.

For example, you might have a single application serving requests to three subdomains– `www.example.com`, `api.example.com`, and `static.example.com`. You can use a dynamic naming strategy with the pattern `*.example.com` to identify segments for each subdomain with a different name, resulting in three service nodes on the service map. If your application receives requests with a hostname that doesn't match the pattern, you will see a fourth node on the service map with a fallback name that you specify.

To use the same name for all request segments, specify the name of your application when you initialize the message handler, as shown in the previous section. This has the same effect as creating a http://docs.aws.amazon.com/xray-sdk-for-dotnet/latest/reference/html/T_Amazon_XRay_Recorder_Core_Strategies_FixedSegmentNamingStrategy.htm and passing it to the `RegisterXRay` method.

```
1 AWSXRayASPNET.RegisterXRay(this, new FixedSegmentNamingStrategy("MyApp"));
```

Note

You can override the default service name that you define in code with the `AWS_XRAY_TRACING_NAME` environment variable.

A dynamic naming strategy defines a pattern that hostnames should match, and a default name to use if the hostname in the HTTP request does not match the pattern. To name segments dynamically, create a http://docs.aws.amazon.com/xray-sdk-for-dotnet/latest/reference/html/T_Amazon_XRay_Recorder_Core_Strategies_DynamicSegmentNamingStrategy.htm and pass it to the `RegisterXRay` method.

```
1 AWSXRayASPNET.RegisterXRay(this, new DynamicSegmentNamingStrategy("MyApp", "*.example.com"));
```

Instrumenting Downstream Calls to AWS Services

You can instrument all of your AWS SDK for .NET clients by calling `RegisterXRayForAllServices` before you create them.

Example SampleController.cs - DynamoDB Client Instrumentation

```
1  using Amazon;
2  using Amazon.Util;
3  using Amazon.DynamoDBv2;
4  using Amazon.DynamoDBv2.DocumentModel;
5  using [Amazon\.XRay\.Recorder\.Core](http://docs.aws.amazon.com/xray-sdk-for-dotnet/latest/
       reference/html/N_Amazon_XRay_Recorder_Core.htm);
6  using [Amazon\.XRay\.Recorder\.Handlers\.AwsSdk](http://docs.aws.amazon.com/xray-sdk-for-dotnet/
       latest/reference/html/N_Amazon_XRay_Recorder_Handlers_AwsSdk.htm);
7
8  namespace SampleEBWebApplication.Controllers
9  {
10   public class SampleController : ApiController
11   {
12     AWSSDKHandler.RegisterXRayForAllServices();
13     private static readonly Lazy<AmazonDynamoDBClient> LazyDdbClient = new Lazy<
           AmazonDynamoDBClient>(() =>
14     {
15       var client = new AmazonDynamoDBClient(EC2InstanceMetadata.Region ?? RegionEndpoint.USEast1
           );
16       return client;
17     });
```

To instrument clients for some services and not others, call `RegisterXRay` instead of `RegisterXRayForAllServices`. Replace the highlighted text with the name of the service's client interface.

```
1  AWSSDKHandler.RegisterXRay<IAmazonDynamoDB>()
```

For all services, you can see the name of the API called in the X-Ray console. For a subset of services, the X-Ray SDK adds information to the segment to provide more granularity in the service map.

For example, when you make a call with an instrumented DynamoDB client, the SDK adds the table name to the segment for calls that target a table. In the console, each table appears as a separate node in the service map, with a generic DynamoDB node for calls that don't target a table.

Example Subsegment for a Call to DynamoDB to Save an Item

```
1  {
2    "id": "24756640c0d0978a",
3    "start_time": 1.480305974194E9,
4    "end_time": 1.4803059742E9,
5    "name": "DynamoDB",
6    "namespace": "aws",
7    "http": {
8      "response": {
9        "content_length": 60,
10       "status": 200
11     }
12   },
13   "aws": {
```

```
14      "table_name": "scorekeep-user",
15      "operation": "UpdateItem",
16      "request_id": "UBQNSO5AEM8T4FDA4RQDEB94OVTDRVV4K4HIRGVJF66Q9ASUAAJG",
17    }
18 }
```

When you access named resources, calls to the following services create additional nodes in the service map. Calls that don't target specific resources create a generic node for the service.

- **Amazon DynamoDB** – Table name
- **Amazon Simple Storage Service** – Bucket and key name
- **Amazon Simple Queue Service** – Queue name

Tracing Calls to Downstream HTTP Web Services with the X-Ray SDK for .NET

When your application makes calls to microservices or public HTTP APIs, you can use the X-Ray SDK for .NET's GetResponseTraced extension method for System.Net.HttpWebRequest to instrument those calls and add the API to the service graph as a downstream service.

Example HttpWebRequest

```
1 using System.Net;
2 using [Amazon\.XRay\.Recorder\.Core](http://docs.aws.amazon.com/xray-sdk-for-dotnet/latest/
      reference/html/N_Amazon_XRay_Recorder_Core.htm);
3 using [Amazon\.XRay\.Recorder\.Handlers\.System\.Net](http://docs.aws.amazon.com/xray-sdk-for-
      dotnet/latest/reference/html/N_Amazon_XRay_Recorder_Handlers_System_Net.htm);
4
5 private void MakeHttpRequest()
6 {
7   HttpWebRequest request = (HttpWebRequest)WebRequest.Create("http://names.example.com/api");
8   request.GetResponseTraced();
9 }
```

For asynchronous calls, use GetAsyncResponseTraced.

```
1 request.GetAsyncResponseTraced();
```

If you use https://msdn.microsoft.com/en-us/library/system.net.http.httpclient.aspx, use the HttpClientXRayTracingHandler delegating handler to record calls.

Example HttpClient

```
1 using System.Net.Http;
2 using [Amazon\.XRay\.Recorder\.Core](http://docs.aws.amazon.com/xray-sdk-for-dotnet/latest/
      reference/html/N_Amazon_XRay_Recorder_Core.htm);
3 using [Amazon\.XRay\.Recorder\.Handlers\.System\.Net](http://docs.aws.amazon.com/xray-sdk-for-
      dotnet/latest/reference/html/N_Amazon_XRay_Recorder_Handlers_System_Net.htm);
4
5 private void MakeHttpRequest()
6 {
7   var httpClient = new HttpClient(new HttpClientXRayTracingHandler(new HttpClientHandler()));
8   httpClient.GetAsync(URL);
9 }
```

When you instrument a call to a downstream web API, the X-Ray SDK for .NET records a subsegment with information about the HTTP request and response. X-Ray uses the subsegment to generate an inferred segment for the API.

Example Subsegment for a Downstream HTTP Call

```
1 {
2   "id": "004f72be19cddc2a",
3   "start_time": 1484786387.131,
4   "end_time": 1484786387.501,
5   "name": "names.example.com",
6   "namespace": "remote",
7   "http": {
8     "request": {
9       "method": "GET",
```

```
10        "url": "https://names.example.com/"
11      },
12      "response": {
13        "content_length": -1,
14        "status": 200
15      }
16    }
17  }
```

Example Inferred Segment for a Downstream HTTP Call

```
1  {
2    "id": "168416dc2ea97781",
3    "name": "names.example.com",
4    "trace_id": "1-5880168b-fd5153bb58284b67678aa78c",
5    "start_time": 1484786387.131,
6    "end_time": 1484786387.501,
7    "parent_id": "004f72be19cddc2a",
8    "http": {
9      "request": {
10        "method": "GET",
11        "url": "https://names.example.com/"
12      },
13      "response": {
14        "content_length": -1,
15        "status": 200
16      }
17    },
18    "inferred": true
19  }
```

Tracing SQL Queries with the X-Ray SDK for .NET

The SDK provides a wrapper class for System.Data.SqlClient.SqlCommand named TraceableSqlCommand that you can use in place of SqlCommand. Initialize an SQL command with the X-Ray SDK for .NET's TraceableSqlCommand class.

Example Controller.cs - SQL Client Instrumentation

```
1 using Amazon;
2 using Amazon.Util;
3 using [Amazon\.XRay\.Recorder\.Core](http://docs.aws.amazon.com/xray-sdk-for-dotnet/latest/
     reference/html/N_Amazon_XRay_Recorder_Core.htm);
4 using [Amazon\.XRay\.Recorder\.Handlers\.SqlServer](http://docs.aws.amazon.com/xray-sdk-for-
     dotnet/latest/reference/html/N_Amazon_XRay_Recorder_Handlers_SqlServer.htm);
5
6 private void QuerySql(int id)
7 {
8   var connectionString = ConfigurationManager.AppSettings["RDS_CONNECTION_STRING"];
9   using (var sqlConnection = new SqlConnection(connectionString))
10  using (var sqlCommand = new TraceableSqlCommand("SELECT " + id, sqlConnection))
11  {
12    sqlCommand.Connection.Open();
13    sqlCommand.ExecuteNonQuery();
14  }
15 }
```

You can also execute the query asynchronously with the ExecuteReaderAsync method.

Example Controller.cs - SQL Client Instrumentation (Asynchronous)

```
1 using Amazon;
2 using Amazon.Util;
3 using [Amazon\.XRay\.Recorder\.Core](http://docs.aws.amazon.com/xray-sdk-for-dotnet/latest/
     reference/html/N_Amazon_XRay_Recorder_Core.htm);
4 using [Amazon\.XRay\.Recorder\.Handlers\.SqlServer](http://docs.aws.amazon.com/xray-sdk-for-
     dotnet/latest/reference/html/N_Amazon_XRay_Recorder_Handlers_SqlServer.htm);
5 private void QuerySql(int id)
6 {
7   var connectionString = ConfigurationManager.AppSettings["RDS_CONNECTION_STRING"];
8   using (var sqlConnection = new SqlConnection(connectionString))
9   using (var sqlCommand = new TraceableSqlCommand("SELECT " + id, sqlConnection))
10  {
11    await sqlCommand.ExecuteReaderAsync();
12  }
13 }
```

Add Annotations and Metadata to Segments with the X-Ray SDK for .NET

You can record additional information about requests, the environment, or your application with annotations and metadata. You can add annotations and metadata to the segments that the X-Ray SDK creates, or to custom subsegments that you create.

Annotations are key-value pairs with string, number, or Boolean values. Annotations are indexed for use with filter expressions. Use annotations to record data that you want to use to group traces in the console, or when calling the http://docs.aws.amazon.com/xray/latest/api/API_GetTraceSummaries.html API.

Metadata are key-value pairs that can have values of any type, including objects and lists, but are not indexed for use with filter expressions. Use metadata to record additional data that you want stored in the trace but don't need to use with search.

Topics

- Recording Annotations with the X-Ray SDK for .NET
- Recording Metadata with the X-Ray SDK for .NET

Recording Annotations with the X-Ray SDK for .NET

Use annotations to record information on segments or subsegments that you want indexed for search.

Annotation Requirements

- **Keys** – Up to 500 alphanumeric characters. No spaces or symbols except underscores.
- **Values** – Up to 1,000 Unicode characters.
- **Entries** – Up to 50 annotations per trace.

To record annotations

1. Get an instance of `AWSXRayRecorder`.

```
1 using [Amazon\.XRay\.Recorder\.Core](http://docs.aws.amazon.com/xray-sdk-for-dotnet/latest/
      reference/html/N_Amazon_XRay_Recorder_Core.htm);
2 ...
3 AWSXRayRecorder recorder = AWSXRayRecorder.Instance;
```

2. Call `addAnnotation` with a String key and a Boolean, Int32, Int64, Double, or String value.

```
1 recorder.AddAnnotation("mykey", "my value");
```

The SDK records annotations as key-value pairs in an `annotations` object in the segment document. Calling `addAnnotation` twice with the same key overwrites previously recorded values on the same segment or subsegment.

To find traces that have annotations with specific values, use the `annotations.key` keyword in a filter expression.

Recording Metadata with the X-Ray SDK for .NET

Use metadata to record information on segments or subsegments that you don't need indexed for search. Metadata values can be Strings, Numbers, Booleans, or any other Object that can be serialized into a JSON object or array.

To record metadata

1. Get an instance of `AWSXRayRecorder`.

```
1 using [Amazon\.XRay\.Recorder\.Core](http://docs.aws.amazon.com/xray-sdk-for-dotnet/latest/
    reference/html/N_Amazon_XRay_Recorder_Core.htm);
2 ...
3 AWSXRayRecorder recorder = AWSXRayRecorder.Instance;
```

2. Call **AddMetadata** with a String namespace, String key, and an Object value.

```
1 segment.AddMetadata("my namespace", "my key", "my value");
```

   or

   Call **putMetadata** with just a key and value.

```
1 segment.AddMetadata("my key", "my value");
```

If you don't specify a namespace, the SDK uses `default`. Calling `AddMetadata` twice with the same key overwrites previously recorded values on the same segment or subsegment.

Troubleshooting AWS X-Ray

This topic lists common errors and issues that you might encounter when using the X-Ray API, console, or SDKs. If you find an issue that is not listed here, you can use the **Feedback** button on this page to report it.

Topics

- X-Ray SDK for Java
- X-Ray SDK for Node.js
- The X-Ray daemon

X-Ray SDK for Java

Error: *Exception in thread "Thread-1" com.amazonaws.xray.exceptions.SegmentNotFoundException: Failed to begin subsegment named 'AmazonSNS': segment cannot be found. *

This error indicates that the X-Ray SDK attempted to record an outgoing call to AWS, but couldn't find an open segment. This can occur in the following situations:

- **A servlet filter is not configured** – The X-Ray SDK creates segments for incoming requests with a filter named `AWSXRayServletFilter`. Configure a servlet filter to instrument incoming requests.
- **You're using instrumented clients outside of servlet code** – If you use an instrumented client to make calls in startup code or other code that doesn't run in response to an incoming request, you must create a segment manually. See Instrumenting Startup Code for examples.
- **You're using instrumented clients in worker threads** – When you create a new thread, the X-Ray recorder loses its reference to the open segment. You can use the http://docs.aws.amazon.com/xray-sdk-for-java/latest/javadoc/com/amazonaws/xray/AWSXRayRecorder.html#getTraceEntity-- and http://docs.aws.amazon.com/xray-sdk-for-java/latest/javadoc/com/amazonaws/xray/AWSXRayRecorder.html#setTraceEntity-- methods to get a reference to the current segment or subsegment (http://docs.aws.amazon.com/xray-sdk-for-java/latest/javadoc/com/amazonaws/xray/entities/Entity.html), and pass it back to the recorder inside of the thread. See Using Instrumented Clients in Worker Threads for an example.

X-Ray SDK for Node.js

Issue: *CLS does not work with Sequelize*

Pass the X-Ray SDK for Node.js namespace to Sequelize with the `cls` method.

```
1 var AWSXRay = require('aws-xray-sdk');
2 const Sequelize = require('sequelize');
3 Sequelize.cls = AWSXRay.getNamespace();
4 const sequelize = new Sequelize('database', 'username', 'password');
```

Issue: *CLS does not work with Bluebird*

Use `cls-bluebird` to get Bluebird working with CLS.

```
1 var AWSXRay = require('aws-xray-sdk');
2 var Promise = require('bluebird');
3 var clsBluebird = require('cls-bluebird');
4 clsBluebird(AWSXRay.getNamespace());
```

The X-Ray daemon

Issue: *The daemon is using the wrong credentials*

The daemon uses the AWS SDK to load credentials. If you use multiple methods of providing credentials, the method with the highest precedence is used. See Running the Daemon for more information.

Integrating AWS X-Ray with Other AWS Services

Other AWS services provide integration with AWS X-Ray by adding a tracing header to requests, running the X-Ray daemon, or making sampling decisions and uploading trace data to X-Ray.

Note

The X-Ray SDKs include plugins for additional integration with AWS services. For example, you can use the X-Ray SDK for Java's Elastic Beanstalk plugin to add information about the Elastic Beanstalk environment that runs your application including the environment name and ID.

Topics

- Elastic Load Balancing and AWS X-Ray
- AWS Lambda and AWS X-Ray
- Amazon API Gateway and AWS X-Ray
- Amazon Elastic Compute Cloud and AWS X-Ray
- AWS Elastic Beanstalk and AWS X-Ray

Elastic Load Balancing and AWS X-Ray

Elastic Load Balancing application load balancers add a trace ID to incoming HTTP requests in a header named `X-Amzn-Trace-Id`.

```
1  X-Amzn-Trace-Id: Root=1-5759e988-bd862e3fe1be46a994272793
```

Trace ID Format

A `trace_id` consists of three numbers separated by hyphens. For example, `1-58406520-a006649127e371903a2de979`. This includes:

- The version number, that is, **1**.

- The time of the original request, in Unix epoch time, in **8 hexadecimal digits**.

  For example, 10:00AM December 1st, 2016 PST in epoch time is 1480615200 seconds, or 58406520 in hexadecimal.

- A 96-bit identifier for the trace, globally unique, in **24 hexadecimal digits**.

Load balancers do not send data to X-Ray, and do not appear as a node on your service map.

For more information, see Request Tracing for Your Application Load Balancer in the Elastic Load Balancing Developer Guide.

AWS Lambda and AWS X-Ray

You can use AWS X-Ray to trace your AWS Lambda functions. Lambda runs the X-Ray daemon and records a segment with details about the function invocation and execution. For further instrumentation, you can bundle the X-Ray SDK with your function to record outgoing calls and add annotations and metadata.

If your Lambda function is called by another instrumented service, Lambda will trace requests that have already been sampled without any additional configuration. The upstream service can be an instrumented web application, another Lambda function.

If your Lambda function is invoked by a service that is not instrumented, or does not propagate the tracing header from an upstream service, you can configure Lambda to sample and record invocations with active tracing.

To configure X-Ray integration on an AWS Lambda function

1. Open the AWS Lambda console.

2. Choose your function.

3. Choose **Configuration**.

4. Under **Debugging and error handling**, choose **Enable active tracing**.

On runtimes with a corresponding X-Ray SDK, Lambda also runs the X-Ray daemon.

X-Ray SDKs on Lambda

- **X-Ray SDK for Go** – Go 1.7 and newer runtimes
- **X-Ray SDK for Java** – Java 8 runtime
- **X-Ray SDK for Node.js** – Node.js 4.3 and newer runtimes
- **X-Ray SDK for Python** – Python 2.7, Python 3.6, and newer runtimes
- **X-Ray SDK for .NET** – .NET Core 2.0 and newer runtimes

To use the X-Ray SDK on Lambda, bundle it with your function code each time you create a new version. You can instrument your Lambda functions with the same methods that you use to instrument applications running on other services. The primary difference is that you do not use the SDK to instrument incoming requests, make sampling decisions, and create segments.

The other difference between instrumenting Lambda functions and web applications is that the segment that Lambda creates and sends to X-Ray cannot be modified by your function code. You can create subsegments and record annotations and metadata on them, but you can't add annotations and metadata to the parent segment.

For more information, see Troubleshooting Lambda-based Applications in the AWS Lambda Developer Guide.

Amazon API Gateway and AWS X-Ray

Amazon API Gateway gateways add a trace ID to incoming HTTP requests in a header named `X-Amzn-Trace-Id`.

```
1  X-Amzn-Trace-Id: Root=1-5759e988-bd862e3fe1be46a994272793
```

Trace ID Format

A `trace_id` consists of three numbers separated by hyphens. For example, `1-58406520-a006649127e371903a2de979`. This includes:

- The version number, that is, `1`.

- The time of the original request, in Unix epoch time, in **8 hexadecimal digits**.

  For example, 10:00AM December 1st, 2016 PST in epoch time is 1480615200 seconds, or 58406520 in hexadecimal.

- A 96-bit identifier for the trace, globally unique, in **24 hexadecimal digits**.

API Gateway does not propagate X-Ray trace ID and sampling headers, or send trace data to X-Ray. If your gateway is downstream of other services in your application, traces will terminate at the gateway and the request will continue with a different trace ID. Gateways do not appear as a node on your service map.

Amazon Elastic Compute Cloud and AWS X-Ray

You can install and run the X-Ray daemon on an Amazon EC2 instance with a user data script. See Running the X-Ray Daemon on Amazon EC2 for instructions.

Use an instance profile to grant the daemon permission to upload trace data to X-Ray. For more information, see Giving the Daemon Permission to Send Data to X-Ray.

AWS Elastic Beanstalk and AWS X-Ray

AWS Elastic Beanstalk platforms include the X-Ray daemon. You can run the daemon by setting an option in the Elastic Beanstalk console or with a configuration file.

On the Java SE platform, you can use a Buildfile file to build your application with Maven or Gradle on-instance. The X-Ray SDK for Java and AWS SDK for Java are available from Maven, so you can deploy only your application code and build on-instance to avoid bundling and uploading all of your dependencies.

You can use Elastic Beanstalk environment properties to configure the X-Ray SDK. The method that Elastic Beanstalk uses to pass environment properties to your application varies by platform. Use the X-Ray SDK's environment variables or system properties depending on your platform.

- **Node.js platform** – Use environment variables
- **Java SE platform** – Use environment variables
- **Tomcat platform** – Use system properties

For more information, see Configuring AWS X-Ray Debugging in the AWS Elastic Beanstalk Developer Guide.